ENTERTAINING ON
A CRUISE SHIP

THE COMPLETE GUIDE

PAUL ROMHANY

© Limelight Press 2009

LIMELIGHT PRESS
Limelight Books. Sackville Street, Shediac.
New Brunswick, Canada

First published January, 2009

Thank you to Jonathan Levey for his editing skills, patience and hard work in helping me put this book together.

Photos taken by Paul and Natalie Romhany.

Dedicated to Natalie for being part of this incredible journey for the past nine years.

Natalie and Paul Romhany on a ship overlooking Monte Carlo

Table of Contents

CHAPTER THREE

CHAPTER FOUR

CHAPTER FIVE

CHAPTER SIX

CHAPTER SEVEN

CHAPTER EIGHT

BONUS SECTION

CHAPTER NINE

Relaxing on a Seaborne ship - here's to your cruise ship career

FOREWORD

I have worked on cruise ships, on and off, for more than twelve years, and as cliché as it sounds, I wish I would have had this book when I started. It would have saved me a lot of time and trouble.

What you have here is the definitive work on working in the cruise industry.

Like Paul, I have worked for just about every cruise line. I have done long contracts and I have done one-day guest spots. I have worked with my wife Lesley as a double act, and I have done the lone stand-up comedy thing. So, I know a little bit about working ships, and yet, as I was reading this book I found myself taking notes and thinking, damn, that will make things easier.

Paul has left nothing out of this book. He explains it all, the good, the bad and the seasick.

If you are just getting into this side of the business or, like me, are already doing it, you will get solid information from the book.

I applaud you Paul, you have outdone yourself with this book.

TC Tahoe
written on board a Carnival Cruise ship 2008

INTRODUCTION

Cruise ships come in all shapes and sizes

When I first started working on cruise ships with my act it was a very daunting task. That was back in 1989 and for many years, after watching 'The Love Boat' on television, I would dream of one day becoming a headline act on cruise ships, and finally when it became a reality I was very nervous and didn't know anything about how to get started and what to expect. Looking back, I wish there had been a book that could answer all the questions that were lingering in my mind. For me it all happened rather quickly. Before I knew it, I was on a ship and thrown in to the deep end, so to speak.

Fortunately, in my case, on that first contract there were other Guest Entertainers on the ship who took me under their wings and showed me the ropes and helped me get my head around the world of cruising. To this day I still work on ships with these wonderful people and have developed some good solid friendships over time.

Most of the work for variety acts has moved out to sea, with their fully equipped theaters and the ever growing need for good entertainment. Most ships have full production shows plus Guest Entertainers, which usually consist of a magician, a comedian, an instrumentalist (banjo, harmonica, guitar, etc.) and a ventriloquist. The production shows on ships today are flashy Las Vegas-style shows comprised of ten to sixteen dancers and singers. As a bona fide cruise ship entertainer, you will become part of one of the last bastions of entertainment for Variety Artists, a place where we get a chance to have an audience and perform our full evening shows.

With this book, I plan to lay everything out for the entertainer who wants to work on a ship, so that by the time you walk on board your first ship you have some genuine idea of what to expect, making your life that much easier. Since there are things that you learn only by experience, I have integrated part of my personal journal into this book. It is my hope from reading my journal entries, you will quickly discover what type of life we entertainers truly live on a ship. I suggest that you start writing your very own journal once you start to get work, because the stories you collect will last you a lifetime. I also strongly suggest that you invest in a good digital camera, and take lots of photos because you will get a chance very few people in this world have, to travel far and wide to almost every country on earth, and to acquire a taste for other cultures, foods and lifestyles.

If I was to give one over-riding piece of advice, it would be this: **make sure that you are ready!** You will only get once chance at working on a ship so don't rush in to it before you feel that you are ready. Instead, read this book, and any other book that may be out there on the subject. Talk to people who are in the industry and ask for their honest opinions and advice.

Cruise ship work didn't happen for me overnight. I wanted to do it for many years but was glad I took my time and developed an original act first, as this act has served me well, and kept me employed for many happy years. To start your self assessment, ask yourself, are you in a position to be away from home and away from your family for long periods of time? Are you healthy enough to withstand the rigorous travel and unconventional lifestyle that comes with working on a ship? And, of course, also ask yourself, do you have the right type of high caliber act to work on a ship? As with any type of performance, you must know your limits and be prepared.

This book is written from my own personal adventures on the high seas, and I am offering inside information that I have come across and collected over the years of working ships. In this regard, included in this book are a myriad of personal stories and experiences that I hope will shed some light on working on cruise ships, thus making it a little easier for those of you desiring to get into this industry, to succeed.

Finally, let me point out that for those of you that do succeed with your dream of becoming an 'in demand' cruise ship entertainer, you will have one of the best jobs in the world, certainly one of the best and highest paid ones on a ship. I never take what I do for granted and everyday am thankful for what I have. The cruise ship life has been great for me. In addition to the thrill I get form performing in the theatrical environment, it has helped me financially, and also the place where I met my wonderful wife Natalie.

You are a Guest Entertainer. This means you don't have any extra jobs on board the ship to carry out, you are simply there to perform your act once per week and to ensure that the ship's passengers are truly entertained. During the past several years that I have been working on cruise ships, I have had the privilege to travel around the world at least a dozen times, visiting almost every country and port in the world. As I write these words, I have just left South America in the Amazon Jungle four days ago, and today I find myself in Dakar,Africa. Next week I will find myself in St. Petersburg, Russia. How many jobs are there where we can see so much of the world?

Cruise Lines offer guests a variety of choices. Today, cruising remains one of the most popular, convenient, and affordable vacation options offered in the travel industry. With more cruise ships sailing to more incredible cruise destinations all over the world than ever before, there has truly never been a better time to cruise!

Paul performing on stage 2008

Taking a bow as Chaplin

CHAPTER ONE

CRUISE SHIPS

There is nothing more exciting than traveling the world on a cruise ship

Brief History of Cruising

The earliest ocean-going vessels were not primarily concerned with passengers, but rather with the cargo that they could carry. Black Ball Line in New York, in 1818, was the first shipping company to offer regularly scheduled service from the United States to England and to be concerned with the comfort of their passengers. By the 1830's steamships were introduced and dominated the transatlantic market of passenger and mail transport. English companies dominated the market at this time, led by the British and North American Royal Mail Steam Packet (later the Cunard Line). On July 4, 1840, Britannia, the first ship under the Cunard name, left Liverpool with a cow on board to supply fresh milk to the passengers on the 14-day transatlantic crossing. The advent of *pleasure* cruises is linked to the year 1844, when this new industry began.

During the 1850s and 1860s there was a dramatic improvement in the quality of the voyage for passengers. Ships began to cater solely to passengers, rather than to cargo or mail related shipments. They began to add luxuries like electric lights, more deck space, and *entertainment*. In 1867, Mark Twain was a passenger on the first cruise originating in America, documenting his adventures of his six month trip in the book "Innocents Abroad." Then in the 1880's the endorsement by the British Medical Journal of Sea Voyages for Curative Purposes, further encouraged the public to take leisurely pleasure cruises as well as transatlantic travel. European ships also began to carry immigrants to the United States in "steerage" class. In steerage, passengers were responsible for providing their own food and slept in whatever space was available in the "hold", (lower level storage area in the ship).

By the early 20th century the concept of the *Super-Liner* was developed and Germany led the market in the development of these massive and ornate floating hotels. The design of these Super-Liners attempted to minimize the discomfort of ocean travel, masking the fact of being at sea and the extremes in weather conditions, as much as possible by providing passengers with elegant accommodations and planned social and game-related activities. The Mauritania and the Lusitania, both owned by the Cunard Line of England, started the tradition of *dressing for dinner,* and advertised the romance of the voyage. Speed was still the deciding factor in the design of these ships. There was no space for large public rooms, and passengers were required to share dining tables. The White Star Line, owned by American financier J.P. Morgan, introduced the most luxurious passenger ships ever seen with the Olympic (complete with swimming pool and tennis court) and the Titanic. Space and passenger comfort suddenly took precedence over speed in the design of these ships-resulting in larger, more stable liners. The sinking of the Titanic on its maiden voyage and the tragic loss of lives in 1912 devastated the White Star Line. In 1934, Cunard bought out White Star. The resulting company name, Cunard White Star, can be found in the advertisements of its ships.

World War I (1914-1918) interrupted the building of new cruise ships, and many older liners were used as troop transports. German super-liners were given to both Great Britain and the United States as reparations at the end of the war. The years between 1920 and 1940 were considered the most glamorous years for transatlantic passenger ships. These ships catered to the rich and famous who were seen enjoying luxurious settings on numerous newsreels viewed by the general public. American tourists interested in visiting Europe replaced immigrant passengers. Advertisement campaigns promoted the high-fashion of ocean travel, featuring the elegant food and on-board activities.

Cruise liners again were converted into troop carriers in World War II, and all transatlantic cruising ceased until after the war. European lines reaped the benefits of transporting immigrants to America and Canada, and business travelers and tourists to Europe. The lack of American ocean liners at this time, and thus the loss of profits, spurred the U.S. government to subsidize the building of cruise liners. In spite of the war's completion, in addition to their luxurious amenities, ships were now designed according to specifications for possible conversion into troop carriers. However, by the 1950's, increasing air travel and the first non-stop flight to Europe in 1958 marked the ending of transatlantic business for ocean liners. Passenger ships were sold and lines went bankrupt from the lack of business.

The 1960s witnessed the beginnings of the modern cruise industry. Cruise ship companies concentrated on vacation trips in the Caribbean, and created a "fun ship" image which attracted many passengers who never had the opportunity to travel on the super-liners of the 1930's and 1940's. Cruise ships now concentrated on creating a casual environment and providing extensive on-board entertainment. There was a decrease in the role of ships for transporting people to a particular destination; rather, the emphasis was on the voyage experience itself. This new cruise line image was solidified with the popularity of the TV series "The Love Boat" which ran from 1977 until 1986. I am honored to say that my wife and I were the very last act on the original ship used in the TV show, "The Love Boat", whose actual name was "Pacific Princess" before she was sold by Princess Cruises in 2002. It was certainly a ship with a long history of amazing magic acts that had performed on her. There were actually two identical ships used for the TV show, *The Island Princess* and *The Pacific Princess*. There is a new Pacific Princess which is a modern ship and joined the fleet in 2003.

Paul with actor Gavin MacLeod from the TV show, "The Love Boat"

The Ship

With the wide-range of cruise lines today, ships now come in different shapes and sizes, and languages. There are small ships that hold two hundred passengers and enormous ships that can hold up to 6000 passengers! I was fortunate to have worked for the Princess Cruise line for six years, and they have both large and small ships. I also work on Holland America, Seaborne, Cunard, Fred Olson, Regent and RCCL to name a few. I am going to use Princess Cruise ships as my example in the resource chapter on size of ships.

The Princess Lines have different sized ships and different names for each 'class' of ship. For example there is The Grand Class ship which has two venues, the main theater and a smaller room for shows. Most of the variety shows are performed in the smaller room, while the large stage productions are in the theaters. Quite often there are two shows going on at the same time, the variety show and the production show in the main theater. The larger illusion shows on ships of course always play the main theater show room. In many cases, the illusionists will leave their equipment on one ship rather than transship, and they often stay on that ship for years.

Princess also has the smaller class of ship, The Tahitian, The Pacific and The Royal. These ships only have one theater and are much more intimate. Some of the sight-lines aren't the best, so you want to keep your magic above waist level.

Today, while I am working on this chapter, I am on a Holland America ship, which has one main show room and it is tiered seating on two levels and a raised stage. In this way, everybody can see me work!

I have also worked for cruise lines such as Fred Olson Line, in order to make sure that everybody can see everything, you really perform your magic performance <u>above</u> waist-height because you are on a dance floor rather than a raised stage. For example, if you performed Kevin James' Bowling Ball Production, it would be missed by most the audience because they would not see the ball drop out the pad of paper.

Be adaptable with your magic because each venue will change from ship to ship. One good thing is that cruise lines will have 'sister' ships, that is, ships that are identical. Once you start working for a company and get to know their ships you will know what will work and what won't work regarding your choice of magic.

The great thing about the internet is that cruise lines have web pages and you can go on a virtual tour of a ship, including the theater where you will be performing. This will give you a good idea of what type of stage you will be working on.

Destinations

In this section, I have listed some of the most popular destinations you can travel to while performing on a cruise ship. My wife and I have been cruising for over nine years now, and we are very lucky to say we have travelled to all of the main ports of call around the world, something we could have never afforded to do had we not been performing on cruise ships.

AFRICA

Extended ocean voyages around the world was the way that many travelers used to see the wonders of the world. On an African Cruise, you can experience the continent the way many visitors used to for centuries. Africa is filled with rivers, canals, and is easily accessible from Europe, the Mediterranean as well as southwest Asia.

Many cruises typically do not stop at Africa ports exclusively. An African cruise might commence somewhere in the Mediterranean and cruise around Africa via the Suez Canal. African cruises are typically longer than an average cruise and can take up to three weeks or more. While you're at Suez, you can take excursions to Cairo and along the Red Sea coast of Egypt, which offers some of the best snorkeling and diving in the world.

Cairo has been a much sought-after destination for hundreds of years. Countries like Egypt, with its Arab, Berber, Coptic and African influences are a spectacular example of the diversity of culture and influences that shape all parts of this wondrous continent.
Most cruises on the Nile originate in Cairo. One option you can explore is extending your tour of the continent by booking another tour before or after your main cruise.

ALASKA

If you are longing to explore the Pacific Northwest, an Alaskan Cruise on the Inside Passage is an absolute must. This itinerary, displays the best that nature has to offer, and a cruise highlights the bounty of the wilderness. As you travel north of the Puget Sound, beyond Vancouver and Victoria Island, past the temperate rain-forest of coastal B.C., you will find where Alaska begins. Some of these trees that you sail past are hundreds of years old.

Unlike anyplace else in the world, Alaska will ignite your imagination with its starry nights and quiet beauty. Like the 15-year, 200-mile journey of the glaciers to Glacier Bay, you will feel an inexorable pull on yourself as well. You might choose to visit during the months of May and September, right before or after the tourist season for great rates while still being able to enjoy the best weather for sightseeing from the deck of your cruise ship.

Alaskan cruises will typically commence in the town of Vancouver B.C. An invigorating feeling fills you at the city of Vancouver, with it's gleaming white Port area with magical white clouds of fog blanketing the harbor is where you will begin your journey north.

ASIA

Asia is a land of hidden treasures. From India to the Philippines, there are dozens of port cities, gateway to the lands of the Orient. Cruising to Asia is a fun and easy way to get around and explore everything that this alluring continent has to offer.

From Turkmenistan in the west to South Korea in the east, this continent is home to the plateau of the world, Tibet, as well as the ancient Hindu Kush. Countries like Pakistan and East Timor defy classification and the mix of cultures in these countries only enhance their exotic flavor.

There are a number of port cities you can depart from on your Asian luxury cruise, with a good choice being Bangkok, Thailand. This city is overflowing with cultural riches, and its miles of temples and sacred structures will simply astound you. Exploring revered temples richly decorated with ornate filigree and filled with golden Buddhas await you. The lush air and majestic scenery only enhance the feeling of awe that will overcome you as you gaze upon the faade of Wat Phra Kaeo. Immaculate paintings and brightly colored statues of Buddhist deities greet you as you enter. The building, over two hundred years old, is one of the most revered sites in Thailand, so appropriate dress is required.

BAHAMAS

The clearest waters on the planet can be found in the Bahamas. Take Bahamas vacations to explore this island nation - made up of a chain of 700 islands, some no more than uninhabited cays and enormous rocks jutting out of the water.

The capitol of Nassau is located on New Providence Island. This is like a sister island to the aptly named Paradise Island - being the two largest islands in the chain. Bahamas cruises will likely drop anchor here in Nassau. Visit the world famous Straw Market, and strike up a lovely conversation with a local artisan while she weaves together her latest creation. Watch the wood chips fly as a local carver sculpts a graceful flamingo, an endangered species that are native to the island.

The most relaxed, idyllic scenery greets you as you walk around this island archipelago. From the stunning sunset on Harbor Island to the deserted beaches of Georgetown, a feeling of pure tranquility will overcome you when you visit the Bahamas.

BERMUDA

Located 600 miles off the coast of North Carolina, Bermuda is a small 21 square mile island in a world all its own. With its three ports, and its remote Western Atlantic location, Bermuda was made for cruising. From its crystal caves to its colonial streets, Bermuda offers a disarming blend of culture and nature to delight every kind of traveler.

Hamilton is one of the port cities so well known that it is known as simply, "town". Front Street is the main event here. Situated in view of the harbor, this charming street is lined with shops and cafes where you can relax at as you watch the ships float by.

Buffeted by breezes that make for excellent bodysurfing and wind-sailing, St. George is a great place to recharge. Take the coastal trail at a leisurely pace and feel at peace as you watch the white-capped waves rise and fall into the ocean.

The island is virtually devoid of tourists in the winter. So it is a good place to visit if you want to enjoy some golf and have the island mostly to yourself, while taking advantage of the great off-season rates.

CANADA

To the north of the United States lies a destination that is often overlooked - Canada. Travel Canada, and you will find you don't have to go far to experience a totally different culture. Take a Canadian cruise to Prince Edward Island and on the way stop at French Quebec City. Canada is strongly influenced by the first explorers to come overseas from France and England. From the image of Queen Elizabeth to the French speaking Quebecois ,

You can depart on your Canadian cruise from a US port such as Boston or New York. Or, if your prefer, you can travel to a city such as Montreal in the province of Quebec. Arrive a few days before your cruise to explore this city, which has a distinctly European feel. Montreal is a very safe, clean city that is easy to explore. It has an inland harbor on the Great Lakes, so it is not often on Canadian Cruises itinerary, but it is a must for the visitor travel ing to Canada.

For the most part, Americans have enjoyed a good exchange rate for many years. Its proximity and approachability make Canada a popular destination for North American travelers.

CARIBBEAN

The Caribbean is an area dotted with islands, located south of the Gulf of Mexico, off the southwestern coast of the United States. From Cuba in the west, all the way to Barbados in the east, you could spend several weeks on a Caribbean vacation discovering all its charms. Start with a leisurely cruise from Miami, Florida and make your way south to experience the Latin Americas of the seas.

Cuba is the largest yet least developed place in the Caribbean Islands. If you enjoy going off the beaten path and exploring, then Cuba is a great way to begin any Caribbean adventure. Havana's crumbling edifices and antique cars give this city a distinct historical charm. With Havana being a port city, you can cruise in with some of the popular cruise lines such as Carnival Cruise Line, Celebrity Cruise Line, Disney Cruise Line, Holland Cruise Line, Princess Cruises, Royal Caribbean, and Windstar. South of Cuba lies the island of Jamaica.

The port of Kingston is must on your Caribbean vacation. From the Botanical Gardens to the *Friday Night Jam*, there is an abundance of things to see and do in Kingston. Scuba diving is often overlooked due to the rich cultural offerings, but a great variety of diving sites exist here, from wrecks to reefs. Most Jamaicans are very friendly and welcome an opportunity to tell you more about their Island. Their heavy accent is not that hard to understand and the locals like it when you try to learn the Jamaican Patois that they speak.

EUROPE
Many diverse countries make up what is known as Europe. A European Cruise is the quintessential way to see it all, from the cobblestone streets of old London to the ancient stones of Spain. There are different types of European Cruises available to explore Europe's plethora of regions.

A European cruise of the Baltic Sea will take you to the countries of Scandinavia, Norway, Sweden, and Finland. If you are interested in visiting St. Petersburg, Russia, including it on you itinerary only makes sense since it is nearby and many cruise lines do offer that option.

The icy northern seas are home to legends of Viking and Valkyries, and the traditions that still live here today are as rich as any other. The sunlit mountain valleys and the rosy faces of the local population will welcome you to a unique experience. The old world charm of Copenhagen, Denmark will cater to your simpler tastes. On your European cruise, you can take a trip back in time on when you visit Tivoli Garden, which is like the father of all amusement parks. You can spend an entire day here walking through its lovely garden setting enjoying its puppet shows, games of chance, amusement rides and delicious restaurants. Stockholm, Sweden is another port city that has not lost its traditional appeal either. Be sure to visit the Vasa Museum, home to the warship that sunk itself due to his heavy armament.

LANZAROTE CANARY ISLANDS

Lanzarote is a lost treasure at sea, situated 60 miles off the Northwestern edge of the coast of Morocco, in the North African continent. It is one of the 7 Islands that make up the Canary Islands. The first adventurers to discover this island was an ancient Roman expedition, which found a pack of very large dogs living here, and named the island Canes, after the Roman word for Dog.

Lanzarote is a fascinating place, from its mix of cultures to its toppled columns to its legends of Atlantis. Being situated in an island chain that enjoys mild weather year-round, Lanzarote is a well-known destination for many cruise liners. Europeans, who share the privileges of EU members, often seek the Canary Islands out for vacations and are free to come and go as they like.

The Canary Islands is an autonomous region of Spain, and in addition to Spanish, both English and German are widely spoken here. Lanzarote is the most northeastern island in the group, and its large commercial fishing fleet is known as the largest of all the islands. Arrecife is the capitol of this gem, and will likely be your port of call if you arrive on a cruise.

MEDITERRANEAN

Mediterranean cruises are the perfect way to explore the coasts of Spain, France, Italy, Greece, and Turkey. Situated between the two continents of Europe and Africa, is the Mediterranean Sea. This Sea lends its name (from the latin term medius) to the lands around it.

Over 1000 islands make the Mediterranean ocean a European paradise for the seafarer. From Venice to Athens, you can experience arriving at your destination like so many others did in times past. On a

Mediterranean cruise you can avoid the hassle of having to arrange lodging and transportation, and being able keep your bags unpacked while you visit different countries is without comparison. A cruise is a magnificent alternative to land travel.

300 Million visitors every year flock to the sun bleached towns and sandy beaches of the Mediterranean. Home to the capitals of western cultures like Rome, Istanbul, and Athens, this sea is the setting for conquests and battles, travels and adventure, mystery and lore. 3 continents and 21 countries border this enormous body of water.

Legends about the great Ulysses come to mind when you think of the ancient times and richness of cultural history this sea has been a part of. As you sail along headed to your next port city, take time to absorb the view and atmosphere. From the calm, idyllic shores of Greece to the height of style in the luxurious yacht haven of Monaco, France, the Mediterranean has offerings to suit every taste.

NEW ENGLAND
The northeastern coast of the North American continent, from Maine to Rhode Island encompasses what is known as New England. Explore this area like the early settlers did and witness the intense beauty and natural charm of the coast on a New England cruise.

Cape Cod is a nature lovers dream, an expansive network of beaches, harbors, nature paths, biking trails and a number of outdoor activities. As you ferry from island to island, you might arrive at the fact that you could spend days here and you might even begin to ponder what it would be like to live here year round. Enjoy whale watching, savor the magnificent views, and get lost in your thoughts at the Cape Cod National Seashore.

Just a short trip from Boston begins the bevy of wind blown beaches, pleasingly devoid of life. Your mind will wander out towards the sea as you watch the waves tumble and crash on the rugged black rock beaches of the Southern coast of Maine.

Quiet and magnificent with a cool northern brilliance, the scenic coastline of Maine takes you back in time. The coast of New Hampshire is a treasured destination for vacationers for miles around. Many come here to enjoy Hampton Beach and the boardwalk, the hub of excitement in the area. Everything is centered around the lovely beach-front where a number of water sports can be enjoyed. Catering to the visitors are charming shops, fantastic restaurants serving the freshest catch of the day, and be prepared to sample some authentic New England clam chowder.

PACIFIC NORTHWEST

If you've ever dreamed of the West, and wondered what it would be like to experience it, explore the Northwest from the sea. A Pacific Northwest Cruise is unmatched in sea travel itineraries. A mysterious fog shrouds the North American coast from San Francisco to Vancouver. Remnants of the great coastal rain-forest remain untouched in large expanses north of BC, Canada. The north-west, home to Indian tribes such as the Makah Tribe of Neah Bay, WA, is the dramatic setting for the culmination of the Lewis and Clark Expedition.

A Pacific Northwest cruise might take you any where from San Francisco to Anchorage, and many cruise companies will have roundtrip cruises to Alaska that begin their voyage in San Francisco. Your cruise ship will sail through the magnificent straight under the Golden Gate Bridge, and you will dock at Pier 35, a convenient starting point to attractions such as Pier 39, The Fisherman's Wharf and North Beach.

In the Puget Sound region of the state of Washington lies the well-known city of Seattle, which is another must see in any pacific coast cruises. Cruise lines stop at many of the piers here, including Pier 30, 66, and the Victoria Clipper, a high speed ferry, departs from Pier 70. Near by the many ports is Pike Place, Seattle's number one tourist spot. The Puget Sound and Seattle are home to stunning views of the Olympic Mountains. On clear days you can see the brilliant snow covered face of Mount Rainier. To the east lies the Cascade Mountain range, so no matter where in the city you find yourself, you are surrounded by picturesque beauty.

PANAMA CANAL

A stunning feat of engineering and a breathtaking display of nature, the Panama Canal is a waterway that begs to be explored. A Panama Canal Cruise has become the best new way to visit Central America.

The Panama Canal connects the Pacific to the Atlantic Ocean, and ever since it opened in 1914 it has become a hub for trade and tourism. Control of the canal was handed over to Panama five years ago, in 1999, by the United States as part of an agreement made in 1977. While not being as developed as other tourist destinations around the world. The Panama Canal has experienced a boom in visitors, and today it continues to grow into a scenic and approachable place with great value.

Cruise ships enter the Miraflores Locks, where hundreds of tourists marvel as the enormous ships are lowered and raised in a feat of engineering. Lake Gatun is where most of the water in the canal comes from. For the adventuresome there is even a nighttime expedition to watch the crocodiles there.

SAN JUAN

San Juan is the glittering imperial city of the Caribbean, located on the northeastern shore of the island of Puerto Rico. Founded in 1521, this fortress-like yet welcoming place is a disarming array of opposites. So, like the indigenous people, you may find that San Juan will enchant you with its exotic charms.

Luis Munoz Marin International Airport is just a short drive Northwest on Route 26 from San Juan, the largest city in Puerto Rico. This city is surrounded by water, the Atlantic Ocean to the North and the Bay of San Juan to the South, making it a strategic location to the Spanish, who used it as a stopover on their journeys to South America. Only in Puerto Rico, which is a territory of the United States, can you can have an old world Spanish feel, but with a unique island charm. No worry about currency conversion here. You can arrive by plane at the seaport and depart on a cruise aboard one of the many fine ships that travel to other exotic locales, further south along the Caribbean.

The people here are a mixture of native Taino Indians, Spanish explorers, African slaves, or the descendants of a combination of the three. Many Puerto Ricans speak fluent English and have strong ties to the United States.

SOUTH AMERICA

Explore the astounding diversity of the 12 Latin American countries as you travel South America. Warm Caribbean waters and the Venezuelan coast beckon you to the north. This country is a fascinating display of extremes, from the impossibly high peaks of the northern Andes to the idyllic coast, perched on the edge of the Western Caribbean Sea.

The Gujana highlight of southern Venezuela gives way to the Amazon River basin and the precious ecological treasures of Brazil. The Andes is a forbidding mountain range home to the secret forts and esoteric monuments of the ancient Inca. It stretches for thousands of miles, beginning in Argentina, curving southwest on the rim of the continent towards Columbia, through Ecuador, down into Peru and ending south in Chile.

The worlds equator crosses the continent in Columbia, Brazil and Ecuador, making these regions, especially Brazil a hot spot for the countless rare species of native tropical life that calls the Amazon Rainforest home. The mighty Amazon River begins as a series of innocuous streams that converge into the most powerful river in the world, serving as the center of the local culture, history and economy.

On the eastern coast of this continent, the highlands of the Andes is the dramatic setting of the Incan empire, which rose to its peak in the fourteenth century. Peru and Bolivia are the two countries, which were at the heart of the Inca civilization.

SOUTH PACIFIC

Visiting the islands of the South Pacific by ship makes sense, since it is aptly known as the Water Continent. To the northeast of Australia, and beyond New Zealand, lies eleven million square miles of ocean. It is here that you will discover the ancient South Pacific Islands. Among the thousands of islands, small and large, of Oceania, as it is also known, thirteen distinct Island Nations are to be found. A South Pacific cruise might originate in Sydney, Australia. Or you can fly into one of the many exotic island ports your journey there.

TRANSATLANTIC

Transatlantic cruises are an enchanting method of travel to Europe from North America, or vice versa. Spend 10 or 30 days at sea traveling round trip from New York to London, from Fort Lauderdale to Venice, or from Miami to Marseille.

Before the arrival of the steam-liner, when sailing ships crossed the Atlantic, this voyage used to take a lot longer. Now, not only is this trip much shorter, it is also much safer and much more enjoyable, thanks to the large number of giant ships making this voyage every day.

Transatlantic cruises are unlike any other you have ever been on. Beginning your journey in a busy port city such as Miami, you feel the bustle of humanity as you board your tremendous ship. The feeling of excitement grows as you reach your cabin and prepare to return to deck to lift anchor.

The crew members will reflect the international flavor of your voyage. Between them and the passenger you will likely hear five languages spoken regularly. Many crew members will speak more than one language, so if you enjoy practicing your language skills you will have even more fun.

WEST CARIBBEAN

A bevy of destinations with exotic names and cultures comprise what is known as the West Caribbean. Take a West Caribbean Cruise to travel with grace and ease on your way to discover some of these hidden gems.

A number of cruise lines maintain a fleet of ships year-round in the Caribbean - this is a highly sought after destination worldwide, 365 days per year. Whether you plan ahead, or are open to unexpected new experiences, you can relish memories of an unforgettable trip to this tropical haven.

A ship departing on a West Caribbean Cruise is easily accessible from a number of southern ports, such as Galveston and Houston, Texas, New Orleans, Louisiana, and Miami, Orlando, Jacksonville, or Tampa, Florida. If you don't have a full week to spare, you will find that a four or five day cruise is every bit as enjoyable.

There are a number of different West Caribbean itineraries with varying destinations,. However, most will commence with, and would not be complete without, a stop at Cozumel, Mexico. Off the western coast of Mexico's Yucatan Peninsula, this 26 by 11 mile island offers a fascinating combination of nature and history to enhance your travel experience.

WESTERN MEXICO

Colonial ruins and spectacular diving await you in the Western Mexico. The combination of leisure and culture make this a top destination for cruises. More and more travelers are discovering the bounties of this amazing country.

Western Mexico is the place where three cultures meet as one, in a captivating display of richness. Sun-dappled Colonial Spanish towns lie minutes away from impressive ancient ruins, and are the pinnacle of modern Mexican culture, with its vibrant ceremonies and festivals.

You might choose to depart from a city such as San Diego on your cruise to Mexico, then head south to Baja, California. The Baja Peninsula (Baja means "below" in Spanish) is 1100 miles long fringe of paradise.

Your first stop might be in the northern coastal town of La Paz, (meaning "peace" is Spanish), a relaxed alternative from the bustle of Cabo San Lucas. Here the beach is tantalizingly free of vendors and stalls, but you can find a jet ski to rent, if you are so inclined. If you are looking for silver there is tons of it here and it is easy to find really nice jewelry at reasonable prices.

WORLD CRUISES
If you have ever wanted to see it all, a world cruise is one way to do it. Three or four months is all you need to go all around the world. No waiting in airports, no luggage check-in, just unpack your things once and prepare yourself for the adventure of a lifetime. Quite often as a Guest Entertainer you will join a world cruise only for a week. My wife Natalie and I did a cruise for three months, which was part of a world cruise, and although it was broken up in to various parts, it was one of the best cruises we have ever done.

Cruise lines, experienced in navigating the seas, have itineraries that will make your head spin with extraordinary possibilities. You might depart from Los Angeles and set sail across the Pacific Ocean to your first stop at the Marquesas Islands. Visit exotic locales such as Tahiti and Bora Bora in French Polynesia, and escape like Gaugin to this island paradise.

A world cruise will take you across the Tropic of Capricorn until you find yourself in Auckland, New Zealand. Next up is the Sydney Harbor, with the well-known skyline dominated by the white façade of the Opera House. Across the Indian Ocean you will find Bali and Borneo, island nations rich in aquatic life and maritime history. The space of an entire month will pass during the first leg of this exciting journey So, enjoy the trip, not just the destination. Bon Voyage!!

Paul and Natalie in Paris 2008

CHAPTER TWO

LIFE ON A SHIP

Cruise ships are the last bastion for variety performers

Crew or Passenger?

Here is the million dollar question that changes for each cruise line. In the majority of my contracts, it states that I am a passenger, in other words I have passenger privileges. I can eat in the dining room, swim in the pool, sit in public areas and so on. However, always keep in mind that you are a non-paying guest and let the passengers have first choice. Don't push in, be polite and you will go a long way in this industry. I don't believe anybody is a 'star', we are just there doing a job!

As mentioned above, in most cases you will be on the passenger list, however there are times when you will be put on the crew list. This is really for immigration purposes only, but in some cases it has caused a bit of a problem.

While I was doing the New York to Bermuda run, all non-US Guest Entertainers were on the crew list which meant I had to be back on board the ship every time we were docked in New York by 1:30 p.m. The other US Guest Entertainers who were on the passenger list didn't have to be back on board by early afternoon. Of course, it cut my day in half during our visit to New York. The reason for this predicament was because during the season a Filipino crew member on board another ship had 'jumped ship' and didn't return to the ship, so immigration cracked down on ALL non-US individuals on board that season.

Whether you are put on the crew or passenger list also depends on how long you are with the ship and where you are cruising. If you are put on the crew list then you will be given a crew ID badge which you use to get on and off the ship. In most instances I am able to ensure that I am put on the passenger list and, therefore get the passenger card. The only reason you might be on the crew list is because it makes the paperwork a lot easier for the crew office, especially when it comes to visas in some countries, such as Brazil. When you are given Guest Entertainer status, always check the guest manual to make sure of rules and regulations for the company you are working for – in most cases this means you don't have to do crew drills. The only thing you might have to do are 'watertight' doors if they put you in a staff area. Watertight doors require you to know how to close and open special doors that shut if the ship gets in to trouble. There are some cruise lines where even Guest Entertainers are required to do crew drills. This would require special training that the ship will provide.

Another incident happened when I got off in Vancouver, Canada. I had planned to stay a few extra weeks there after one contract, however immigration officials told me that I was a crew member and didn't have shore leave! I argued with them ... rule Number ONE - NEVER ARGUE WITH AN IMMIGRATION OFFICIAL! As a result they gave me 24 hours to leave the country. I booked a cheap ticket to London, went there and played a game of golf for the day, then flew back to Canada without incident. Always check to see if you need to be issued shore leave when getting off in a port if you intend to stay, even though you may be on the passenger list. If all else fails, and I hate doing this, tell them you are a guest celebrity on the ship. Using that word 'Celebrity' might just help! (It's the ONLY time I ever use it).

Generally people who work under the Hotel Manager such as Cruise Staff, Youth Staff, Musicians, Excursions, Entertainment Department, gift shop, photo shop are generally listed as staff.

Waiters, Cabin Stewards, plumbers, carpenters, deck hands etc are under the Crew category.

The real difference for the above is the privileges they each get. This includes where they can eat, if they can use the nightclubs, etc. It doesn't affect you as a Guest Entertainer unless you want to meet somebody somewhere or have dinner with somebody.

With all its rights and privileges, still, it will be well worth your while to check in to your status before signing your contract.

Embarkation
When you join a ship, the technical term is called embarkation. If it is a seven day cruise, then passengers will embark every seven days. In the majority of cases, the cruise line will fly you to your destination a day before you are to join the ship. You will be met by the local Port Agent, who is responsible for your transport to the hotel and to the ship the next day. In some cases the Port Agent hasn't turned up to pick me up, so I always make sure I have my agent send me the Port Agent's details: including phone number, e-mail and emergency phone number, plus the name and address of the hotel where I will be staying. From experience, I like to have all bases covered when it comes to arriving in a foreign country. Nowadays I always e-mail the Port Agent ahead of time, to let them know I will be arriving so they are there to pick me up. Having said that, I caught up ship once where the Port Agent did not show up. I dialed the number, given to me by my agent, only to be told that they hadn't been the companies Port Agent for about five years.

You will find, more often than not, that there will be other crew members joining with you and they are usually picked up from the hotel between 7-8a.m. In some cases because I am a Guest Entertainer they don't want to see me too early, so I often find out where the ship is docked and catch a taxi a little later on, giving me more time to relax in the hotel. At the same time, this also gives the ship a little more time to process all the crew and get my cabin ready.

On the day you are scheduled to join the ship, they do like you to board at a certain time, so be sure to check this before leaving. If it is a turn-around day, where passengers are getting on and off, it can be very hectic. In such cases I often go with the crew straight on the ship. Upon arrival at the ship's terminal, go straight to the cruise ship's information desk and explain that you are a Guest Entertainer and have your joining documents ready to show. You will then be directed on board.

If there is no information desk, then head straight to the gangway and advise the security officer on duty that you are embarking. They will call the reception on the ship and get you settled.

You will either be asked to visit the Crew Office (crew purser) where all of the embarkation formalities will be completed, or told simply to go to the main reception area where you will be given your key. I always make a point of visiting the Cruise Director's office to introduce myself, hand over my promotional photo and get the schedule of performances.

Side note: There have been times where I have flown very long flights, from Vancouver to New Zealand, and by looking at the schedule, found out I was performing that very night. This doesn't happen often, but be prepared because it can happen.

The cruise ship rules also frequently state that you are to attend the passenger safety drill with passengers. If this is your first time on ships I strongly advise you do this!

Disembarkation

When you leave the ship the technical term is called disembarkation. Arrangements for leaving the ship differ from port to port and the crew office will know more about the details of what time you are to be picked up and taken to the airport. If you are on the passenger list, then the 'Practica' will look after you. The Practica is the ships name for the person who is in charge of guest relations. They are usually located at the front desk. Often when you sign in, they will get you to fill out a form which will ask you for your leaving details. Cruise lines get deals on flights and often these deals come in under the wire, so don't panic if your flight details don't arrive until the very last minute.

Sometimes disembarkation can be a long process, as you may have to go through customs and immigration. Be prepared for a long day.

A few things to make sure you have before leaving:
• Paid all your on board bills.
• Returned your crew ID to the purser, if you are on the crew list.
• Hand in your blue or yellow card (a safety card given to you when you join).
• Leave your key in your cabin.
• Pay your room steward his or her tips. If you are in a passenger area this is generally $3.50 US per day. In crew area it will be less. Check with other entertainers what they are tipping once you are on the ship.
• "Signed off" the ship's crew articles, if on crew list.

Accommodation

With the cruise lines I work for, they always put me in a private double cabin and with my own bathroom facilities. The cabin is either located in the passenger area or in a staff area, depending on the ship. My contract also states that I get an outside cabin. This means I get a cabin with a window, as opposed to an inside cabin. Towels and linen are always provided. Each morning your cabin steward will come and change the towels and usually once a week they will change the linen.

Accommodation on each ship varies, in many cases they tend to put all the entertainers together in one area which makes for fun times and a good way to get to know the other acts. On the cruise line I am currently performing on, Guest Entertainers are all staying in passenger areas. Therefore, the room service is the same as it is for regular passengers. If you are in put into a staff area, then you will not get the chocolate placed on your pillow at night, and the cabin steward will usually come clean your cabin once a day, unless you ask otherwise. We have always had a TV in our room, sometimes with a DVD player and fridge. On contracts where we have been booked for six months or longer, when there was no fridge, we often purchased a little $80 fridge and have it in our cabin, as it always seems to comes in handy on the long runs.

There is always a phone in the cabin, and if I am able to buy a calling card at crew rates from the crew office, I can phone home at a low-cost from my cabin. I remember in the early days I had to line up with the rest of the ship's crew to use one phone, on one of the ship's lower decks. I could be waiting over an hour to use it. There are advantages to being in a staff area. For passengers to use the regular phones in their cabins, it can cost up to $4.50 per minute. For crew it is only seventeen cents, depending on the location you are calling. Many cruise ships now offer a service where you can use your cell phone via a satellite on the ship, however I have found this to be very experience.

I worked on one ship where my wife could call a land line number and it would be put through to the ship, not costing her a lot of money to call me. This is generally the case with cruise ships that are English operated such as Saga Cruises. For her to call me from a land line to my cabin is normally very expensive, so it is easier for me to phone her if I can get a crew calling card.

Again, rules for phone calls vary on different ships. On the Queen Elizabeth II for example, you don't have access to 'crew' areas so there are no discounts with the phones (i.e. no crew phone cards). However, they do have a discount on the use of internet so I was able to use SKYPE to make my calls from my computer. On Princess and Holland

America I am able to purchase a crew phone card and internet card which makes life so much easier and less costly for keeping in contact with home. To be honest, this is one of the main reason I enjoy working for these two companies, because I like to be able to check e-mail and phone home from my cabin on a regular basis. I take my laptop and because most ships now have wireless internet it makes life being away from home so much simpler.

On board Facilities

As I mentioned, as a Guest Entertainer you are able to use the on board facilities. These can include:

Gift Shop

This is where you will also sell any of your DVD's and/or CDs. The shops on board sell everything from medicine to clothing to expensive jewelry. Always check to see if you are entitled to discounts, in most cases you are. I often find it much less costly to purchase my duty-free drinks on board and take them home from the ship, rather than purchasing them at an airport. Also, I have found that perfume is a great buy on board the ships. If buying alcohol to take home after you leave a ship, ask for a box to pack it in, because you can no longer take it in your hand luggage if flying to your destination.

Exercise Facilities

Ships will always have a gym with the latest exercise machines. In some cases you may have to book your time to use a machine, but this is never really an issue. Keep in mind that passengers have first option, as they are paying for their cruise. Also, if they recognize you and you are always 'hogging' the treadmill they WILL complain!

There is also usually a jogging track or 'walk-a-mile' program and other sports equipment. Some of the larger ships have tennis courts, basketball courts, rock-climbing and ice-skating rinks! A recent RCCL ship I was on also had a roller-blading rink. Most ships offer yoga, pilate and aerobic classes. Sometimes they are free, but in most cases these classes are charged to your account. If you look in the ship's daily schedule it will always say whether they are free or not. Keep in mind that the ship is a tipping environment, and they many cruise lines have now started to add 15% gratuity on top of the regular fee for an activity.

Bars

The age of bars on most US ships is 21 and they are very careful about asking for ID if need be. Some ships I have been on have a rule that no entertainers can sit at the bar itself. These are reserved only for passengers. Always check out these types of rules <u>before</u> sitting down to have a drink.

Nightclubs

If you are a late night-person then the place to head to is the nightclub. These are often modern clubs with loud music and flashing lights where the party-goers head. I know of several magicians who enjoy going out at night and will often take a few close-up tricks and just hang out at the bars and nightclubs. Often there are theme nights such as 70's night or Rock'n' Roll night. These are way to loud and smoky for me, also, I'm not a big drinker so I very rarely go to the nightclubs.

Cinema

Ships are a great place to catch up on the latest movie. Because I travel so much, most of the latest movies I see are on ships. This always causes a problem when my wife and I are at home together, and we want to rent the latest video. After all, I've everything at sea! Nowadays, on the larger ships, they have a cinema 'under the stars', so you can lay out at night with your popcorn and watch a movie on the large "outdoor" screen while wrapped in a blanket ... very cool. The only problem with so much of these 'new' ideas of entertainment is that it they are taking people away from the live shows.

Casinos

Modern on board casinos boast the latest games and tables. Again, always check the rules for Guest Entertainers as some lines will not allow entertainers to gamble, or if they do you can only play certain games. This also includes Bingo and such games.

Spas

The spas on board ships today are incredible. Specially-trained professionals offer a full range of hairdressing and beauty treatments. You can have everything from a haircut to a full body massage while wrapped up in seaweed with hot rocks on top of you. If you are transshipping a lot (i.e. flying from one ship to another) and you that find your muscles get tired and sore, then nothing can beat a good massage. On the ship I am currently sailing on, they even have those 'massage' chairs you see at airports. I find that with all the traveling and lifting that I do, even a chair massage goes a long way in relaxing me. Again, check out crew-related discounts in the spa. If you mention you are a Guest Entertainer you will often get a discount, however, it usually only applies on port days, not days while the ship is at sea.

Services within the spa include: Hairdressing, coloring, foot and nail services, facial treatments, synergistic and aromatherapy treatments, thalassotheraphy, slimming treatments and even hair removal and teeth whitening!

Dance Classes

The ship is a great place to learn how to dance. Whether you're an old pro, or you have two left feet, ships have trained dance teachers who will teach you the latest steps. These are usually held on days when you are not in port.

Dentistry

Some cruise lines such as Holland America have a dental professional on each ship. If you want a brighter smile, they also have the facilities and the expertise to complete a professional whitening procedure.

Swimming Pools

Indoor, pools, outdoor pools, jacuzzis, hot tubs ... you name it, ships will have it. I am always conscious of making sure I am not in a crowded area if sunbathing and I tend to enjoy swimming during a time of day when most people are getting ready for dinner, when it's not so crowded.

Laundry and Dry Cleaning

Again, this varies from cruise line to cruise line, something you will need to check. Ships are equipped with passenger laundries where you can do your own washing. However be warned ... they can be dangerous. Many comedians joke about going to the laundry room and seeing fights and arguments as passengers try to get hold of a washing machine or dryer.

Depending on the ship, you might be allowed to use the officers' or crew's laundry room, which is not be so bad, but always check to make sure you have this privilege. If you wish, you can send your laundry out for cleaning, then Guest Entertainers are charged at the crew rate for their laundry and dry cleaning. Again, check the regulations for the cruise line that you are to be working for.

Communications

I have touched on e-mail and phones, but you can also send postcards via the ship's front desk, as well as change currency and take out cash from a credit card. They will take your postcard and charge it to your account. Prior to leaving the port the postcards are handed to the Port Agent who will take them ashore and mail them off. For larger items, I always prefer to find a post office in the port and mail them myself.

Discounts

This varies from cruise line to cruise line, so again, either ask your agent or check the Guest Entertainer Manual of your specific cruise line for the discounts you are allowed. The general rule for most ships is that there is a 25% bar discount for Guest Entertainers and a 20% discount in the boutique shops on board. At the end of each cruise when you get your bill, make sure that the discounts have been taken off the final account. It has happened on so many occasions where the final discount was wrong, or simply not taken off. For whatever reason these days, the bills are always wrong and most Guest Entertainers have to end up going down to the reception at the end of a cruise to sort the problem out. I believe that the problems on ships are often due to simple lack of communication between departments!

There are the top-end cruise lines where you don't have to pay for any drinks at the bar, but that is the minority. As mentioned earlier, there is also a 21-year minimum age requirement for purchasing alcohol on most cruise lines. Everything you purchase is put on to your account so ships are a cashless society. However, I always take a few dollar bills on board, and leave them as tips.

Medical
In most cases the company does not provide medical coverage and I strongly recommend that you arrange your own medical, health and life insurance plan. In my contract it states that in the event of illness or injury during the term of the contract, Guest Entertainers agree to look exclusively to their medical and health insurers for payment of medical benefits and cannot, in any way, hold the cruise line company liable for such payments.

Visits to the ship's doctor can be very expensive which is why medical insurance is important, especially when traveling overseas. If your are placed on the crew list, then more often that not, a visit to the doctor will not cost anything. In such cases, if they want you to get an injection, such as Yellow Fever or the Flu Injection, then they will not charge. It all depends on the particular doctor that you have and the ship's policy.

Ships generally have one physician, two registered nurses and a crew physician. While not a full-service hospital, the infirmary is well-equipped to handle most emergencies, as well as routine medical procedures. If you happen to get ill during the voyage and the physician is unable to care for your needs on board, you will be transferred to medical facilities on shore. In the even on an emergency, the infirmary does include an Intensive Care Unit, equipped with cardiac monitoring equipment.

Many common prescription medications are available through the ship's dispensary. Meclizine for seasickness, Tylenol and aspirin.

Security Awareness
Security on board cruise ships has become high priority after 9/11. I was actually on a cruise ship, having just left New York, the day before 9/11 and the majority of our passengers were from New York. It was one of the hardest cruise assignments I have ever had to do, simply because everybody wanted to get back to New York. However, all flights and ports were closed, so we ended up heading to Boston. That is one cruise I will never forget.

Cruise ships now have MARSEC (Maritime Security) Levels 1, 2 and 3. These are different levels of importance that show the threat level to a ship or other Maritime interest. There are 3 levels of maritime security. Each level must be responded to by specific security plans. I will discuss what you might expect, because some magicians may carry knives and/ or guns for their act. If you do, then you <u>will</u> be searched and they weapons may be taken from you!

Level 1
<u>Status</u>: Normal operating conditions
<u>Plan</u>: Maintain security measures
- Control of access to the ship.
- Screen all individuals and all items they carry, for weapons and other dangerous devices.
- Designation of Restricted Areas.
- Screen of ship's stores and luggage.
- Monitor the entire security of the ship.

Level 2
<u>Status</u>: Heightened/increased risk of a security incident.
<u>Plan</u>: Increase security measures.
(Level 2, continued)
- Increase security patrol.
- Increase access controls.

- Increase over-the-side lighting, so that the areas along the sides of the ship are fully illuminated.
- Increase screening of individual people, luggage and stores.
- Increase restrictions for visitors.

Level 3
Status: Probability of an act of terrorism
Plan: Maximize security measures
- Launch continuous security patrols.
- Over-the-side lighting in all areas.
- Underwater inspections.
- Visitors refused on board.
- Security searches of the ship.
- Post a trained personnel at all entrances to restricted areas.
- Stop the loading of stores.

Relationships
As a Guest Entertainer, we really do have the best life on a ship. I wanted to add the following section in to give you a better idea of what happens on ships in regards to other people and their views about Guest Entertainers.

When I first started out, I was single, and while not a big party person or a big drinker, I would occasionally go to the crew bar or be invited to the officers *mess*. The officers mess is where they eat on board a ship. The crew mess is where the crew eat, and the food there can be quite disgusting. Life on board a ship is very different than life on land. The best comparison I can come up with is that it is like going back to high school.

You find out very quickly that people gossip, spread rumors and everybody knows everybody else's business! My main rule is simply NOT TO GET INVOLVED. I keep a slight distance, although I am always friendly and talk to other crew members. However, I learned very quickly that it is best to remain professional at all times, and keep your business to yourself.

This is only my personal opinion. I know several magicians and other entertainers who enjoy going to the crew bar to mix and mingle and chat. I have made many friends on ships over the years, but I chose not to go to the crew bar. Remember that the waiters and cabin staff who see you in the crew bar will then have to serve you.

You will quickly discover that some entertainers can be very demanding. When this applies to your show I understand why, because the company is paying you a good salary and you want to do your very best. However, the problem comes when the entertainer starts demanding a better cabin, and that they are *above* everybody else. I am here to tell you that we are ALL on the ship to do a job! My rule is simple, have respect for other crew members on the ship and they will have respect for you!

Generally, you will find that departments tend to hang out together, such as the "shoppies," the salon people and even the entertainers. One of the highlights of cruising for me is meeting other great entertainers and hanging out over dinner, swapping stories about the business.

It does have it's downside in that you cannot be home for long periods, but this can be worked out. My one piece of advice is to have a project on board to do, such as write, work out in the gym with a goal in mind, or work on some new effects for your act. Make the most of your downtime on the ship.

The Crew Bar
This again is different on every ship. In most cases you can not go to the crew bar because crew areas are out of bounds. There are some ships where you are allowed to visit the crew bar. The crew bar is a place where the crew head to relax, get very cheap drinks and they often have theme nights where you can dance the night away. As mentioned earlier, always check to see if, as a Guest Entertainer, you are allowed to visit the crew bar. This is one of the few places where you can really let your hair down and mingle with other crew members.

As a Guest Entertainer, you can use the passenger bar if you want to mix with other Guest Entertainers or passengers. Some staff members are allowed to use various passenger bars, so you can always arrange to meet them there.

Make the most of the fact you are traveling to amazing ports. Get outside, do your own thing, get involved in being an escort on tours which will help you to see amazing sights. The biggest privilege is that as Guest Entertainers we are able to get off the ship during the day, and visit the most incredible ports. Rather than get caught up in the 'ship' lifestyle, take advantage of the fact that you are on a luxury liner traveling to these wonderful places.

As Guest Entertainers we have more privileges than most staff, my advice is not to abuse them! Keep in mind that you are a guest on the ship, and that you represent the cruise line, so people will be observing you and your behavior.

It can get very cold in Ushuaia

CHAPTER THREE

THINGS YOU NEED TO KNOW

From Greece to France to Italy ... ah, the life of a cruise ship magician!

CRUISE SHIP JOB DESCRIPTIONS
The following are non-Guest Entertainer cruise jobs. It is important that you are aware of what each person in the entertainment department does.

Cruise Director
The Cruise Director is responsible for all on board entertainment. This position involves supervising and scheduling staff within the Entertainment department, as well as administrative duties. The Cruise Director also serves as the Master of Ceremonies for many activities. In the past few years, the job has evolved to more of an administrative position (especially on the bigger ships).

Assistant Cruise Director (ACD)

The Assistant Cruise Director assists the Cruise Director in all of his/her responsibilities: coordinates passengers' activities programs, supervises Cruise Staff, etc. He/she is expected to socialize with passengers and participate in on board activities. Quite often, the ACD is the main liaison between Guest Entertainers and the Cruise Director.

Cruise Staff / Activity Staff

Cruise Staff members are expected to socialize with passengers, play games, dance, call bingo numbers, get passengers involved in social and entertainment activities, and provide customer service. On occasion, they may be called on to escort shore excursions in the various ports of call.

Youth Staff

The Youth Staff is on board to organize the time of the junior cruisers on board (ages of 3 -17). The Youth Staff does this through sports, games, activities and more. Youth Staff have to be fun and outgoing, and definitely need previous experience working with children!

Disc Jockey (DJ)

Strong knowledge of various music genres from all decades is required. Microphone/MC skills and experience is also required, as well as an outgoing, and very lively personality! The DJ may also be required to handle some cruise staff activities.

Stage Manager

The Stage Manager is responsible for all aspects of the main theater and all shows therein. Their duties include scheduling, running shows, and supervising the performers and technicians on board the ship.

Sound Technician

The sound technicians are typically required to run complete audio, including set up and mixing on a professional sound console in the main theater for all shows and performances.

Lighting Technician

This is the lighting controller for all shows on the ships. This person typically needs in-depth experience, though it is not always required. Must have troubleshooting skills, programming knowledge as well as repair and maintenance skills.

Stage Staff

Assists backstage in whatever way necessary. Entry-level position, which in many cases paves the way for sound and/or lighting tech positions. Some theater knowledge is required.

Requirement of Shows

Each cruise line will have different show requirements for their Guest Entertainers. what I offer is simply a guideline –

Length and number of shows

I checked the guidelines in the manual for the cruise line that I work on, and they state that a minimum repertoire of two distinctively different thirty minute, and one fifteen minute show is required. On longer cruises it may be necessary to perform three of four different thirty minute shows. On the ships I work, I have never done two different thirty minute shows, rather one full forty five minute show, and a split show with another act, or two different forty five minute shows. On the cruise I am on at the moment, as I am writing this book, I am performing two different forty five minute shows, and one close-up show. The close-up show was something that I suggested to the cruise director, as it gives me another chance to push my DVD's, plus I thoroughly enjoy performing close-up magic.

How many shows you are required to perform depends entirely on the length of cruise. If you are doing the short seven day cruises then more often that not you will only be required to do one full forty five minute show, as well as another show, thus sharing the bill with another act. On the longer cruises of say twenty four days, you can be assured that you will need to do two different full forty five minute shows. This requires a lot of work, and it is important that your second show is as strong as your first.

I was on a cruise ship recently where the contract said I needed to do six different twenty five minute shows in three weeks. I told my agent that I didn't have that many different shows so he was able to contact the cruise line and they said that what I had was enough. Prior to taking a contract, make sure you have enough material, if you don't then let them know. The worst thing is to accept a contract that requires more work than you can do, and turn up and then have to let them know you don't have enough material. This doesn't play well with the cruises directors.

Speaking from experience I prefer just to do my one main forty five minute show, as it contains all my number one material, rather than try and split it up between two shows. After experimenting with my act I realized how important it is to make sure your first show is very strong. In this way people will talk about you, get to know you and come back for your second show. You will hear other entertainers say they have an A and a B show, in my opinion if you want a long career in Cruising make sure both your shows are A material. If you can do a close-up show, then by all means mention it to the cruise director as it all helps in the long run, keeping your name in front of the passengers when they fill in their comment cards.

The general rule of thumb is that you will do your main forty five minute show twice in one night. So be prepared!

Your schedule
Your schedule will vary from ship to ship and from cruise to cruise. Generally speaking, on a seven day cruise you will be required to work one night with your main act. This you will do twice, once at the early show, usually 8:30pm, and the other at 10:30pm for two different audiences. On the larger ships they are now getting us to work more, so we will work one night with the two shows, then repeat the show again the next night for the crowds who missed it. The large ships now carry up to 2,800 passengers so you are required to perform an extra show. On

the seven day cruise you may also be asked to perform an extra ten to fifteen minute spot on the last night, along with other Guest Entertainers

Because I have two different full forty five minute acts plus the close-up show, I tend to get the longer runs which also means the better contracts where the ships travel to more exotic locations around the world. It makes sense to keep me on a ship longer as I can do two different nights of entertainment and the close-up show on a sea day. However, having said that, next week I will be leaving the ship I have been on for three months and transshipping to another ship for a little over a week where I will be on during the last part of the cruise, and during the beginning of a new one. Then I will fly to join another ship for a little over a week, then fly to another ship for only one night's performance before flying home. Unfortunately, there is no set rule for how many times you will perform and you usually only find out when you arrive on board the ship. My advice is to make sure that you are prepared before launching your cruise ship career, otherwise it will be short-lived, and chances of getting re-booked will be very slim.

There somehow seems to be an invisible network amongst the Entertainment department in the cruise ship industry, and word travels fast. If you do something negative for one cruise line, another line will certainly hear about it, and may cancel your bookings. Remember that Carnival cruises owns about 70% of the cruise industry including: Carnival Cruise Lines, Windstar Cruises, Cunard Lines, Holland America Line, Princess Cruises, Costa Cruises and The Yachts of Seabourne. That is a huge market and the entertainment department is now overlapping with these companies, as they all come under one umbrella. You can't afford to get a bad name in the cruise industry.

Performance Material
I have always made sure that my material was never 'adult' orientated or 'blue', unless asked to do the midnight show – in which case you can perform routines that are a little more adult orientated. Make sure you find out the demographics of the cruise line that you will be working for. Because of my Charlie Chaplin act, they tend to put me on longer

cruises, which suits me fine because they have the better travel itineraries.

There is a joke amongst entertainers when asked the average age of the passengers they say, "between dead and deceased!" I am currently on a twenty four day cruise as I write this, and the average age is sixty plus. On the shorter cruises, such as those in the Caribbean, you will find the average age much lower with children traveling. One of my good friends works for a cruise line where he is required to do a thirty minute family orientated show and a thirty minute midnight adult show, so he obviously has his material suited for each of those those audiences.

According to marketing data, the cruise ship attracts a vacationing crowd from a cross-section of North America, the UK and sprinkles of other nationalities. Therefore, your material will need to be of an international appeal. I have appeared on cruise ships where the majority of passengers didn't speak English. Magicians at least have a sleight advantage over comedians in that we have the visual aspect of our shows to help help address conditions. I was hired on one cruise to do my Chaplin show, because the ship of 2,800 passengers were all Korean and they had hired the ship for an Am-way conference!

My advice, in this regard, is very simple. Choose material for your act that is suitable for all ages.

Music for the act
You have the ability to work with a live band on the ship. If you plan on working on ships a great deal you may wish to utilize this lost resource although the way things are changing the option of having a 'live' band is becoming less available. There was a time, when working on ships, that my advice would have been if you currently use no music at all, consider the use of the live band on the ship. However, with cut backs these days, don't rely on having the luxury of a back up band! As a backup I would have all my music on CD, mini disk or ipod.

Some of the music acts obviously require the band or orchestra to back them and in such cases, they bring their own musical arrangements. The more self-reliant you are in your act, the more you will keep working. There was a time when ships kept two different orchestras on ships, one for the main show lounge and the other for the smaller lounges where most of the variety acts worked. When I give the Production Manager my music, s/he gets a mini-disk and a CD of it, just in case something happens during the show and a machine breaks down. This I tell you from experience, because it HAS happened! If you use a video montage in your show, as I do, make sure you have the sound track on CD as a back-up as well.

Nowadays, I travel with my laptop, which makes life so much easier for me. If I need to change the show in any way, I can easily record a new audio CD of my show and everything is in order so the production manager isn't skipping from one music track to another. I like to make everything as easy as possible so I can concentrate on my performance rather than worry about technical aspects of the show going wrong. Remember also that you may be transshipping (going from one ship to another) and often have little rehearsal time. Therefore, having cue sheets and your music all in order will make for much smoother sailing.

Cue Sheets

Always have your cue sheets ready to give the production manager. These will include any music cues and lighting cues. You will always get time to rehearse and this will be the time to go over any cues. The stages on the ships today are incredible and have everything.

Also, be sure to prepare cue sheets for light and sound technicians. Early upon your arrival on the ship the stage manager will contact you. He or she will want to know what special requirements you need and how much rehearsal time to schedule. You should be familiar with your technical requirements. Talk to him about the kind of lighting and sound you need and any backstage help you will require. At rehearsal you should be able to supply written cue sheets that explain how and when all the technical things happen during your act. For recorded music I use a programmable mini-disc unit. If you use recorded music I recommend that you put it on the highest quality playback method you can. If you use extensive and complex lighting, I recommend you bring DVD of your act to show the lighting technician how you'd like it to look. Light fixtures change from place to place, but the same mood and affect can be created from various sources. In the resource section at the back of this book you will find an example of a cue sheet I use.

Live animals

Some acts do use live animals on ships, to do this you need to get pre-approved by head office of the cruise line you are working for so they can sort out the paper work well in advance. To travel with livestock is the responsibility of the Guest Entertainer.

Theater Conduct

It is important that you are familiar with stage *deportment*; how to enter, exit, and take a curtain call. This is all part of professionalism, and basic theater 101. First impressions matter, but never more than when you are on stage. During the first 30 seconds, your audience will size you up. They make judgments about you that will color their attitudes about what you do. The first moments are critical. You need to strategically decide how you will present yourself immediately upon your introduction.

Likewise you should give careful consideration to the end of your act. How will you finish? How will you exit the stage? Cruise ship shows all have emcees, so you will be called back to the stage for a bow.

Usually, an act will finish their last routine and take a bow as the MC announces the act's name. The band will play a quick and bouncy piece of music as the performer walks off stage. The emcee will then ask the audience to "call the performer back," with another round of applause. At this point the entertainer walks back to the stage to receive the applause.

The theaters on cruise ships today are more equipped than most theaters on land, with the latest sound equipment, lighting and video equipment. Try and view your act as theater and make use of all the technology available to you. In my act I use a video montage to introduce my Chaplin act. I have also performed close-up magic on the main stage and had it projected behind me on a large video screen. On a cruise you will be expected to know how conduct yourself and your act in a real theater setting. This is not always something a magician that is used to working solo is familiar with.

You will be required to deal with other professionals like the an emcee, stage manager, sound engineer, light technician, orchestra leader and other professional entertainers that you will share the stage and dressing room with. You should know stage terminology, blocking and what light designs you will need. If all this is foreign to you, get some experience before trying the ship market.

Contract

A Guest Entertainer Independent Contractor Agreement will be issued each time a Guest Entertainer is contracted to work on board. The contract should be reviewed carefully and signed accordingly. The contract will specify how much money you are being paid on a weekly basis and your travel dates. Contracts will vary, in all cases if I am on a ship for less than a week, I still get paid a full weeks wage. If I am on for eight days then I will get paid 'pro-rata' that is, eight days pay.

You will also get a *joining* letter. This letter will come in useful when passing through immigration, as they may ask to see it. Quite often when traveling through US immigration I am taken into another room while immigration officials confirm with the cruise line that I will be actually joining the ship. This contractual agreement will also specify your flight details, the port agent details of the country you will be flying to, and your return flight. There are times when you don't get your return flight until you are on board. Always have a copy of your contract and boarding agreement with you. You will need to show the boarding agreement to the security officer when you get to the gangway on the ship. At the end of the book, under references, I have included a sample contract.

Contract Payment

Each company differs on their pay system. There was a time when I would be paid on the ship on a bimonthly basis, but this is no longer the case. In my case my agent gets my money on the 15th and 30th of each month and he then transfers it to my account. I prefer this because then he can take out his commission and it saves me having to send him the money. I know there are still ships where they act gets paid on board and also some acts who have the money deposited directly in to their bank accounts. Your agent will let you know how they operate.

During a ship's dry-dock, refit, or maintenance period that falls within the duration of a contract, it is at the company's discretion to either pay the Guest Entertainer on a pro-rata basis or provide a round trip airfare to the Guest Entertainer's "home" airport and back to the ship. When I finish this contract next week the company is accommodating me for two nights in Gibraltar before I transship to another ship for a week. They will pay for my hotel, food and any travel while I am staying in port.
Guest Entertainers are paid for the day they embark the ship, but not for the day they disembark the ship. Travel days are not usually reimbursed unless otherwise agreed.

For US citizens the cruise line must report all earnings and a 1099 form will be issued at year end. All Guest Entertainers are responsible for payment of government taxes.

In my situation I am a non-resident of any country having left New Zealand almost six years ago on a full time basis, and so I am in the fortunate position of not paying tax. How this works, is that I am considered a non-resident, I no longer live in New Zealand, or any other country. I don't know how it works in other countries, but as long as I am away for more than six months a year from New Zealand, I can claim this status. I have set up a US bank account so that I can have a US visa which I find very handy when paying ship related accounts.

Cruise Director

While on board the ship, it is the Cruise Director who looks after the Guest Entertainers and is the person in charge of scheduling performers and putting together the daily 'newspaper', describing what times the activities will be. More often than not, it is the Cruise Director that will be introducing you, so have a very short and precise introduction prepared so that s/he can use it to bring you on stage. They don't like to read long winded introductions so my advice is to keep it short and simple. The cruise director is also the person who will be reporting back to head office about your act and how it was received. You will never really know what the Cruise Director is thinking, and in my time on ships I think I have come across the best and the worst.

You get the Cruise Directors who are very professional and genuinely care about their Guest Entertainers, yet on the other hand you get those that don't care at all. In one case, I had a Cruise Director who didn't even bother to turn up and introduce me, so I had to do it myself AND take myself off stage. The next night he never showed up and so another Guest Entertainer introduced the act. Without a doubt the worst Cruise Director I have ever worked for, was just plain lazy and didn't care. When I approached him on the matter his comment was *"I could get more money working at McDonalds"* ... I told him maybe he should go there and work instead. I made a noise complaint one night, because there were parties next door in the cabins every night going on until three in the morning. This went on for almost two weeks until I complained. We had the dancers in the hallway and none of the guest acts could sleep. When I complained, the Cruise Director told me not to hassle his dancers, then I found out that HE was the one holding the parties!!! Sometimes you can't win.

In short, I try to keep out of the Cruise Director's way. I simply go on, do my job, be polite and that is it. They do have a very busy life on a ship and they run a large department, so as little hassle from Guest Entertainers makes their lives that much easier.

Dress Code

One of the advantages of being a Guest Entertainer is that we have passenger status while on the ship, allowing us into public areas where other crew members are not allowed. We get to mix and mingle with passengers and over the years you will keep meeting the repeat passengers and you can develop some very nice relationships. On ships, keep in mind that they usually have dress codes, such as semi-formal and formal nights. You are still employed by the cruise line, and like being employed in any job you are an ambassador for the company, therefore you are expected to adhere to the dress code for the evening and also dress in a neat and appropriate manner during daytime hours.

On formal nights, most men will wear tuxedos and the ladies are dressed in evening gowns. On other nights, I always wear a dress shirt and dress pants.

Casual: No shorts, tank tops, swim-wear or workout attire.
Informal: Sports jacket for men.
Formal: Jacket and tie for men. Tuxedo suggested. In some ports of call, due to cultural differences, tank tops or shorts worn by women in public is considered inappropriate.

Electricity

Cabins are equipped with standard 110v (North American) outlets and 220v (European), accommodating your appliances brought from home. Always bring an adapter just in case you need it for your electrical equipment.

Gratuities

You are expected to pay gratuities to your cabin steward at passenger rates at the end of the cruise. This is generally $3.50 per day if you are in a passenger cabin. On some ships where we are in staff areas then the gratuities are slightly less because they only come in once a day and you won't get the full service that you would if you were stationed in a passenger area.

If you eat in the dining room then you must tip your waiter and busboy. As a rule, if I chose to eat in the dining room I always tip after my meal. However, this isn't very often, as I usually eat in the Buffet or Bistro area.

On the ships now they often have an automatic charge of $10 per person per day gratuity added to your bill. As a Guest Entertainer you do not have to pay this unless you chose to. This is what the passengers pay and it covers all gratuities including the dining room. As I mentioned above, I never eat in the dining room and so only my cabin steward gets a gratuity. If we chose to eat in another restaurant on the ship, rather than the buffet, then of course we leave a tip.

Dining

You are allowed to dine in the passenger dining room and in the buffets. Still, priority to passengers must always be observed. Usually the maitre D' will often have a special table put aside for Guest Entertainers, although on several ships they have placed us with passengers. There are usually two main sittings, one at 6pm and the other at 8:15pm. Nowadays, on the modern ships, they promote open dining so you no longer have to have a seating assignment. Also with the larger ships there is much more choice of dining from 24/7: Lido, Pizzeria, Italian Restaurants, Chinese Restaurants and even a Steak House! Of course, each ship differs with their range of restaurants. On the larger ships there will be a cover charge in some restaurants. For example, the steak house charges $20.00 per meal, while the Italian restaurant charges $25.00 per meal. All crew and passengers pay the same amount to go to these speciality restaurants.

On vessels with alternate dining facilities, a cover charge will be charged to all staff, Guest Entertainers, and officers, which is usually no more than $2.00. When you join a ship, ask if there is a list which outlines the various charges, or ask another Guest Entertainer who can tell you. Dining in the Officers' Mess is by invitation only.

Money Matters

A ship is a "cashless society", making cruise life as simple as possible. Within 24 hours after boarding you must present a credit card (Visa, American Express, Master Card or Discover) to activate and for settlement of your account. You simply present your Guest ID Card and sign a receipt for each of your on board purchases. Another option is to give a $100 cash deposit rather than give the ship your credit card details. You will need to leave something in order to use make purchases on board or use the internet.

You may also deposit cash or travelers checks' in advance to cover your purchases. Travelers Checks may be cashed at the Front Office. Some ships also offer cash advance services. This means that guests can draw up to $1000 in cash, per day, against their activated credit cards.

Photographers

As a magician on board a ship, there are plenty of photo opportunities. Thus, ship's photographers can prove to be a great asset. Often, they will give you a special price or discount on photos. They can produce a very professional 8 x 10 promotional photo. Photographers are always around the ship taking photos, and if you have a digital camera they can even put your photos on to a disk or other media format. I always update my promotional photos on the ship as the quality is just as good as you would get on land, and at a much better price!

Passports and Visas

In order to work legally on board a ship, you must be in possession of a valid and current passport effective beyond your term of contract. In the majority of cases you will also be responsible for ascertaining whether an entrance visa is required and for acquiring this special document. The same will apply for any inoculation requirements. I always check with my agent who can contact head office to find out if I need a Visa to enter a country or not.

I remember my very first contract in Brazil, when I didn't have the correct Visa. I flew from Vancouver, Canada to Houston, then over to

Miami, then waited eight hours at the airport before flying to Rio. Once I arrived I was taken aside by immigration and kept for eleven hours in a small room where nobody was able to tell me what was going on, as they didn't speak any English. They just left me there, with me thinking I was heading to jail for not having the right documents. It wasn't until I saw an airline steward walk past, who spoke English, that I was able to understand the situation and get help in order to purchase a ticket back to Miami! Once I got to Miami I phoned the emergency number at the cruise line's head office and explained what had happened. This put them at ease since they wondered why I never turned up on board the ship, and had been missing for a few days. In response, they reimbursed me for all of my travel and hotel expenses, and were able to route me to another port where a visa wasn't necessary.

If you are planning on making a career from working on cruise ships, then I highly recommend getting a 'Seaman's Book.' This will prove that you are working steadily on ships, and also in some cases provide you withe extra baggage allowance. It also makes it much easier in some cases when you need to apply for a visa. The company I work for currently will be making it mandatory that every Guest Entertainer obtain a *Seaman's Discharge* book. You should certainly speak to your agent about getting one and they can look up where to apply for them.

Note about Visas:

India visa – For those living in the U.K., it is no longer possible to obtain a same day visa for India at the embassy in London, nor the consulates in Birmingham and Edinburgh. It now takes a minimum of three working days to receive the visa, so acts either need to apply by post (takes longer) or go to London, Birmingham or Edinburgh and be prepared that they will not receive the visa and passport back for at least three working days.

Check passport expiry dates as many airlines and countries for example will not allow a passport holder to fly or enter the country if the passport is due to expire within 6 months.

Seaman's Books and Brazil – For those on ships heading to Brazil the cruise lines often ask that the act possess a UK Seamans Book (Bermudan or Bahamian Book may suffice but UK is the one they often ask about first) as there have been instances before when Brazilian authorities have gone on board and found acts on the passenger lists, and they have discovered that they are actually on the ship in a working capacity, at which point the Seamans Books can avoid problems for the individual and the cruise line. It can be obtained by post or in person through various port agencies in the UK, details on the application form from this link :

http://www.mcga.gov.uk/c4mca/rss-cd-form-msf4509.pdf

A seaman's book has also got many an act out of scrapes with airlines when checking in with extra luggage, so all in all is worth the time and expense to obtain, especially at a time when the cruise lines budgets don't allow them to pre-purchase extra luggage all the time. The attached link is for acts who have a contract in place with UK registered vessels, i.e. on Fred Olsen or Saga (or maybe Carnival UK Group now as well, based in Southampton who look after QV and QM2) so if you are going to Brazil on a cruise line based in US we will ask them if they can apply for the book on behalf of the act, as this has been arranged before. Acts also need to produce a yellow fever certificate if going to Brazil, and the inoculation needs to be in the system at least 10 days before the act goes to Brazil, so again it is something that should be updated with a booster injection if the act has a few days of free time between contracts to utilize.

Visas for USA and Australia. As well as visas for the likes of India, China and Vietnam, be careful because Australia and the USA can catch people out. Many acts get caught out not realizing that non-residents of Australia or New Zealand passport holders need to obtain two visas for Australia. Both of which can be obtained online at:
www.uk.embassy.gov.au

The first is the ETA – Electronic Travel Authority, a tourist visa basically, valid for one year and allows passport holders to enter and re-enter Australia as many times as they like, as long as never there for more than 90 days at a time. The second came into being in January 2008 and is the MCV – Maritime Crew Visa – and is required for any act working on a ship that enters Australian waters, if they do not possess an Australian or New Zealand passport. Again it can be applied for online at :

http://www.immi.gov.au/sea/mcv/index.htm

and is valid for three years, free of charge and takes about 48-72 hours to come back with a 13 digit reference number.

USA - from 12 January 2009 all passport holders heading to United States to stay, or simply in transit, must complete ESTA – details pasted below but in a nutshell it is not a visa as such, but it will be mandatory. It only needs to be done once rather than for each visit to the States, and needs to be done at least 72 hours before you fly.

Apply for the Visa on line - www.esta.cbp.dhs.gov

ESTA and Travel Authorization

ESTA is short for Electronic System for Travel Authorization. ESTA is an application system for all travelers from Visa Waiver Countries only. The Visa Waiver Program has made visiting the United States very easy for millions of visitors with a machine readable passport. Now the same visitors must apply for a Travel Authorization in advance in addition to have a machine readable passport or e-passport. The application process is online and operated by the U.S. Department of Homeland Security. The Travel Authorization is not a visa. In fact, a person from a non-visa waiver country should not even attempt to apply for a Travel Authorization. The purpose of ESTA is to let DHS pre-screen all Visa Waiver Travelers before they leave their respective countries. US bound travelers are recommended to apply for the Travel Authorization at least 72 hours prior to departure. An approved Travel Authorization is not a guaranteed entry, but a prerequisite to travel to the United States by air or sea carrier.

Advantages of applying for a Travel Authorization before it becomes mandatory:

- Know that you are approved to travel to the United States.
- Know that your personal data is cross checked against a number of U.S. official databases but without any findings.
- The Travel Authorization is valid for two years and can easily be updated for future visits.
- If denied, you will have ample time to apply for a B-1 Visitor Visa or B-2 Tourist Visa.

Who needs to apply for a Travel Authorization?

- Any traveler that intends to visit the United States under the Visa Waiver Program via air or vessel.
- Any traveler transiting through the United States under the Visa Waiver Program.

Any traveler also includes children and infants who visits/transits on the Visa Waiver Program.

When should you apply for a Travel Authorization?

- It is currently voluntarily to apply for a Travel Authorization
- After January 12, 2009 all travelers must be approved to travel to the United States via air or vessel.
- Travelers transiting through the United States must also possess an approved Travel Authorization after January 12, 2009.
- If your application for a Travel Authorization is denied, you must apply for a B-1 Visitor Visa or B-2 Tourist Visa which can take weeks or months.

Advice for Obtaining Visas Quickly: There are now companies that specialize in getting visas and passports quickly, they charge a nominal fee and it is worth every cent. I had to wait over six weeks once to get a visa in my passport to go to Brazil, and by the time they came back I had missed a weeks work on the ship. That is when I learned there are companies in most major cities that can speed up the application process.

Be sure to check these companies out and get them to arrange the necessary documents.

Performance Appraisals

The Cruise Director will regularly submit written performance appraisals on the Guest Entertainer and these will be placed on file for future reference. The appraisals, along with passenger comment cards will determine whether or not a future contract will be offered.

Cruise lines also get passengers to fill in comment cards and some even specify individual acts. If you fail to keep above a certain average on the comment cards then they will start looking for another act. That's right, it can be that tough on some of the high-end cruise lines!

I have always wondered how this feedback system would work in the real world, in hotels and theaters where the audiences had to fill in comment cards after they see a particular show. Remember also, that many passengers are *repeat cruisers* who have *seen it all* and *done it all*, or so they seem to think. So, if you seek longevity in the field of cruise ship entertainment, it is important to try keep your act novel and <u>highly</u> entertaining.

Sales of DVDs and Other Products

This can prove to be a very lucrative side-line if you have a DVD or product(s) for sale. I sell my own DVD on the ship for a set price, which can vary from cruise line to cruise line. If you have a product to sell then you must check with your agent to see how to go about selling it on the ships. My suggestion is to create something to sell because it is a great *passive* income. As a side note, I have set up a company called *Magic Master Class* where we sell a generic DVD where you can purchase a magic teaching DVD and burn as many copies as you like and design and print your own covers to make it unique to you. To find out more email me at paul@chaplinmagic.com or visit www.paulromhany.com

In most cases, Guest Entertainers usually sell their products through the gift shop only. To do this you usually have to:-

1. Submit a sample for approval to the Entertainment Department prior to any sales.
2. The gift shop will <u>not</u> accept CDs or DVDs for sale until they have received authorization from cruise line head office.
3. All products must be of a professional quality and appearance.
4. Direct sales of products to passengers is <u>not</u> permitted.
5. Promotional displays of CDs and DVDs are only permitted in the Gift Shop. Therefore, they may not be displayed in public rooms, on pianos, etc.
6. At this time of writing, the cruise line I work for has a fixed price for CDs which is usually $15.00, and $20.00 for DVDs.

How to Pitch Your Product

You will be amazed at the amount of performers who have one or more products to sell. There are a few key ways to pitch your products to passengers, the most obvious is during your performance or having the cruise director pitch it to passengers after your show. People always want to take something home as a memento of their cruise, and on board ship you literally have a captive audience. The best cruises to sell products on, are usually the shorter cruises. This is because every seven days your audience changes, giving you more people to pitch your product to.

During the show, it helps to give away one DVD to a person who assists you on stage. In my show I have two people on stage and I always give away one DVD and a bottle of wine, supplied by the Cruise Director. I have spoken to others on the theory of 'giving' away your DVD during your show and some feel that giving it away makes the product 'less valuable' in the public's mind. Why should they pay $20.00 for the DVD if the performer is *giving* it away ... is it worth the $20.00? The best to determine the most effective approach, is to simply experiment until you find the best way for you to make more sales.

Contrary to general policy, some ships I am able to stand at the back of the theater with a table set up, selling my DVD after the show. This always results in more sales. To do this, make an arrangement with the gift shop, who take a percentage of the sales, and I also make sure to tip the sales assistant who helps me 'man' the tables and sell the DVD's.

During the close-up show that I do on board, I also pitch my products. I even perform one of the effects on the DVD and talk briefly about the DVD and what is on it. I know of one act who has a TV and DVD set up in the gift shop and runs his DVD non-stop.

Travel/Excess Baggage
Guest Entertainers provide and pay for their own transportation to and from the ship, unless air transportation is required. So from your home to the airport you have to cover the travel costs as well as from the airport to your home. As a general rule, the cruise line will provide round-trip air transportation from a major airport, where the ship is docked, nearest the Guest Entertainer, to the point of departure. For those living outside the US, individual air transportation arrangements will be agreed upon and arranged.

As mentioned, as a Guest Entertainer, you will provide and pay for transportation to and from the airport at the point of origin. (i.e from your home to the airport), and you will use the cruise line's passenger transportation between the airport and the ship when available. On your contract it should specify that you are to be picked up at the airport upon arrival, by the ship's agent. This agent will then take you to your hotel or to the ship, depending on when you arrive.

For certain ports of departure it may be necessary to arrange air travel the day before the ship's departure, in which case the cruise line company will provide hotel accommodation overnight in the appropriate port. Choice of accommodation is at the company's discretion. There have been instances where I have arrived at the airport with no port agent to pick me up, so I would secure my own taxi and find a hotel, nearby, being sure to keep the receipts and to give them to the Cruise Director, or send them to my agent. This is another reason I always make sure I know the port agent's phone and cell number, and the name, address and front desk phone number of the hotel where I will I staying in prior to joining the ship. Again this should be your agent's job to find out the necessary details. Having this valuable information can save you a lot of headaches when you are traveling.

In the case of the cruise company I currently work for, you must advise the company of any excess baggage and/or freight requirements at least thirty days prior to your contract commencement date - especially if you are performing large-scale illusions that need to be shipped prior to your departure. This excess baggage and freight *does not* include personal effects such as televisions, and DVD players etc.

You cannot leave any baggage, freight or personal effects on board at the end of your contract, without securing permission from the ship's Entertainment Department.

Also, it is important to note that the transfer of baggage and freight between vessels must first be approved by the entertainment department. I know, that with some cruise ship magicians, they are allowed to store their illusions on the ship, if they take a few week's break. This makes sense as it saves the company the additional cost of shipping them on and off. There have been instances where I have been engaged for a six month contract with a two week break in the middle, in such instances, rather than take everything off the ship, all my magic props I arrange with another act who is on board to keep one of my prop filled bags in their room.

Having professional flight cases for your magic can make life a lot easier for you when traveling, especially if you fly a lot between ships. The cases are designed to protect, and they sure show the scars for protecting all its precious contents. Most of my own cases are made by *Encore Cases*. The owner of Encore is a performer himself and understands my needs quite well. I recommend them to you. (www.encorecases.com)

Traveling with a Guest
One of the benefits of working on a cruise ship is that as a Guest Entertainer you are able to bring your own guest with you, be it your partner, wife, relative, etc.

Each cruise line has different rules and regulations regarding: whom you can bring on, for how long they can travel with you, and if there is a cost involved. I know some cruise lines that allow you to bring a guest on at no additional cost. The must of course, sleep in your cabin. On the line that I generally work for, there is a minimal per day fee of $15.00, plus any port taxes.

Below are a few of the rules and regulations that I was able to find in relation to bringing their own guest on board ship.

1) All guests of Guest Entertainers are required to sign a 'boarding agreement', waiving any and all claims indemnifying the company in regard to their travel.

2) Guest travel is a privilege and not a right. Do not discuss any financial arrangements of your guest's passage with other passengers.

3) Your role as a Guest Entertainer and the presence of fare-paying passengers must take precedence at all times and should not be allowed to interfere with the comfort of the passengers, nor should it interfere with the work routines of other staff.

4) Your guest will stay in your cabin accommodation.

5) Your guest should adhere to the passenger dress code and behave in accordance with the company's code of conduct. You don't want to get in trouble for any of your guest's behavior, this may get you fired! Just like yourself, your guest may enjoy the use of the public rooms, however, always keep in mind that the passengers are paying full fare for their cruise, so be sure to show some courtesy and common sense.

6) Guests share the same dining privileges on board as normally enjoyed by the Guest Entertainer. Thus, they take their meals in the ship's restaurant or in another dining area normally used by the Guest Entertainer.

7) At the end of each cruise, your guest should tip the normal gratuity to the cabin steward, at the recommended passenger rate.

8) In the case of the company I work for, ship discounts do not apply to the guests of Guest Entertainers. Instead, they are to pay full price at the bar and in the gift shops.

9) You are ultimately responsible for your guest on board ship, you must make sure that all bills are paid.

10) The company will not be liable for any medical costs incurred by guests. In this regard, I suggest that your guest always purchases medical insurance prior to boarding the ship. On many ships, they insist that your guest has *proof* of travel and medical insurance.

11) Each individual cruise line will have their own specific rule on what the minimum age a guest must be. In some cases you can bring your children, but for the company I work for, the minimum age limit is 18.

12) There is generally a cut-off date that applications must be sent to head office to enable your guest to board ship. You should be able to get a form for your guest to travel from your agent, who will get it directly from the cruise line. In some cases, applications not received thirty days prior to your ships departure, will not be accepted.

13) The company is not responsible for your guest's visas, passports, air transfers, or hotel arrangements.

14) The guest of a Guest Entertainer is usually not allowed to gamble on board a ship. Of course, if you are a "double act" and have an assistant, then they will be under contract (just as you are) and the company rules that apply to you will apply to them. You will be booked as a "double act" and share the same cabin. My advice is, if you want to travel with somebody, <u>make sure</u> you know them very well. Natalie always travels with me on longer contracts, and I wouldn't have it any other way. It's great to be able to share the wonderful and amazing experiences with

somebody so close to me, and she is a great help to me in relation to my shows, (both before and after).

Escort Tours

One of the advantages you have as a Guest Entertainer is that you can submit your name to serve as an escort on port tours. This is a great way to travel as it allows you to see some of the highlights of the various ports. During our own voyages, Natalie and I always like to escort tours out. To do this, all you need to do is introduce yourself to the 'tour manager', when you join the ship, and ask if they have a sign-up 'escort' book for tours. By signing up, you will get to the same ship's tours that passengers usually pay big money for - for free! The only job requirement is that you turn up half an hour early prior to the passengers on the morning, or on the afternoon of the tour, help the tour people get the passengers organized, then get on the bus with the passengers.

Keep in mind that you are not a tour guide, so you don't have to have any knowledge of the places you are visiting. Simply make sure the same amount of people that started the tour, finish the tour. I have had several cases where I have "lost" a person or two on the tour I escorted. In the majority of cases they didn't hear the meeting time to return to the bus, and have wandered off. I always make sure, with the official tour guide, that the "lost" person will be okay, and that somebody will be sure to find them. I have to admit that it is easy to get 'tour' burnout, due to the fact that you are dealing with passengers all the time, and that after a while you will feel the need to *do your own thing* in the many enchanted ports where your ship sets anchor.

We have done everything from swimming with sharks and stingrays, to snorkeling in some of the best waters in the world, to visiting the ancient wonders of Egypt - all at no extra cost! However, when you are on a ship for a lengthy contract, it makes it all worthwhile if you do a few of the ship's tours as an escort, because you can also get tired of just visiting cities and shopping malls after a while.

Do Your Homework

I am assuming that if you have bought this book, then you are interested in working on cruise ships and have started your research into this type of work. Before applying for cruise ship work make sure you know your act and the demographics that you believe your act is aimed towards. If you specialize in family entertainment, then look in to cruise lines that specialize in booking that type of performer, such as Disney Cruises. If you perform large illusions, then you will want to work on the larger ships that have the storage space to store such illusions and offer the larger theaters. The shorter cruises are what we call 'party' cruises and usually host first time cruisers, so you will need to know how to cater to these crowds. Know your act, know your limitations, and be prepared.

Get as much information about the various cruise lines as you can. Use the internet and look at the different types of ships that are available, most of them now have web sites which will provide you with a 360 degree view of the theater. Have a look at the brochures that are available from travel agents. Most importantly, make sure that you are ready <u>before</u> you embark on performing magic on cruise ships as a career.

I can't stress enough the importance of having enough material so that, if called upon, you can perform an extra show, or perform a close-up show or even an extra fifteen minute extra, spot if required. Your agent should be able to tell you what is required, but make sure you let them know exactly the length and type of show you perform. If you only have one show, then make sure your agent knows this. There is nothing worse than being booked, only to have the cruise director get angry at you because you only have enough material for one show.

How Much Money Can I Make?

I am guessing that many of you have skipped directly to this section. If so, I understand ... being paid for your work and your time away from home is important to most. So, here are some numbers to consider. Fees range from $1,500-$3,000 per week for Guest Entertainers, keeping in mind that your agent will take between 10-15% from your wage. A good ventriloquist friend of mine was recently paid $4,000 a week for one cruise! Of particular note I heard recently that acts from Australia are getting paid on one cruise line only in Australian dollars. So rather than being paid $2,500 US dollars, they are getting $2500 Australian dollars. At the time of this writing, the value of the Australian dollar is much less than the US dollar. Always make sure you know what currency you will be paid in. Once, I was fortunate enough to do a job that was paid to me in English pound. This meant that my wage was more than <u>double</u> for the weeks that I worked on the ship. It worked out in my favor!

One of the main advantages to working on a ship is you will be able to save your money. All your accommodation and food is taken care of, so the only thing you might spend money on might be alcohol and some food items if you are in a port.

The TO DO List
Here is a sample checklist of things to make sure you have prepared, prior to your departure at sea.
1. Passport - make sure it is current.
2. Visa(s) - always check to see if you need special visas to visit certain countries. Have these ready, kept inside your passport.
3. Your contract. Often you will need this to show immigration officials when you travel, because chances are you won't have a ticket to leave a country, so they will want to see some form of official letter which tells them you will be *joining* the ship on a certain date.
4. Extra passport photos. I always carry a few extra photos just in case.
5. Any documentation from the agent or ship regarding your travel to and from the ship. I always have the port agent's number, in case I arrive and nobody is there to pick me up. (which has happened more than once!)
6. Cue sheets for the act, plus a detailed checklist for all of my equipment and personal items.
7. Biography and publicity photo for the Cruise Director. They will need a <u>recent</u> photo, and usually like to have a very short biography that they sometimes print in the ship's daily newspaper.

Note - I also make sure to have back up documents, (hard copy and disk format) just in case I should lose something.

How To Find Work on Ships

There are several ways to find work on cruise ships. Some cruise lines hire directly. A promo pack consisting of photo/resume, cover letter and demo DVD, addressed to the Entertainment Director, may be all that you will need. Cruise lines that contract out for entertainment will usually forward your material to the agency that secures their entertainment.

In such cases, it would be wise to send your promotional package directly to this agency for consideration. There are several agencies that specialize in the cruise ship market. For references to some of the top agents in the business, refer to the chapter in this book. Again, send a promo pack. Remember that most agents will take 10% -15% commission in return for securing you work.

When submitting a promo pack remember to keep your demo DVD short (no one looks at more than ten minutes). An edited live performance is usually preferred over a studio tape. Keep cover letters and resume's to one page each and include a recent 8x10 color and black and white photo.

Contracts vary in length from cruise ship to cruise ship. If you are a self contained cabaret act you might be flown in for only one night or be offered as much as a six month contract.

Are You in a Position to Cruise?

Here is a topic that you won't read about in other books and one that you seriously need to consider! You have to be realistic about cruising and understand that it isn't all glamour.

Cruising is an exciting way to perform and travel the world while getting paid for it, but *it is not for everyone*. It requires a certain mind-set that accepts the limitations of being away from friends and family for extended periods of time, living and working in a confined space and being away from many of your day-to-day creature comforts (car, telephone, your favorite soap opera etc.) For those willing and able to deal with these issues, a cruise ship can be a wonderful place to live, work and perform!

I have mentioned before that you really do need to be in good shape to withstand all the traveling, especially if you are a fly on act. Experiencing the time changes and the constant flying and carrying your luggage around IS NOT HEALTHY! Are you prepared for this? It is a known fact that entertainers HAVE DIED from heart attacks on ships because of the strain of travel. Make use of the gym on the ship, watch what you eat and be health conscious. It is far too easy to adopt a lazy attitude towards your own health while on a ship. I just want to warn you now, to look after yourself and make sure you are up to the stress, challenges and lifestyle of life on board a ship. As I write this part of the book, I have just flown over fifty two hours, from Barcelona to New York, to Los Angeles then finally to New Zealand.

Another point that is worth looking at is can your wife, partner and family cope? Most of the crew members are away from home for six to nine months, some even longer. Many have a wife or husband that stay at home with the children. A six month cruise is a long time to be away from your family and in my opinion, far too long to be on board a ship. I have been on ships where crew members do four month contracts and they all seem so much happier than those who do nine months. Over the years, it seems that the contracts have gained in length for crew members. As a result, the standards have dropped! On the ships with shorter contracts, the crew members are still at that stage where they do a great job, and overall, remain much happier.

Before embarking on your high seas adventures, ask yourself, as an entertainer, are you prepared to be away from home for three months if required? For a single person it's a great life, you can meet people, you don't worry about what is happening at home i.e, is your wife happy, are the kids okay? Ironically, in spite of the large numbers of crew personnel and guest passengers, being on board a ship can be a very lonely life, since you never really make close-friends. Instead, people are always coming and going. Of course you will bump into these people again and again, but you are always saying goodbye.

When I was single, I enjoyed being on board ships for long periods of time, some contracts lasted for six months straight. However, when I met my wife Natalie, on a cruise ship some nine years ago, things changed. (for the better!) I suddenly found my life's companion, but we had to make decisions about how to make our relationship work.

You CAN make it work, but certain sacrifices (from both partners) will need to be made. Natalie gave up her career as a Property Development Manager, for many years to travel with me. Now I am prepared to do more work on land so that she can get her career going again. I'm not going to counsel you on relationships, but just want to bring this point up because it's something you may not have thought about. From the very start, Natalie and I talked about how we can make it work with me traveling and her at home. Our solution was for me not to accept the longer duration contracts, which I'm very happy about because it gives me more time at home, where I can concentrate on other satisfying projects. Nowadays, I only take contracts that are three weeks or less, then stay at home for a few weeks, then back out at sea, and so on. When you first start out cruising you will find it very hard to say NO to your agent because they will offer you A LOT of work if you do well. If you don't do well you will get a DO NOT RETURN. The agent just won't book you, simple as that!

After you have been in the cruise ship industry for a while, and have become more established with your agent, you will be in more of a position to turn down work. If it means having a healthy relationship, then my personal advise is for you to turn down the work!

To summarize, before going any further with the cruise ship life, make sure it is for you. Are you in a position to be away from home, and is your relationship strong enough to survive being apart. There are some silly sayings like *"what happens on a ship stays on a ship."* I personally don't buy into that rubbish. Whatever you do on a ship will come back and bite you in the behind! So, stay away from situations that you will regret!

Everybody has their own beliefs and morale standards, I just think it is important to take these things into consideration when thinking about making your livelihood as a cruise ship entertainer. There are too many stories of entertainers whose relationships have broken up because the performer is at sea all the time and never at home. You CAN get the best of both worlds, but be realistic about it. Set your working goals and your conditions ... then STICK TO THEM.

If you are in a position where your partner can travel with you, then this is by far the best because you both get to share in the excitement of travel and experience cruise ship life together. I know some well known magicians such as Shawn Farquhar, who did such a good job for the cruise line that they paid for his entire family to travel with him. They even gave him a larger suite! There are several top magicians who have been in the industry for many years and have earned the respect from the cruise line. As a result, they have been offered these types of deals. They are an example of those that make it work.

TRAVEL TIPS
The following are just a few pointers I've gained over the years, when it comes to packing for a cruise:

• There are general standards for evening wear on ships, these are 'semi-formal' and formal. I always take a sports jacket and two pairs of dress pants plus a good looking and smart dress suit for formal nights. Most men wear tuxedos and the ladies evening dresses on formal nights, so I pack a tuxedo as well.

• I cover each suit with a plastic dry cleaning bag. Then fold each outfit over and place in my suitcase, hanger and all. They WILL NOT WRINKLE. Unpacking is a breeze... just open your suitcase and start hanging things in the closet!

• Clothing that is slightly creased or wrinkled can often be freshened up by steaming. Just hang those items in your cabin's bathroom, while taking a hot, steamy shower and often the wrinkles will fall out. If all else fails, many ships have ironing stations in their self-service passenger launderettes or, for maximum convenience, send the offending garments to the ship's laundry for pressing.

• I place all my bathroom equipment in one of those toiletry bags designed to hang over the closet rail, or hook onto the door. Ships bathrooms are VERY small and this type of hanging system makes life much easier. Plus, your cabin steward will love you!

• I also pack some of my dress shirts in tissue paper, just like they were in the store, this also keeps them from wrinkling.

• I have a few necessities in my overnight carry on bag that I take on board my flight. Also in this bag is my 'commando' act, in case my main show is lost.

• Here's an idea I learned from a cruise ship entertainer, and it really helps to save space. You may have seen those special bags designed to suck out all the air and shrink your clothing. This is GREAT for smaller items such as socks, underwear, etc. My wife Natalie, always takes her own pillow so we use those bags for larger items as well. Your cabin steward will always have a vacuum cleaner and you can use that when you are packing to leave the ship. If you don't have those special bags then simply use a plastic garbage bag and some duck tape to seal it, once the air is sucked out. Trust me ... it works. This also helps to keep your clothes dry, should your luggage get wet.

• You might also spray your suitcases with Scotch Guard, for additional waterproofing (both inside and out).

• Locking your luggage. There are certain rules in countries where you can no longer lock your luggage. However, there are locks now available which <u>are</u> allowed by airlines, since they can be opened by security if necessary. These locks are more costly, but worth it.

• Duct Tape - NEVER LEAVE HOME WITHOUT IT!

• I always label all of my bags, as they have been lost before. Also, make sure that you know what your luggage looks like. If it is lost then you will have to describe it to the airlines, color, size, shape, etc. Remember, tags <u>do</u> come off, so I make sure that I have two tags on each piece of luggage at different places. If an airline is unable to trace the owner, or if luggage hasn't been claimed after at least three months, it ends up at the Unclaimed Baggage Center in Scottsboro, Alabama--a veritable Land of Lost Luggage. Only two hours from Birmingham and two and a half hours from Atlanta, the Unclaimed Baggage Center is a treasure hunter's dream destination. Over 500,000 people per year make the long trek to "shop" amid more than a million lost items, including watches, jewelry, electronics, and designer clothing. You don't want to be one of them, so take proper precautions mentioned above.

• I am very weary of catching colds, especially on ships and on planes. Something I do that seems to help in preventing this is to carry with me some antiseptic cream. I take a cotton and put some cream around the inside of my nose prior to flying. This seems to dissuade bugs that are present in the from air getting any further. On one trip, from Vietnam, I actually wore a surgical mask while on the flight because it seemed that everybody was sneezing and coughing! A little extreme, perhaps, but with the way flu's spread I was not going to take any chances.

• Drink LOTS of water while flying. I learned this the hard way, as I actually collapsed on stage one night after a very long flight and developed leg cramps due to dehydration.

• The minute you feel seasick, get an injection! In all of my years at sea, I was only seasick once, but that time was the worst feeling in the world. I went straight to the doctor, got an injection and since then have never been seasick. To be honest, it's not a big issue anymore on these cruise ships. They have stabilizers which helps stop the motion of the ocean, and captains will do what they can to avoid bad weather. If you think you are going to head into bad weather and you don't want to take chances, then the ship's boutique will always sell some Dramamine or anti-nausea patches that you can wear on your wrist or arms.

• Because you will be traveling to many different ports, located in many different parts of the glove, having a range of some "basic" language skills is a great advantage. When I first joined ships I had no experience with other languages, but over the years I have made it a point to be able to speak a little bit of French, Italian and Spanish. While I am by no means fluent in any of these languages, I do know enough so that when I travel I can say a few things and ask a few important questions.

• Don't Miss the Ship! Always, and I do mean ALWAYS check the exact time that your ship leaves the port. In most cases you need to be back on board at <u>least thirty</u> minutes prior to the ship's departure. Prior to going to bed at night, a 'Patter' or a list of the next days events will be placed in your cabin. This newsletter will also have some information such as the port agent's contact details for that particular port, the time of departure, and often highlights of key places to visit while in port. I always take this newsletter with me. Be forewarned ... if you miss the ship you will be responsible for getting to the next port at your cost. This can sometimes also result in dismissal!

Some Safety Tips About Cruising
If you have never cruised before, then here are a few safety tips to check prior to embarkation.

1. Check out the Ship's Report Card.

Whenever you get 1,500 or 2,000 or even 5,000 people together in one place, you are bound to share a lot more than a good time. Ships get report cards which you can view. The best reports come from the Vessel Sanitation Program of the Center for Disease Control and Prevention (CDC), which routinely inspects ships for cleanliness, repair, food preparation and storage, water quality, hygiene, pest (management and many other things). Check out your ship's report card on the CDC website if you are interested. It will let you know the results of the last inspection and exactly what grade the ship received. This is always a very interesting and enlightening exercise.

2. Keep your guard up.

It is natural to let your guard down on a cruise ship and in different ports of call. Life is good, the water is warm, the booze is flowing, the food is scrumptious, the ship seems like Paradise Island. You are living large, and that's precisely when you're most apt to get into trouble.

You need to be aware of your surroundings on a ship, just as you would in a big city. Keep your distance when tempers flare. Don't accept drinks from strangers. If your gut tells you something is wrong, it probably is. And don't keep it a secret, either; notify the Purser's Office the minute you suspect trouble.

I had an instance when there was a huge argument and screams of terror , came from the cabin located only a few doors down from me. I put my head out into the hallway and saw other people's curious heads out there, but nobody did anything. I phoned the front desk who immediately got security to the scene. It turned out that a man was beating a woman and (thankfully) they did something about it.

3. Use the ship's safe.

I tend not to take any expensive watches or jewelry with me on my cruises. Nowadays, most cruise ship cabins are equipped with a small safe. All my passports, wallet and cameras are kept in this safe unless absolutely needed.

4. Watch what you eat.

With the myriad options on board available for dining on a cruise ship, you can certainly be adventurous. Just don't be reckless. If, in the United States, you are lactose intolerant, you will continue to be lactose intolerant on the ship. If stateside seafood makes you puff up and itch, so will the on board seafood.

Shipboard water is usually safe, but once on shore, you should always insist on bottled water. And make sure it is a *sealed* bottle!

Know how your food is prepared, too. Is it heavy on the mayo in the hot Caribbean sun? Is the steak served tartare? And if you are served something you don't like - for heaven's sake, send it back. Once during a port call in Ocho Rios, Jamaica, I was served some almost-still-clucking chicken - not what I was expecting at a purportedly five-star restaurant! So be aware, and don't be afraid to ask that your food be prepared the way you like it.

5. Watch the booze.

Booze will always compromise your judgment, perception, and behavior. While everyone likes to have a few umbrella drinks aboard ship, don't let them get out of hand. Alcohol is a reason for 'firing' so always be aware that "somebody" might be watching.

6. Be careful on land.

Be careful on your shore excursions. The cruise lines organize the shore trips because they are moneymakers for them; in return, you get some assurance of quality and security. You can save a buck (or many) by going it alone, of course, but beware. Make sure you negotiate any taxi ares and fees upfront. Most cabbies will be honest when the cards are on the table, but if you do not agree in advance, the sky will be the limit and you may find yourself in a police station for failure to pay the fare.

8. Report anything suspicious.

While the crew-to-guest ratio looks pretty high in the brochure, much of the crew actually works behind the scenes and is not permitted any guest interaction; moreover, many may not even speak your language. Most of the senior crew will be looking out for guest safety, but they cannot be everywhere at once. Ultimately, your safety is your own responsibility. Just think safe, and it will be smooth sailing all the way.

Surviving a Cruise with the Norwalk Virus

To this day, I don't know how I got infected. Maybe I picked it up on our flight from Newark or on the layover in London. But by the time I boarded the riverboat in Mainz, Germany, I had a full-blown case of the Norwalk Virus: chills, diarrhea, nausea, and stomach cramps.

Gastrointestinal viruses such as Norwalk are becoming increasingly common among cruise ship passengers. They're caught by eating food or drinking liquids that are tainted, touching contaminated surfaces or objects and then putting your hand in your mouth or coming into direct contact with someone else who is sick.

The cruise industry is quick to point out that infection can happen anywhere - in a plane, a restaurant, an airport terminal. And this may be true. Equally true, however, is that the reports of cruise ship passengers spending part of their voyage in the infirmary are on the rise. So whether they catch the stomach flu before they board, or during the journey, is probably academic to most passengers.

Fortunately, according to the Centers for Disease Control, Norwalk is mercifully short. Symptoms last between one and two days. Which, in a way, makes it the ideal traveling illness. By the time you know you're sick, the worst of it is over and you haven't lost much vacation time.

There is no known treatment for the Norwalk Virus. Doctors recommend drinking plenty of water and resting, but there's no vaccine, no antibiotic treatment, no elixir to cure this debilitating stomach flu. You just have to sleep it off.

Still, in spite of its brevity, you suffer when you've got the Norwalk stomach flu. Big time. You feel as if you're sore all over, just like the day after you start a new exercise routine, and every muscle in your body aches. It's as if a bomb went off in your stomach; food isn't an option, and even the much-needed water feels like acid being poured down your throat. Every half-hour or so, you rise quickly from your bed to evacuate your bowels. But for that day or two, the illness also puts everything into stark perspective.

The suddenness of your affliction with Norwalk is eclipsed only by the suddenness of your recovery. To be sure, the Norwalk Virus is a dreadful illness that I wouldn't wish on anyone else. The cruise industry is correct to be worried about its effect on business, and should be doing everything it can to prevent its transmission. To help combat Norwalk, cruise ships now have hand sanitizors placed in key locations around the ship. Make sure you use these!

Paul in Paris 2007

CHAPTER FOUR

CRUISE LINE CONTACTS

Carnival Cruise Lines
3655 NW 87th Avenue,
Miami, FL 33178-2428, USA
Phone (305) 599-2600 website: www.carnival.com

To get work as an entertainer you can go direct. Generally you will need two shows, usually both about 25-30 minutes in length as they prefer to have split shows. Visit their website at:
www.carnival.com/CMS/Fun_Jobs/Shipboard-Entertainment.aspx

As one of the largest and most popular cruise lines in the world, Carnival Cruise sails to more than 60 exciting and beautiful destinations, all around the world. This includes ports of call in the Caribbean, the Bahamas, Mexico, Hawaii, the Panama Canal, Europe, Alaska, and more! Every Carnival Cruise Ship is truly a thrilling destination all in itself, offering luxurious accommodations, fine dining, world-class entertainment, and a plethora of other on board activity. Carnival provides entertainment options for the entire family and passengers of all ages, including the well-equipped casinos, themed bars, lounges, and nightclubs, the state-of-the-art Spa, the Carnival and fitness center, a seemingly endless variety of duty-free shops to be found along each ship's stunning main boulevard, and so much more!

Dedicated to the absolute best in comfort, service, convenience, quality, and most of all FUN, every cruise ship in the Carnival Cruise fleet comes with a friendly, highly trained, experienced, and dedicated staff. And this staff is hired to ensure that you have the most outstanding cruise vacation experience will ever had! On a Carnival Cruise vacation, your ship is your destination, and it's many fascinating and breathtaking ports of call that you get the opportunity to visit are just an extraordinary added bonus!

Celebrity Cruises
1050 Caribbean Way, Miami, FL 33132-2096, USA.
Phone (305) 539-6000. Website www.celebrity.com.
They also have an employment website at :
www.celebrity.com/aboutceleb/

You can send your promotional material to:
Celebrity Cruises
Human Resources Department
Attn.: Entertainment Department
1050 Carribean Way
Miami, FL 33132-2096, USA.

Since its conception in 1989, Celebrity Cruise Line has built a fleet of cruise ships that has set new standards for the entire cruise line industry. Celebrity's goal is to not only meet the highest expectations of each and every passenger, but to exceed them. Their highest commitment to exceptional quality, superior design, spacious accommodations, grand style, friendly and attentive service, and exceptional cuisine, truly puts each Celebrity cruise ship in a class all its own.

Currently offering eleven world-class luxury vessels, Celebrity Cruise Line is committed to providing a cruise vacation experience quite unlike any other, offering a host of fine amenities and other luxuries that were previously unheard of in the cruise industry. Whether you're dining on an original gourmet dish from renowned Celebrity chef Michael Roux, trying your luck at a game of roulette in the lavish casino, taking in one of the nightly world-class stage shows, indulging in a full-body massage in the opulent Aqua-Spa, or simply sipping a delicious martini in a stylish bar while gazing out at the stunning sea scape views will ever so gracefully passing by, a Celebrity Cruise is one vacation that you truly have to experience to believe!

Costa Cruise Lines

200 South Park Road, Suite 200
Hollywood, FL 33021-8541, USA
Phone (954) 266-5600
Website www.costacruise.com

Note: This is an Italian-based line, bought out by Carnival Cruises. It is very Italian-oriented, comprised mainly of European passengers.

Costa Cruise Lines invites you to come and experience a *real cruise vacation*...Italian style! Costa Cruises has emerged over the last century from a humble fleet of freight liners, transporting mainly fabrics and olive oil between Genoa and Sardinia, Italy. It now lays claim to being the largest and one of the most popular cruise lines in all of Europe. Costa's eleven magnificent cruise ships sail to stunning destinations all throughout Europe and the Mediterranean, the Caribbean, and South America.

Costa Cruises is truly a unique and delightful cruise vacation experience that you will not want to miss! It combines some of the newest and most innovative features in the cruise industry today, along with a friendly and comfortable atmosphere, superb cuisine, and spacious accommodations, all of which are synonymous with the rich Italian tradition.

Crystal Cruises
2049 Century Part East, Suite 1400
Los Angeles, CA 90067. USA
Phone (310) 785-9300
Website: www.crystalcruises.com

This is one of the TOP cruise lines that cater specifically to the wealthy passenger market. These passengers are very well-travelled and have "been there and seen it all." All acts are individually marked by passengers. To be considered, you can send your promotional material to:

Crystal Cruises
Attn.: Entertainment Manager
2049 Century Park East, Suite 1400
Los Angeles, CA 90067 USA

Voted the world's best small ship cruise line for ten years in a row, Crystal Cruises offers their guests a truly unique and enchanting cruise vacation experience. Explore the cultures of the Far East, marvel at the treasures of Europe, and discover the beauty of Alaska. Crystal Cruise Line offers its guests the ultimate in style and luxury, featuring an opulent Six-Star cruise ship fleet and a wide array of itineraries that include more than 175 different ports of call in 56 countries. Crystal Cruise's magnificent cruise vacation experience will exceed even your wildest expectations, with unbeatable Crystal Cruise service, impeccable accommodations, delicious gourmet dining options, world-class entertainment, as well as a host of other fine on board features and amenities that anyone with a sense of refined taste, is certain to enjoy.

Cunard Line Ltd.
6100 Blue Lagoon Drive, Suite 400
Miami, FL 33126. USA
Phone (305) 463-3000

Website: www..cunardline.com

Princess Cruise entertainment department is booking entertainment for Cunard. I suggest going through an agent, although you could mail your promotional package off directly, first, to see if you get a response.

Cunard Cruise Line is home to two of the most famous cruise ships in the world. the renowned Queen Elizabeth II and Queen Mary II. Dating all the way back to the early 20th Century and the golden era of cruise travel, Cunard still operates the grandest and most stunning ships in the cruise industry. Sailing to spectacular destinations all over the globe. these ships still echo the majestic prowess of some of the greatest and most legendary cruise ships of all time.

Cunard offers a host of incredible on board features and fine amenities, including comfortable and spacious accommodations, an array of decadent dining options featuring gourmet cuisine from world-famous chefs, countless on board activities and enrichment programs, in addition to a highly trained and dedicated staff that are always there to make sure your every wish becomes a reality. In 2007 the new QEIII joined the fleet, with the Queen Victoria joining in 2008.

Discovery Cruise Line
Attn.: Human Resources
1755 NW 70th Avenue, Miami. FL 33126 USA
Phone (305) 597-0336
Website: www.discoverycruise.com

Classical and elegant design are the hallmarks of Discovery World Cruise Line. Combining all the modern features and amenities that have helped to make cruising the popular vacation option that it is today with all the timeless grandeur and refinement of the greatest cruise ships of yesteryear, Discovery World Cruises offers their guests all they will need to feel right at home while on the cruise vacation of a lifetime!

Founded in 2002, Discovery World Cruises' one and only vessel, the magnificent 20,000 ton MV Discovery, is big enough for cruising to faraway places, yet small enough to enter remote ports and harbors that larger vessels have to pass by. Holding a mere 650 passengers at a time, the MV Discovery offers first-class accommodations and service, and sails to a number of exotic destinations throughout South America, Australia/New Zealand, the South Pacific, the Caribbean, The Galapagos Islands, and even Antarctica. During the summer months, Discovery offers Mediterranean, Northern Africa, Iceland, Greenland and Canada Cruises.

Disney Cruise Line
200 Celebration Place,
Celebration, FL 34747 USA
Phone (407) 566-7577 (direct line to entertainment department).

Website: www.disneycruise.go.com
Disney conducts live auditions four times per year. You can check out the website at:
www.corporate.disney.go.com/careers/auditions_cruiseline.html

From the hearts and imaginations of the dream-makers of the Walt Disney Company, comes some the most exciting and imaginative cruise ships at sea today. Come aboard Disney Cruise Line's Disney Magic and Disney Wonder and discover two ships as grand as the greatest ocean liners of the past, with all the modern innovations and conveniences you would expect to find on cruise ships today, plus so much more! Disney Cruise Line offers staterooms that are among the largest at sea, a delectable array of dining options, swimming pools, lavish entertainment, separate activity areas for adults, teens, and kids, and even all of your favorite Disney characters on board to keep you company! Combining a thrilling cruise adventure with an enchanting magical touch that only Disney can provide, a Disney Cruise is the perfect vacation option for both the young, and the young at heart!

Fred Olson Cruises
Marine Personnel Department
Fred Olson House, Crown Street
Ipswich, Suffolk, IP1 3HS UK
Website: fredolsen.co.uk.
I have worked this line before. Please note that, on a three week duration cruise you are required to have SIX DIFFERENT shows! I suggest that you only attempt to book this particular cruise line if you have enough strong material, as they are 100% marketed to please their British audiences.

Holland America
300 Elliott Avenue W.
Seattle, WA 98119 USA.
Phone (206) 286-3499
Website: www.hollandamerica.com
Note that their policy is <u>not</u> to book mentalists or hypnotists. You can apply via website at :
www.hollandamericaentertainment.com

Holland America Cruise Line has been carrying their passengers to breathtaking and exotic destinations all over the world for more than 130 years. Today, Holland America is proud to offer a spectacular 13-ship, 5-star luxury fleet. Having recently introduced the magnificent and innovative Vista-Class family of ships, Holland America Cruise Line is currently sailing to more than 280 spectacular ports of call, in countries all over the world, and on all seven continents!

Holland America is committed to providing each of its guests with the ultimate cruise vacation experience. As soon as you step on board you will notice right away what makes Holland America one of the most loved and most luxurious cruise lines sailing the high seas today. Offering the very best in world-class dining, the most comfortable and spacious accommodations at sea, extravagant entertainment, a rejuvenating spa and salon, first-rate casino, special kids-only programming, plus a vast array of other fine amenities and activities for people of all ages to enjoy, the incredible ships of Holland America Cruise Line truly set themselves apart as superior members of the cruise industry.

Mediterranean Shipping Cruises (MSC Cruises)
Naples, Italy - Head Office,
MSC Naples
Via A.Depretis, 31
80133 Naples, Italy
Mail your promotional material to the above marking it to the attention of the Entertainment Department. MSC Cruises uniquely blends maritime traditions, culture, and famous Mediterranean cuisine to deliver the ultimate cruise experience while displaying a real commitment to the finest hospitality afloat. Currently offering six magnificent cruise ships, MSC Cruises has made true Italian service the heart of its business, and its key point of differentiation in the cruise industry. Visiting destinations throughout Northern Europe, the Mediterranean, the Caribbean, South Africa, and South America, MSC Cruises prides itself in allowing each one if their passengers to make their MSC Cruises vacation into whatever they want it to be. From the moment you wake up, choose however much or little you feel like doing. With a full range of exciting and relaxing activities for guests of all ages, in addition to some of the finest accommodations and dining options at sea, MSC Cruises are perfect for cruisers of all ages!

Norwegian Cruise Line
Ship Personnel Dept. 7665
Corporate Center Drive
Miami, FL 33126 USA
Phone (305) 436-4000.
Website: www.ncl.com
For current jobs you can visit:
www.164.109.173.140/ship_employ/shipboard_index.htm

Norwegian Cruise Line (NCL) is comprised of a magnificent 12-ship fleet. With Norwegian Cruise Line, it's all about choices, and having a lot of them! With NCL's the innovative "Freestyle Cruising" program, you essentially get customize your own individual cruise vacation to be whatever you want it to be. Decide where and when you want to eat, how you want to dress, and in what activities you would like to participate. Traveling to destinations all over the globe, each of Norwegian Cruise Line's ships offers the utmost in exceptional service, quality, and activities for the entire family!

The grand ships of Norwegian Cruise Line feature everything: from large and luxurious staterooms, several spacious pools and hot tubs, luxurious rooftop Garden Villas, a large movie theater, a full service library complete with an array of literary and musical selections, state-of-the-art conference center facilities, well-appointed casino, the best in live entertainment, an amazing spa, more than a dozen restaurants, theme bars and lounges, trendy night-clubs, virtually unlimited shopping, to a spectacular sports deck complete with basketball, volleyball, soccer, and a full-size jogging track!

Oceana Cruises
8120 NW 53rd Street
Miami, FL 33166 USA
Phone (305) 514-2300
Website: www.oceanacruises.com
These are great ships and are sister ships to The Tahitian, Pacific and Royal at Princess Cruises. These used to be part of Renassaince Cruises until they went bankrupt after 911.

Oceania Cruises was formed in 2002 by cruise industry veterans, Joe Watters and Frank Del Rio. Oceania's commitment to providing the best in class cuisine, luxurious on board features and amenities, as well as destination-oriented itineraries, all at an outstanding value, have all come to define Oceania Cruises as the five-star product of choice for traditional premium and luxury category cruisers, of all ages!

Oceania Cruises offers two intimate and luxurious, 684 passenger cruise ships. Regatta and Insignia provide a cozy, small ship atmosphere, with all the luxury and choice you would find at the largest and finest resort. Oceania's 5 Star dining menus were crafted under the meticulously watchful eye of world-renowned master chef, Jacques, Oceania Cruises' Executive Culinary Director. Regatta and Insignia are currently offering an incredible variety of itineraries to the Mediterranean, Scandinavia, Mexico, the Caribbean, and the Panama Canal. These itineraries have also been tailored to include many overnight port stays, allowing passengers time to immerse themselves in the history, culture, and local flavors of all these extraordinary places.

Orient Cruise Line

I haven't included any contact details here because this line is now owned by NCL and so the Entertainment Director books talent for both the NCL and the Marco Polo. My wife and I have worked the Marco Polo. It is a very old ship but also a classic ship. Come cruise the world with Orient Cruise Lines and the infamous Marco Polo. As the current one-and-only cruise ship representing Orient Lines, this incredible 22,000 ton/mid-size ship, that is approximately 580 feet in length, was built with a strong, ice-breaking hull. In addition, it is a vessel with multiple uses. Perfect for trolling around the chilly Antarctic seas, as well as the more moderate Mediterranean sea. The Marco Polo has all the warmth and intimacy of a private yacht, yet still offers her maximum of 826 guests a wide selection of fine amenities and exciting on board activities options, making her good for endeavoring longer journeys. Originally built in 1965, at the Mathias-Thesen Werft in Germany, Marco Polo was completely refurbished and essentially rebuilt in 1993. Some unique features on the Marco Polo are eight inflatable Zodiac landing crafts stored inside the ship for expedition use, as well as a takeoff and landing area for helicopters located on the top deck. Orient Cruise Lines and the incomparable Marco Polo are currently offering exciting itineraries throughout the Mediterranean and Greek Isles, the Baltics, South America, the Panama Canal, and the Antarctic!

P & O Cruises

77 New Oxford Street

London WC1A 1PP England.

Also, PO Box 5287, Sydney, 2001. New South Wales, AUSTRALIA.

www.pocruises.com

As Great Britain's leading cruise line, P&O Cruises has been revolutionizing modern passenger cruising, as we know it today, for more than a century. Today, the P&O Cruises fleet is still growing at an unbelievably rapid pace, and each one of its magnificent vessels boasts some of the most impressive on board amenity and activity options being offered anywhere in the cruise industry today. Cruising to some of the most beautiful and spectacular destinations in the world including the Mediterranean, the Baltics, the Norwegian Fjords, the Caribbean, Asia, and Australia, each P&O cruise ship offers a bountiful array of exquisite dining options, the very best in live entertainment, large and luxurious staterooms, plus a host of other exciting on board activity options for passengers of all ages to enjoy while at sea!

Princess Cruises

24844 Avenue Rockefeller

Santa Clarita, CA 91355-4999 USA

Phone (310) 553-1770

www.princesscruise.com

Princess Cruises invites you to come escape...completely. As one of the world's most magnificent cruise lines, Princess Cruises offers an experience truly incomparable to anything you could ever imagine. From humble beginnings in 1965 with a single steamer cruising only to Mexico, the Princess Cruise fleet now carries over 800,000 people per year to beautiful and exotic destinations on all seven continents! With an extraordinary commitment to providing each of its guests with a paramount level of outstanding service, amenities, and luxuries beyond belief, Princess Cruise Line's goal is to provide the ultimate in affordable luxury, with an emphasis on having big ship choices with small ship intimacy and comfort.

Princess Cruises currently operates a stunning nineteen-ship luxury fleet, and lays claim to one of the largest and most modern fleets at sea today! With its exclusive Personal Choice Cruising program, Princess Cruises places an extremely high emphasis on allowing each and every passenger to customize their own individual vacation into whatever they want it to be. Each Princess Cruise ship offers its own version of a host of different delectable and unique dining options, each with its own special flare and ambiance. It also offers the finest in world-class entertainment, and an array of exciting activities to suit any personality: from shuffleboard to professional scuba-diving certification. No matter the size of the ship, all public spaces aboard all Princess Cruise ships are designed to feel intimate and are decorated in a contemporary style, allowing passengers to enjoy themselves in an informal, relaxed on board atmosphere that celebrates all of today's unique and diverse lifestyles.

Radisson Seven Seas Cruises
600 Corporate Drive
Suite 410
Fort Lauderdale, FL 33334 USA.
phone (954) 776-6123
Website: www.rssc.com

When it comes to modern cruise ships, Radisson Seven Seas Cruises offers five of the most refined and luxurious ships in the cruise industry today. Their 6-star small to mid-size ships, including the new all-suite, all-balcony Seven Seas Voyager, were designed to hold a smaller number of people at one time. In this way, those aboard can have more space to sit back, relax, and indulge in all of the finer *little things* that life has to offer. The ambiance on board each Radisson Seven Seas cruise ship is personal, individual, and accommodating - "upscale but not uptight." From Ballroom dancing and Le Cordon Bleu French cooking lessons, to its professional Bridge lessons, Radisson Seven Seas truly offers something for everyone. Radisson Seven Seas Cruises currently visits more than 300 destinations on six continents, including the Caribbean,

Europe, the South Pacific, Canada, South America, the Panama Canal, Alaska, and even Antarctica!

Royal Caribbean Cruises Ltd
1050 Caribbean Way
Miami, FL 33132 USA
Phone (305) 539-6000
Website: www.royalcaribbean.com

As one of the most popular cruise lines in the world, Royal Caribbean Cruises has firmly established an esteemed reputation of excellence, priding itself in providing its customers with the most extraordinary cruise vacation experiences in the cruise industry. Traveling to hundreds of thrilling cruise destinations, all over the world, Royal Caribbean Cruises offers its passengers a chance to see and do more things than they could ever imagine on any vacation.

Royal Caribbean is committed to setting new standards for cruising, activities, adventures, and fun for the entire family, and they do it all with their award winning Gold Anchor Service!

Royal Caribbean Cruises' stunning fleet of nearly two dozen stately vessels features some of the finest dining, nightlife, activities and attractions for passengers of all ages. This includes ice skating rinks, swimming pools, numerous themed bars and lounges, and the now infamous Royal Caribbean rock-climbing wall! This also includes Royal Caribbean's specialized Adventure Ocean Youth Program, which consists of specially planned programs and activities for children ages three to seventeen. Whether you're a first timer or an experienced cruiser, you will feel right at home on any Royal Caribbean cruise ship. With an array of on board activities, shore excursions, and dining options for all tastes, every passenger aboard a Royal Caribbean ship is sure to find numerous things that they will enjoy doing throughout the duration of their time on the high sea!

Seaborne Cruise Line
"The Yachts of Seaborne"
6100 Blue Lagoon Drive
Miami, FL 33126 USA
Phone ((305) 463-3000

Another TOP end cruise line where entertainment is not a priority. The ships are AMAZING and the service is INCREDIBLE. My wife and I love working these ships. They only hold about 200 passengers and again, these people are well-travelled and have seen it all. To successfully perform on this ship you need at least TWO different fifty minute shows. Come aboard with Seabourne Cruises, and experience the true definition of ultra-luxury cruising. Imagine, combining all the comfort and intimacy of your own private yacht, with all the amenities and opportunities for adventure that you would find on any large cruise ship. These possibilities become a reality with Seabourne Cruise Line. Since its conception in 1987, Seabourne Cruises has offered its passengers a dramatic alternative to the typical resort or cruise vacation.

Seabourne Cruises is dedicated to delivering the highest levels of personalized service to an exclusive group of guests aboard intimate, comfortable, and highly luxurious cruise ships. Since all of Seabourne's ships are smaller in size, carrying a maximum of 208 (very lucky) guests, they have the capability to travel to some of the most beautiful and exotic places in the world, many of which their lager counterparts can not fathom venturing to. Some of these magnificent destinations include Northern Europe, South America, the Caribbean, Australia, the South Pacific, and more, all coupled with Seabourne Cruise Line's spectacular, refined, and award-winning on board experience.

Silversea Cruises LTD.
110 E. Broward Blvd.
Fl. Lauderdale
FL 33301. USA
Phone (954) 522-4477
website: www.silversea.com

Again, one of the top-end cruise lines. Silversea Cruises was founded on the idea that everyone should have the opportunity to experience what a true luxury cruise vacation is like. It is the magical experience of discovering the world, and enjoying the special ambiance of an immaculately run cruise ship that drives everything that Silversea Cruises does. Since its inception in 1994, Silversea Cruises has been dedicated to defining the elite luxury cruise experience, going above and beyond what is expected to achieve the distinction of being the world's best. Silverseas offer thoroughly modern cruise ships with every technical innovation. They also offer spacious ocean-view suites with sumptuous furnishings and appointments, and most with a private veranda, as well as inspired cuisine includes the finest wines and spirits found at sea. Silversea Cruises wants to make you feel like you are in the one of the finest floating hotels earth, while having all the comforts of home at your beckon call.

Silversea Cruises is currently offering a wide array of extraordinary itineraries aboard its four incomparable luxury vessels: Silver Cloud, Silver Wind, Silver Shadow, and Silver Whisper. Destinations include breathtaking ports of call located in the Mediterranean, Northern Europe, the Far East, the South Pacific, South America and the Amazon, the Caribbean, Mexico, Africa and the Indian Ocean, as well as Alaska and the Pacific coasts of the United States and Canada.

Star Cruises
Star Cruises Terminal,
Palau Indah, Pelabuhan Barat,
42009 Pelabukan Klang,
Selangor Darual Eshan,
Malaysia. Phone (60) 3 3101 1313
website: www.starcruises.com
Star Cruises is one of the largest lines in Asia and still growing. They
have been known to hire magicians who use tigers and large animals and
their ships are equipped with great stages for illusionists.

Relaxing in Aruba 2006

Cruise Line Entertainment Bookers

Bartels, Inc. 1545 McIntosh Trail Senoia, GA 30276 USA Tel: 770-599-6802 suzanne@bartelsinc.net

Blackburn International Allan Blackburn Le Montaigne 2 Avenue de la Madone 98000 Monte Carlo France Tel: (377) 93 30 67 98

Blue Moon Talent, Inc. Ken Fine 1153 Bergen Parkway, Suite M-181 Evergreen, CO 80439 USA

Blue Moon Talent, Inc. Parris Lane 1205 N. Buffalo Dr. #202 Las Vegas, NV 89128 USA

Bramson Entertainment 630 Ninth Ave. - Suite 203 New York, NY 10036 USA Phone : (212) 265 - 3500 Fax: (212) 265-6615

Broadway Bound Inc. 830 Broadway 3rd Floor New York NY 10003 United States Of America Tel: (212) 674-8631 Fax: (212) 475-1567

Don Casino Productions 20880 West Dixie Highway Suite 105 Miami FL 33180 USA Tel: (305) 935-0137 or (305) 935-9094

Elaine Avon Ltd. Montage 127 Westhall Rd, Warlingham Surrey CR3 9HJ UK Tel: 01883 622 317

ESI Entertainment Minneapolis, MN United States Of America Tel: 952.470.9000

First Class Entertainment, Inc. Howard Beder 483 Ridgewood Road Maplewood, NJ 07040-2136 USA Tel: (973) 763-0591 Fax: (973) 763-0570 talent@gotofirstclass.com

Excellent Entertainment Suite 2, The Business Centre, 120 West Heath Road London NW3 7TU UK

Garry Brown Associates 27 Downs Side Cheam, Surrey, UK SM2 7EH
Tel: 0208-643-3991   Tel: 0208-770-7241   Tel: 0208-643-8375
gbaltd@compuserve.com

Hire Notes 2200 South Pioneer Way Las Vegas, NV 89117 United States
Of America (Bands and piano players only)

Jean Anne Ryan Productions 308 SE 14th St Fort Lauderdale FL
33316 USA Tel 305 523 6399

Karst Talent P O Box 1784 Palm Springs, CA 92263 Tel (702) 480
4722 Fax (760) 323 4599 Karsttalent@yahoo.com

Matrix Entertainments Ltd PO Box 222 Esher, Surrey KT10 9YB UK
(Tel: 01372 464 829)

Mike Maloney Entertainment PO Box 371059, Las Vegas, Nevada
89137. USA Tel: 702-243-7456

Molyneux Musick 312 9th Avenue South, Nashville, Tennessee 37203
USA Tel: 615-254-5411

Morag Productions P.O. Box 80-1736 Aventura FL 33280 USA Tel
305-937-2586

Nite Raiders Entertainment Las Vegas, NV / Myrtle Beach, SC,
Calgary AB Canada Contact: Dana Leslie Nease North America
Entertainment Rep. Email: dana@niteraiders.com

Oceanbound Entertainment 418 Francois Otterburn Park, QC J3H
5X1 Canada Toll free: 1-888-714-0964 Tel: 1-450-714-0964 Fax:
1-514-227-5475
Openwide International 7 Westmoreland House, Cumberland Park,
London NW10 6RE UK Tel: 0208 962 3418. Fax: 0208 962 3440

Prima Artists 3 Sovereign House, West Hill Road, St. Leonards, E. Sussex, TN38 0NH, United Kingdom +44 1424 203 500 cruising@prima-artists.com

ProShip Entertainment 5253 Decarie Boulevard Suite 308 Montreal, Quebec Canada H3W 3C2 TelL : (514) 485-8823 Fax : (514) 485-2675

Ray Kennedy Production Company 244 South Academy St Mooresville North Carolina 28115, USA

Roger Kendrick Cruising Entertainments National Westminster Chambers 6 Orchard Rd St Annes on Sea Lancashire FY8 1RH UK UK Tel 01253 726046

Showbiz International Cruising Ltd. Rossall Point Fleetwood, 83 Princes Way, Nr Blackpool, Lancashire. FY7 8DX UK
Telephone : 01253 777711 Fax: 01253 773358

Sixth Star Entertainment &Marketing 21 NW 5th Street, Fort Lauderdale, FL 33301 USA Tel: (954) 462-6760; fax: (954) 462-0737

Stiletto Entertainment 8295 S La Cienega Boulevard, Inglewood, California CA 90301 USA Tel: (310) 957 5757. Fax: (310) 957 5771

Spotlight Entertainment 2121 N Bayshore Drive, Suite 909 Miami, FL 33137 USA Tel: (305) 576-8626 Fax: (305) 573-5457

Suman Entertainment Group 12426 West Dixie Hwy., Unit A North Miami, FL 33161 USA TEL (305) 981-3135 Michael Suman Producer - Live Entertainment

CHAPTER FIVE

THE BUSINESS SIDE OF SHOW BUSINESS

Now we come to the real crunch ... there is an old saying which is "Show Business is 10% show and 90% Business" ... this certainly applies to the cruise ship performer as well. What follows are some ideas and thoughts, that I wish to share with you, on the importance of viewing the "entertainment" that you offer, as a business. Take them, or leave them - it's from my own personal experience from being in show business for the past 25 years. If you find that some bit of advice helps, then I will be very happy.

Professionalism

The following are my thoughts on what I call the 'professional' part of performing on cruise ships. This plays a very important role in your job as a cruise ship entertainer, and it will help you to keep getting booked - year after year. Some of this information may have already been mentioned in earlier chapters. If so, it is worth repeating.

Your attitude, while on the job

Keep in mind, you have been hired for a specific purpose, and that is to deliver a professional show – not to party. More often than not, you will invited to a dinner or to the bar on a ship and will be offered drinks. My own golden rule is to never drink alcohol while working; you have been hired as a professional to do a job.

The key word here is *professional*. Once you start working ships, you will soon realize why a lot of people drink, and drink heavily. It is cheap, it is social and, if you are traveling by yourself, this can be something that soon becomes an addiction. There are many stories of entertainers who have become addicted to drinking because they have worked on ships for so long and it has often been the cause for dismissal. Ships can and <u>do</u> test for alcohol, so don't let it get in the way of your performance. If you do have already have a drinking problem, then ships are NOT for you! There are several of my good friends that work on ships, who used to have problems with alcohol. Fortunately and to their credit, they did something about it and now even go along to the AA meetings on board their ships, to prevent a relapse.

Dress

This really depends on personal taste. However, I always try to look professional, so I have a suit that I wear or I at least dress neatly and at least look smart. People are always judging you not only on stage, but off as well. First impressions are important. It is important to convince everybody that you are a professional and that you know your business. Your audience will often judge you by the way you dress so, whatever you wear, dress neatly and look smart. My motto is *"Dress for Success"*, both on and off stage.

Hygiene

Make sure you smell nice. Always wear a pleasant after-shave, but be careful not to wear too much. Use non-scented deodorant and carry breath refreshers with you at all times. If you smoke then your clothes, breath and hair will smell of stale smoke. To a non-smoker this can be very unpleasant. On some ships you will be asked to host a dinner table, which means you also have to know how to be polite and well-mannered, even if people are saying stupid things to you or ask you the same questions over and over.

Because I often work where there is food and drink, it is important that my appearance is neat and tidy. I always carry an electric razor, a comb, mouth spray and some after-shave in my kit ,backstage.

In addition to your appearance, be sure to keep your magic neat and tidy. If you use white rope, always make sure it looks clean. I learned that from Billy McComb, who watched me work at the Magic Castle and each night would sit down with me and share his insightful ideas. I had never thought that my rope was dirty because nobody had told me, but I was sure glad Billy had the care and the courage to say something! It's the little things, like that, which make an act more 'book-able' and presentable on ships.

Off-Stage

How you conduct yourself off stage is just as important as the way in which you conduct yourself on stage. Remember that people talk, and if you are 'dressed for success' and have a professional attitude, then word will spread that you must be good. Be meticulous and always remain on the ball.

Your appearance should be neat and well-groomed. Conduct yourself in a manner that makes people genuinely enjoy your company. People do have expectations on how successful entertainers should dress and act.

In the magic business, networking plays a major part of getting more gigs. Once people find out what you do for a job, they become very interested and will ask questions.

Be prepared to answer questions, know about your subject and have some stories about your job. Passengers often like to talk to entertainers and you will find yourself sitting at a dinner table with them, so be prepared. On some ships the entertainers are asked to do a 'coffee' show which is a question and answer time with you, another great place to push any DVD's you might be selling.

Knowledge about your craft and having the confidence to mix and mingle will help you become a better performer for cruise ships. Remember that you are your own best advertisement.

I also like to observe and listen to what people have to say. One of the best pieces of advice I was given when starting out was 'to be a good listener'. Being a good listener is a great tool for learning.

Finally, keep in mind that passengers DO fill in those comment cards and if you mix and mingle well, this will impact nicely on their comments about you and your show.

Performance
I will touch briefly on this, as I've talked about being ready to work on ships in previous chapters. Confidence and personality play a major role in any type of performance situation, magic included. This does not mean you have to be cocky; in fact there is nothing worse than an entertainer on an ego trip. The best cruises are the ones where all entertainers are friendly and egos don't get in the way. As I am writing this chapter I am on a ship with 3 other acts, all of whom have been in the industry for at least 20 years and have done it all and seen it all. They realize they are here for a job and egos are not a problem. It's great because we all eat together and hang out, making it a much more enjoyable experience for all.

When you are confident in what you do, then you can start to have fun with your performance. Confidence comes by rehearsing, practicing and being prepared.

Be honest with yourself and do not take on work you cannot handle or are not ready for. If you feel you are not ready for ships then do not take it. My suggestion is to start working your act out until you are 100% confident it works well, then, once you have all your promotional material together, start looking for work.

Don't let people intimidate you. Do what you really enjoy doing. Your positive attitude towards what you do is very important. Be proud of your abilities as a performer and magician and above all, HAVE FUN.

Preparation

Being prepared not only relates to your performance, but it relates to other aspects of the engagement as well. Once a board your ship, know exactly where the theater is, how to get there from your cabin and what time your shows are scheduled. In addition, walk around the entire ship and observe the age group of your soon-to-be audience. If you have the chance, always watch the other shows, in order to get an even better idea of the audience's likes and dislikes.

As an adjunct to the contracts supplied from the ship, I also have my own booking sheet. A booking sheet is a great way of making sure that you are truly organized, and that you have <u>all</u> the details you need to know.

On ships you will always be given a rehearsal time. Never be late, and make sure you have everything you will need for your rehearsal so that you don't have to run back to your cabin! My music, for example, is on both CD and MiniDisk ... always be prepared. You are generally given two hours for rehearsal. Don't be scared to use the entire time, making sure everything is perfect and the stage and sound technicians know exactly what is required to run your show smoothly.

Have a back up show

You just never know. Whenever I travel, I always carry my back pack with me. This back pack is comprised of smaller-size items that will enable me to do an entire comedy show in the event that my non-carry on luggage, with all my normal props, gets lost en route. I call this my commando act. Although the props are very small, they can play to a large crowd. It consists of the following effects:

1. *Color Change Silks*
2. *Rope Routine*
3. Richard Osterlind's *Bank-Night*
4 *Big Ten Routine* which I am now selling through:
www.hocus-pocus.com
5. *Linking Finger Rings*
6. *Dream Prediction,* again my own invention and is for sale.

This can provide me with forty five minutes of very strong magic and fun filled comedy, making for a highly entertaining show. As mentioned, this is my backup show, should I lose my bags, and it works well.

The new Pacific Princess in Tahiti on our way to North America 2005

BOOKING SHEET

Cruise line:_____

Date of ship's departure: _____

Time and date of shows: _____ a.m. / p.m.

_____ a.m / p.m.

Length of show(s): _____

Number of people theater seats: _____

Target audience (range of age and nationality): _____

Voyage of ship (destination): _____

Cruise Director phone: _____

Name of Cruise Director: _____

Stage Manager phone: _____

Name of Stage Manager: _____

Total fee: _____

NOTES:

The business side of show-business

As I have stated before, the business side of cruising and of performing, plays a very important part in determining your success as an entertainer. You can be a great performer, but if you lack crucial business skills, such as: negotiating, effective telephone techniques, organization skills, etc., then you will not be able to reach your full potential.

In this regards, your attitude toward selling and promoting yourself is vital to your business and securing work. Thus is, if you want to get more work, you are going to have to get out there and sell yourself. Or, as Nike says, *"just get out there and do it!"*

To start off you will have to *do it* all by yourself – unless you are fortunate enough to be promoted by a credible manager from the very start. However you should make sure you are fully prepared <u>before</u> you approach an agency. It is up to you to put your promotional material such as video and website together.

Realize that not every cruise line will want to hire you. The way to look at it is like this: if an cruise line doesn't want to hire you, then eliminate them from your mind as a potential booking – at least for the time being – and move on to pursuing another cruise line. An agent that has either seen you work or at least seen your promotional DVD should have some idea of what cruise line(s) will suit you.

The important thing is to keep selling your services and that you realize that some prospects will say no. Also, it is important to keep in mind that when they say no, they don't mean you are a horrible person. Instead, they are just reflecting the idea that your style may note be suitable for their particular cruise line and demographics.

How many times have you been approached to buy a product and you've said no, simply because you didn't see a need for it, and then a year later you find you need the product? It's the same with show business, don't give up! Pace yourself, but be persistent!!

I have a separate office in which I conduct all my entertainment related business. In this office are a computer, telephone, filing system, stationary, office supplies, and all my books on magic and business. After all, I am running a business and I need to be as professional as possible. The same business-like approach should also work well for you. Being organized will make running your business a lot easier and more efficient and ultimately, result in your ability to contact more of the "right" people to secure more bookings.

A large agenda is very important for tracking all appointments and engagements. As well as keeping it backed up on my computer I also like to have a regular book with appointments. In my own hard copy agenda, I pencil in all inquiries and ink-in when the engagement is confirmed. Next to the telephone is a large pad for writing notes and daily messages. During times when you are not at home to answer the phone, either your well-scripted voice mail message will take the message of a live person who will be sure to write all details on this pad. When you <u>are</u> home, the way you answer the phone is very important. This is often the first time a potential client or agent has contact with you, so you will need to appear confident and cheerful.

You want to make an excellent lasting impression over the phone; it is one of your most valuable assets. It is important that you come across as a professional who knows his or her business, and is not new to it all. I use a cordless phone at home, which enables me to move about when talking to clients, in case I need to get near the agenda or check the calendar or computer.

All correspondence should be dealt with promptly and professionally. Even though I am away on cruise ships most of the time performing, I still answer all e-mails as quickly as possible. Having a mobile phone is vital if you are running a business so that potential clients can contact you quickly, and not loose trust, nor simply move on to book the competition. I have an i-phone and I can instantly check emails from my agent as well. If you are traveling on ships, be sure to get a cell phone that is quad-band and will work world wide.

Keep all your correspondence and business cards that you collect. Yes, you will collect A LOT. This information will help you make up a list of prospective clients. I send out a newsletter, every so often, to keep my contacts informed of my travels. Recently, this newsletter has morphed in to a BLOG which now has over thirty thousand readers.
BLOG: http://romhanyreport.blogspot.com/

Accounting and book-keeping is very important. You must keep books and all receipts for tax purposes. You will need to log all business-related expenses and be able to verify them. All my accounting is done on my computer. At the end of each financial year, my accountant prints all my expenses and earnings.

Sending out invoices in a timely manner is also important. With computer programs today, such as Microsoft Office, you can get professional looking templates to create letterheads and invoices. I also like to send out thank-you notes and make a follow-up phone call to my agent, after each ship contract, just to make sure that everything went well from the cruise ship's perspective.

Reliability
It is very important that you are reliable and dependable. If an agent hires you, then they need to know that you will turn up. Working for an agency can generate a great deal of work, but only if they are certain you are professional, and will turn up on time, and do a great job.

A word of advice - ALWAYS DOUBLE CHECK your departure dates and the times you leave. You DON'T want to miss the ship because you got am and p.m. mixed up. This happened to me when I first started in the cruise business.

PROMOTING YOURSELF
Once you are confident with your abilities, and feel that it is time to start trying to get work on a ship, you have then come to the next ingredient for a successful performer - namely promoting yourself. This includes

preparing a well written Bio, promotional DVD, brochures, and business cards.

But, before you can go out there and visit agencies, bureaus and potential clients, you will need not only to have some basic promotional material, you will also need an understanding of your market and the *type* of ship you believe will suit your particular act. To get a better understanding, read the chapter in this book which discusses each different type of cruise ship company and their potential age based market.

Your Promotional Package
The agent or cruise line will want to see a good professionally shot DVD of your act performed in front of a live audience, usually no longer than nine minutes in length. Some agents may want to see an entire forty five minute performance in front of an audience, so be prepared to have a follow up DVD of your entire act to send them. They will also want a biography and a good head shot. In this business your promotional DVD is the one main item that will get you work! Keep in mind that agents and bookers have seen almost EVERY type of act under the sun, so you want to make sure you can offer them something that is unique, (original and PG rated). You won't get booked if you film yourself doing a kids birthday party. I will discuss how to put together a DVD later in this chapter. According to one agent that I heard from, if you send in your promo clip as VHS video format, they won't even look at it! Those days are GONE, and whether or not your promo clip is in video or DVD format reflects on your style and on your act (i.e.. outdated or current). It doesn't hurt to have video clips on your website or up on youtube.

When approaching agents make sure you have:
1) Ten minute DVD of your act - make sure it is GOOD quality footage, and not outdated (style of hair and dress are sure giveaways!)
They may want to see a longer DVD.
2) 8 x 10 promotional photo - usually a good head shot is sufficient.
3) Biography of yourself - not too long - short and to the point
4) Cover letter: Introduce yourself, how you heard of them, why you think your act will entertain their guests (i.e.. age/income,

demographics). Closing statement thanking them for their consideration and letting them know you will follow-up shortly.

5) A brochure, if you have one with a list of clients, testimonials etc.

Business Cards

Business cards are important for the performer because you will find you do a lot of networking on ships. One of the great things about being a cruise ship magician is that it enables you to meet potential clients for your "land-based" magic work, in particular corporate functions and private parties. I would estimate that I would go through several hundred business cards a year. The business card will announce you as a professional entertainer, and it will stay around, so the person will be reminded of you at a later date when their need for your services arises.

There are many ideas that a printer or designer can give you regarding what to put on a card that will make people want to hold on to it. One of the best business cards I saw was from a professional speaker was one that folded in half and when folded looked like several hundred-dollar bills folded in half. It was something that a potential client was sure to keep. You might consider incorporating a calendar, optical illusions, games or charts of important information. I have developed mine using the well known trick *Out To Lunch Principle*. For more ideas be sure to check out my book called, "Lunch Is Served." It has over sixty routines in it for business cards.

An effective business card presents four or five pieces of information: your name, your logo, what you do, your phone number, and web address. The idea of turning a business card in to a resume is old and outdated.

I always carry a small stack of cards everywhere I do business and ask if I can leave some behind (ideally, with the key staff member that liaises with their guests/clients).

Alan Watson, a magician friend of mine, goes through fifty thousand cards per year and doesn't pay for a single one. What's his secret? He has found a sponsor who prints his cards with his name on one side and the sponsors on the other. As a result, Alan is constantly working and prospective clients know who he is.

One final secret about business cards ... it's great to print ample supplies and hand them out endlessly, to stack the odds of generating calls in and, ultimately bookings. However, it's even more important to "collect" the business cards of others so that you can add this info in to your database and then, be pro-active - make calls out (lots of them!). Don't just wait for the calls to come in.

Success as a entertainer depends on the quality of your performance, the number of years you have been in business – success very rarely comes overnight – your ability to meet the right people, your willingness to make phone calls and the quality of your promoting.

Brochures
With the advent of the Internet, the brochure is quickly becoming outdated. However I still produce a brochure that I send out to new clients which also has my web information on it. The agent likes to leave a potential cruise line with a DVD and a brochure with photos in it.

With the internet today, you can get brochures printed very inexpensively on high quality glossy paper that look very professional. Be sure to visit: www.vistaprint.com for the best printing bargains around.

Finding out (and appealing to) the needs of a particular market are important when planning an effective brochure. You will need to investigate the market in your targeted geographic region(s), and what the specific needs of the buyer are. Your brochure does not have to be wordy; it simply must appeal to the buyer's needs, and make them want to inquire about your services. The brochure is important, but remember it is only part of your marketing success.

When planning a brochure, there is so much involved when it comes to choosing the right type of font, making sure that you say the right things, and that you sell yourself properly. If you insist on designing and producing your own materials, please learn how to do this properly. You need to have an understanding of what sells a magic act for the cruise ship market.

<u>A brochure should have the four following ingredients:</u>

1. Easy to read, and pleasing to the eye in terms of page design.
2. Professional photographs and/or artwork.
3. Good typography (font styles, font size, white space to print ratio etc.).
4. Excellent writing and the integration of a strong (yet subtle) sales psychology approach. Be sure to include both the features and the benefits of your services in a way that will move the buyer to action (i.e.. get them to call you, sooner than later).

Don't evaluate the services of designers and copywriters on the basis of cost. In these areas you get what you pay for. You are paying for creativity and the ability to make your printed pieces produce positive results.

Photos

Your publicity photo is VERY important on a cruise ship. You will always need to have several with you when you join a ship and always 8 x10 size.

There are two different types of photos you could use. One is the action photo, and the other is a studio photo. It is important that you use professional photographs, and to use a photographer who has taken theatrical photos before.

A photo should tell passengers and cruise agents the type of personality you have. If you want to come across as a fun, warm like-able person, then have a fun photo contained in your promo kit.

There is nothing worse than seeing a photo that was taken twenty years ago. Keep your photos up-to-date. Recently I had to update my photos because I bought a new pair of glasses that changed the shape of my face (the photos cost more than the glasses - and these glasses were not cheap!).

As mentioned earlier, one of the great things about cruise ships is they have professional photographers on board, and they can provide you with a fantastic publicity photo at a very reasonable cost.

There are different ways to use photographs, such as integrating them into postcards, business cards, brochures, mailers, or posters, to announce your upcoming presentation(s).
A good black and white photo is advisable, however if you can afford color photos, then it would be worth the extra cost. Be sure to check out your local Wall-mart or Kodak shop as they now print photos at a very low cost.

Websites
Today a website is very important, more so for land-based work than cruise work. Once you get yourself established within the cruise industry your agent will look after you and, chances are, include you on their agencies website. However, if you want to introduce yourself to an agent, then a good start is to ask them to view your website.

A website is a great way to establish yourself as a professional performer. It is a way for you to get your message out to regular and potential clients by producing a 'blog', which is a newsletter published on a website. The website is one of the most valuable business tools you can have as a magician. Not only can you have pages dedicated to a client list, Bio, photos and videos of you in action, but, you can also post booking forms, and even a place for people to add comments about their own experiences (hopefully positive), if they have seen you work.

Another fun page to add to your website, if you work on cruise ships, is a photo page of you with passengers. People will constantly come back to your site, and tell friends to check it out as well. This could also result in future land based work.

My personal preference is to hire a professional web designer whose previous work you have seen, and whom you know will give your site that professional look. Too many people use free internet design programs like Front Page, which look as though are generic and don't stand out. I have two different sites people can view, one is an all Flash site with animation and the other is a Non-Flash site for those computers that aren't able to view Flash.

I design my own websites using Dream Weaver and Flash, as I am self-taught and have a solid understanding of how to design effective websites.

I strongly advise purchasing your own domain name. It is much easier to put on business cards and easier for people to remember, and look you up. It also helps you rank more highly in the search engines such as Google and Yahoo.
To see my websites visit:
www.paulromhany.com and **www.chaplinmagic.com**

Your website should include the following:
- A good photograph – to establish credibility. Be sure to include photos of you in action, plus a good head shot.
- A logo, theme or 'lead' – this will instantly let people know what you do. In my case, my theme is *Chaplinesque Comedy Magic*.
- A summary of what makes you different than everybody else.
- A client list with testimonials. People like to hire successful people.
- Multi-Media page, where you post samples of video, photos and audio. This gives the potential client a chance to see you in action and see the positive audience response. I also include access to a high-quality photo and a poster that advertises my performance, allowing clients to download these if they want to print these materials themselves, then

distribute them on their own. Quite often, on cruise ships, the cruise director will have visited my website and downloaded these promotional tools prior to me embarking on the ship.

- Articles and other 'tit-bits' that you may have written or had published about your business and/or entertainment services in newspapers and magazines.
- Contact information making, it as easy as possible for people to get hold of you.
- Product page. Websites are a great way to make a little extra income. Why not sell your teaching DVD (the one that you sell you sell on ships) also on your site!

How to get free publicity

While not directly related to cruising, I think it's important to add this section to any part of a book that deals with the business of show business. Having some good publicity in your promotional package will impress the bookers.

I am a big believer in getting free publicity. My motto is simple, if you don't ask, you don't get ... but "be careful what you ask for, because you may get it". This has resulted in countless free radio, newspaper and television advertising for me.

Here are some ways to generate free publicity:

1. Every time you perform before a group, offer to submit a short summary of your show and history for the organization's newsletter. Don't forget to send them your photo. It gets you in front of those you just performed for, as well as to those who missed you the first time around. Many groups also send their newsletters to the media. Be sure the last paragraph tells people what you do and how to get in touch with you via your website.

2. Call the advertising department of every newspaper and magazine you want to get into and ask for a copy of their editorial calendar. It's a free listing of all the special topics and special sections coming up during the calendar year. It will tip you off to sections where your

story idea might be a good fit, so you can query the editor weeks, and even months, ahead.

3. Call a reporter from your local newspaper and invite him or her to lunch, or to coffee. Offer yourself as a resource and ask, "how can I help you?" Feed them tips and story ideas. Become such a valuable source that they will keep coming back to you for more information, and eventually write about you.

4. Consider starting your own television show on your local cable TV station's community access channel. The station will provide the camera equipment for a small fee, and you can produce either one single show or an entire series of programs. Air time is free, yet highly valuable. Call your local cable company for details.

5. Build a network of other entertainers who are working or have worked ships. In this way you can receive and provide help that is often mutually beneficial. When a fellow entertainer cannot take an upcoming cruise assignment, perhaps you can. And of course, vice versa.

6. Whenever someone asks you to write for their e-zine or online magazine, visit their web site first and see if they have a resource section where you would be a good fit. Ask to be listed for free, in exchange for providing an article or ongoing articles.

7. If you publish a printed newsletter, be generous with providing free subscriptions for the national and local media. You'll be amazed how many reporters start calling you for interviews. If you can't afford to pay people who submit articles for your newsletter, then be sure to tell them that they will be seen by national media, who get your free subscription. Write articles for electronic magazines and include a paragraph of information at the end that encourages readers to click the link to your web site.

8. Don't forget newspaper and magazine columnists. They're always hungry for fresh ideas. Keep in touch with them and pitch them ideas regularly.

9. Call local radio talk show hosts and invite them to call on you when their other guests cancel. They will be thankful for your offer. I am often asked to appear on the magic based talk-show at itricks.com.

10. Contact your trade association and ask them to refer reporters to you. Many reporters who don't know where to find sources start by calling trade associations.
11. Always refer to yourself as an "expert" in your marketing materials, at your web site, in information that explains your workshops, in your introductions, and in your media kit. The media always seek out experts and interview them.

Natalie enjoying a drink in our cabin on a ship

CHAPTER SIX

IN THEIR OWN WORDS

You meet so many amazing people while performing on ships

Here are some unedited stories and words of advice, from friends of mine who work on cruise ships.

You Never Know Who is in Your Audience

Matthew Fallon

With every show you perform, on board ship or not, be true to yourself, your art and your audience. You never know who is watching. A number of years ago, Mistia and I were performing on board Celebrity's ship "Mercury" doing Panama Canal and Caribbean runs. One night, after our show, we were on our way to dinner and approached by a middle-aged man who expressed that he thoroughly enjoyed our performance. This is always wonderful fuel-for-the-tank, and we thanked him gratefully. He then continued on to ask if I knew much about the history of magic. "I do not know as much as I'd like but I am an avid studier!" I replied. He asked if we would mind coming to his table in the main dining room just before 9:00 p.m. to meet an older man seated at his table. The middle-aged man said that the older was sharing with his table mates that he enjoyed our show and that his father, too, was a magician, a quite famous one, who performed for royalty and the wealthy many years ago. The middle-aged man seemed skeptical of the older man's stories and wanted my opinion.

Later that night around 8:45p.m, Mistia and I made our way to the main dining room. I was extremely curious who this man's father may have been and, being quite open to hearing most anyone's story, my anticipation was building.

We found the correct table by number and recognized the middle-aged man who first approached us before dinner. He immediately stood up with a smile and introduced us to everyone seated with him. He finished introductions with an out-stretched hand, gesturing to an older man seated with his wife. I remember thinking to myself, "...if that man doesn't look a lot like Max Malini..." This older man introduced his wife Babs and himself, Ozzie Malini. My jaw dropped. Goosebumps all over. Mistia and I were standing across the large, round table from the two of them and I gently put my arm around Mistia pulling her with me to get closer. Ozzie complimented us on our performance and mentioned his father was a magician named Max Malini. Immediately, the middle-aged man who invited us to this encounter asked me, "Have you heard of him?" Wide-eyed and all smiles, I answered, "Wow, oh, yes." Ozzie and Babs were just finishing dessert and coffee and were then going to the evening's show. Ozzie asked us if we could get together to talk afterward. "Absolutely!" I said. We agreed on a place and time.

Sitting with Ozzie was an incredible gift. He was soft-spoken and shared many memories of his father: a couple of coin sleights, his performances for royalty and the wealthy and his travels. I wish I had a tape recorder. I came to learn Ozzie and his wife lived near us in Southern California and he kindly invited us to get together at their home as he was excited to share so much with me.

After returning home from our contract, I phoned Ozzie and, unfortunately, his health was not 100%. He was in and out of the hospital and a number of months passed during which Ozzie was not up to meeting in person so we would talk for a bit on the telephone. Looking forward to getting together again soon we would end each conversation with a not-too-distant date to call and try again. It was when I made an unscheduled call that Babs answered and said Ozzie had passed away just a couple of days prior. She was glad I had called as she wanted to invite us to Ozzie's memorial service. It was a small, beautiful family affair that we felt honored to be a part of. Solely by chance and coincidence were we given the opportunity to meet Ozzie Malini on board that ship. Ozzie was the son of a true Legend in magic whose love and support for our art was as strong as his father's. He was very generous with his time, knowledge, stories and advice. Ozzie Malini was a wonderful man.

Matthew and Mistia Fallon are a dynamic illusion team who have performed on ships for a number of years with their highly energetic and entertaining illusion show. The show also includes some wonderful aerial acrobatics by Mistia. You can see more of them at: www.fallonmagic.com

Mistia, Natalie, Paul and Matt in Barcelona 2007

Cruise Industry Advice

by TC Tahoe

Things you need to know:

1. Have a valid Passport. This is a must! Your passport must be valid for at least the next three months. It is also the responsibility of the artist to have all necessary travel visas and inoculations.

2. READ THE FINE PRINT!!! If you are offered a contract with a Cruise Line MAKE SURE you understand the details.

a.) How you will be paid (Cash/Check on board ship or end of contract? etc.) Do they deduct taxes? Are you paid in US funds - some ships might not!

b.) Do they pay for airline tickets, transfers and hotels to and from ship?

c.) Accommodations. Will you have a passenger or staff cabin? (Passenger is better) private or shared. You will probably be required to pay tips to your room steward and dining room waiter.

d.) Will you eat off the passenger menu or " crew food " in the Mess?

e.) How many different performances a week and what length.

f.) Are you considered to have passenger status or crew ? If you are crew, expect to do boat drills.

g.) Extra duties. Are you an Entertainer only, or are you expected to do Cruise Staff duties such as selling BINGO cards, greeting passengers during embarkation, escort tours etc?

It should be noted that almost every cruise ship contract is written in a way that allows the employer to cancel out if they feel that an entertainer's work is inferior or inappropriate. Your performance should reflect the demographics of the ship. Shorter cruises (3 - 4 days) tend to be a younger crowd while cruises longer than seven days attract older passengers. Additionally, cruises to the Caribbean and Mexican Riviera generally attract a younger passengers, cruises to Alaska, Europe, Asia and the Panama Canal a little to a lot older.   Most cruise ships offer the same show twice an evening. Once after first seating dinner (approx. 8:30) and again following second seating (approx. 10:30). Additionally , many ships may offer a midnight cabaret show (adult), a pre-dinner cocktail hour show or a welcome aboard show. Shows on board ship rarely are longer than one hour. The amount of material a performer needs will depend upon the length of cruise and the ships' entertainment format. Most variety acts need to have between 60-90 minutes worth of quality stage material.

Cruise ships vary from small 120 passenger yachts to 3000 passenger super liners. As a result, stage and backstage areas vary drastically. Many of the new mega-ships have theaters and show lounges that rival those found in Las Vegas or Atlantic City while older, smaller ships may only have a spotlight and a dance floor for a stage. Variety acts such as Magicians, Comics, Instrumentalists as well as Vocalists round out the Show Room entertainment. If your show requires music accompaniment - remember that most ships do not use live orchestras any more Make sure you bring your music in a couple of different formants. CD, cassette tape, or mini disk. Rehearsal time is usually limited so make sure you meet up with the technicians ahead of time. And bring at least TWO cue sheets one for the light tech and one for the sound. On board entertainment is coordinated by the Cruise Director. He or she is in charge of the entertainment and cruise staff including writing evaluations of performers every cruise. The C.D. will usually host the evening entertainment and, quite often is also a performer. As an entertainer on board ship, you are constantly in the public eye.

From the moment you leave your cabin you are on display. As a result, cruise lines have very specific rules of dress and conduct. Most of these are common sense, while others may not be as obvious. You will receive a copy of the ships rules upon joining the vessel - read them, understand them and follow them. Almost all ships require proper attire at night. Formal , informal and casual nights are scheduled throughout a cruise. It is also advisable to determine if there are "theme nights" such as "Country Night" or "50's Night." Although all cruise ships have stabilizers to limit the motion - SHIPS DO MOVE, especially during rough weather. Nothing is quite as miserable as seasickness. If you THINK you are susceptible - find out BEFORE you sign a six month contract!

Hospital Story
By Den West

My wife Bobbie and I had a three month contract on a Princess Cruise ship in 2005 and were on the ship with Paul and Natalie Romhany. It was a world cruise so we were on together for quite some time and became good friends. The ship was sailing around the South Pacific and one day while on our way to Tahiti, there was a medical evacuation. This is where a passenger becomes so ill that they have to be taken off the ship, sometimes by helicopter, to a local hospital. The night after the medical evacuation, my wife Bobbie and I are having dinner and see a lady sitting by herself, obviously very upset, so we approached her to make sure she was alright. It turned out that her husband had become very ill and was rushed to hospital and she was to disembark the ship the next day in Tahiti and didn't know how her husband was doing or where she was going to stay. She was very scared. and obviously very upset, and a long way from home.

After talking to her she recognized us from our show. We asked her if she would like us to visit her and her husband in the port and she got very excited saying her husband would love to see us as they had enjoyed our show so much and it would be a lovely surprise. To be honest, I don't think she really thought we were serious but we found out where the hospital was and where she and her husband would be. Later that night we ran in to Paul and Natalie Romhany, and told them the story. They told us they would like to join us so we planned to meet in the morning and head to the hospital.

The next day we all met, got a taxi to the local, only, hospital and when we arrived we could see the condition were not the best. We found the room and as soon as we entered the expression of joy on both the husband and wife's face made it all worthwhile. The wife told her husband of our meeting, but didn't expect us to turn up. We stayed for an hour, I gave a mini-concert in the hospital room as I played guitar while Bobbie and I sang, and Paul did some close-up magic for them.

Both Paul and I agreed it was one of the most rewarding gigs of our career. Later we heard that the husband became well enough to fly back to the U.K where he had a successful operation.

Bobbie and Den West are one of the most respected couples on the high seas. They are two the greatest people you will meet, and have a very dynamic act. Den is a multi-instrumentalist, and his lovely wife Bobbie has a powerful voice. This is why they are one of the busiest acts around today.

Front left, Natalie, Den, Paul and Bobbie

Tips and hints for cruising

Eric Bedard

Over the years of cruising and traveling to and from ships, I have learned a few pointers to make the journey and/or cruise more enjoyable.

Often times you land in a city in the middle of the night and need to sleep in the next day so you are well rested as you could be scheduled on the Welcome Aboard Show. Then you discover that the curtains don't close all the way in your Hotel room. If you take one or two of the hangers that have the pants clips on them, you can use the clips to hold the curtains shut. Just put in your earplugs and you are good to go.

Some times you are scheduled to take the shuttle with the crew, which usually leaves at 7:00 am or earlier. Then when you get to the ship, you often can't get on until all of the passengers are off the ship. (I stood in the blazing heat for three or four hours before I learned).
Instead of getting up after three hours of sleep, get your rest, have a nice breakfast and then take a cab to the vessel around noon or so; you can submit the receipt directly to the cruise line and in most cases you will be reimbursed. This is the case with Princess whom I cruise with exclusively, so you should check with other Guest Entertainers for other cruise lines so you don't get in trouble.

A few packing tips: When packing dress pants, roll them up tightly. They open up without wrinkles and many times you can wear them after they hang for an hour or two.
Also saves a lot of room in your baggage.
If you go to Shoppers Drug Mart in Canada or Walgreen's in the US, you can buy "Space Travel Bags". Pack each one like they are a drawer. Undergarments in one, work out clothes, shorts in 2nd, and shirts and tee shirts in the third. After packing them, you zip them up and roll out all the air. Great for saving space and if you happen to take a ghetto speed boat to meet your ship on an island in Bali, it insures that all of your clothes will be dry when you get there, even if you are not!

I am sure that most travelers have learned to have lots of Zip Lock Baggies with them, but in case you are new to traveling & cruising: carry lots of these with you. Put all of your toiletries in them when traveling so there is no leakage and they are great for storing props. You put all of the small items for each routine in its' own baggie so instead of having whole bunch of loose props, you have 5 or 6 baggies. Oh and carry a small flashlight with you in your pencil/marker case so if you are back stage just before the show and the back stage lights get turned off, you can still check on props or see your way around.

My buddy and fellow magic dude, Sukuma Avery told me this one: Carry a bottle of Fabreeze with you and if you are ever in a situation where you have a shirt that gets a little sweaty and is a little ripe smelling, you can spray the arm pits with Fabreeze and let it air out and wear it one more time, in case you can't get to the Laundry before you go on.

And another great tip from another fellow magic dude, Trevor Watters, is to carry some of those Ass Gaskets (Trevor's name for them) with you when traveling. You know when you are in a nice restroom and they have those thin tissue, disposable seat covers for you to use. Well these fold up really small, (you can actually carry one in your wallet) and you should always have a few with you. In many countries, especially in Europe, the Med and the Orient, the washrooms can be very interesting and you will be grateful to have these Ass Gaskets with you.

Also, when traveling, always carry some toilet paper or tissue paper with you as in many countries they don't have any in the public washrooms. Another must is to carry a small bottle of hand sanitizer with you at all times. I got the Norwalk virus(two times in a week) in December of last year and was quarantined for 7 days in my cabin; and I spent a lot of time in that tiny washroom. So, sanitize your hands often; use paper napkins to open and close washroom doors and avoid shaking hands with pax if possible. A polite way to do this is to do what Chickie Spears does and that is to offer your knuckles for a slight bump as many people do nowadays.

Cruising Tips

Jim Coston

1. Although it's not as easy to do now as it used to be (before cruise line consolidation), try to debut your show somewhere where you can afford to fail.

Working at sea is very different than working on land. Even if you have significant experience shore side, adjusting your act to the needs of a ship audience can take some time.

If your first cruise ship contract is with a major company (RCI, P&O, Princess, HAL, Carnival), and you don't do well, you've most likely hurt your chances to return and that denies you access to a dozen or more ships!

When I began back in 1981, there were dozens of smaller cruise lines where you could polish your craft before tackling "the big guys". Quite often you were Cruise Staff / Entertainers and if you you didn't do well, who cares??

Today, there are still a few around (Discovery, Sea Escape etc.). Do yourself a favor and learn to "work the room" somewhere where your future doesn't hang on every shows' success.

As tempting as it may be to "start at the top" it is far wiser to pay your dues and work your way up.

2. If you are just starting out, consider doing shorter (2 - 5 day) cruises where you are less likely to need a full second show. Many performers have one strong show and have nothing left in the bag for a second appearance.

A shorter cruise allows you to repeat your performances more often and you can slowly add new material to flesh out a second show.

If you DO have to provide two full shows, and feel one set is significantly weaker than the other, I believe you should do the stronger material first. I've seen more than one performer opt to "save" their strongest material for their second show only to see their contract cancelled before they have their chance perform!

If you endear yourself to the audience initially (after all, first impressions...) you can often parlay that good will in your second show.

3. Before signing a contract, READ IT! Not all cruise contracts are the same. Will you have passenger privileges (full or modified)? Will the Cruise Line cover all Airfares & Transportation? Will you be on the Crew List? Will you be required to do "extra duties'? Will you be covered medically?

And if they say you will have a Staff Cabin .... check the spelling of Staff (Staph) <grin>

More than just a musician - Jim Coston is an entertainer. By combining traditional Dixieland Jazz with a selection of Broadway show tunes, popular standards, classical favorites, novelty tunes and just a touch of bluegrass, Jim Coston brings the banjo into the new millennium with and eclectic evening of music and comedy sure to please audiences everywhere.
Jim Coston has been a featured headline Cabaret Act on over 80 different cruise ships worldwide. Additionally, he has been featured at numerous Theaters, Fairs, Conventions, Corporate Events and Nightclubs across the USA as well as local and national Radio & Television appearances.

Observations After My First Year

Chris Michaels

All mainland entertainers are facing fewer venues and less opportunities to play an actual "showroom". Cruise lines offer beautiful theaters, bands, lighting, and audiences that come to be entertained. While it can be a tough market to break into, the rewards are great.

This last October 9, I celebrated my first year anniversary as a guest entertainer with the Holland America cruise line. It's been a learning experience for me, after this first year I have made (and corrected) mistakes.

GETTING THAT FIRST JOB!
You really have to ask yourself: "Am I ready?" There are many bases to cover before that first cruise.

What does your resume have that is going to set you far above all other DVD packages the cruise office receives every day? If you are not a graphic artist, have an professional help prepare your presentation for you. Years ago, I went to a local county fair and asked to look over the entertainment promotional materials they had received. I made notes of which packages caught my eye, which ones I would open first. Look successful from the onset and you will be successful.

Ask yourself: What is going to set your act above any other out there? What is yours and yours alone? What are the guests going to be talking about at breakfast the next morning?
After your first cruise, entertainer friends might be asking for your help. How do they get your job on your ship! While many of my (musician) friends are great players, they don't have an act! A comedic (entertainer) juggler will be remembered over a technical juggler. Too many jugglers do the same jokes, too many magicians do linking rings and too many

singers do "My Way". An audience will talk about the things they haven't seen or heard before.

After getting the initial booking:

FIRST THINGS FIRST!
If the ship sails at 5:00 p.m. don't arrive at 4:55 p.m.!
Get there with extra time for everybody.
Check in at the front desk, then drop off your suitcases to your room. Second, check in and meet your cruise director. He or she is your "boss", let them know you are on board. They should have your performance schedule and onboard phone numbers of the Stage Manager and Musical Director. Third - find your show equipment and props. If they have been sent ahead, be sure they are on the ship before you set sail! On this very cruise, I was walking up the gangway and noticed my five cases sitting on the dock, NOT ON BOARD! The cruise director made a few frantic calls and made sure everything was loaded just 20 minutes before we were to set sail.

After you have played a cruise line a few times, you might offer to the C.D. (Cruise Director) that you would be available for other duties. This is at your discretion. Some smaller cruise lines have been known to take advantage of a guest entertainer's time. Days at sea can seem long, sometimes it's fun to take an hour and be a guest on a "Game Show" or do a "Coffee Chat".
A "Coffee Chat", is an informal question and answer session. It's a great chance to talk one on one with your audience and even "plug" your CD, DVD or items for sale. I usually bring a few small instruments and even give a quick lesson to those interested. Dress up, a little nicer than the guests. Remember you are representing the cruise line, your agency and yourself!

I've only had a few occasions where I was called to do extra duties. Once a singer was sick and I was asked to change ships and do a short variety show. Moving equipment, charts and costumes was a pain, but made my act more valuable to the main office. Today I was asked to dress up as Frankenstein for Halloween. Why not? The CD's weekly report to the head office could include you being as a "team player", going above and beyond your contract show duties.

AIRLINE MILES

Pick just three major airlines and join their frequent flier programs.

When a cruise ship buys for your airline ticket they will probably book you on the cheapest flight available.

Those cheap flights are sometimes booked on smaller airlines such as Air Canada, NWA, Air France or Hawaii Airlines. If you are booked with a smaller airline, go to their website and do a search under "Partners". Find a one of your three "chosen" frequent flier airlines in their partner family. For example: Delta has the Skyteam Global Alliance, United has the Star Alliance and American has their Advantage programs.

For example, a few weeks ago I flew to Montreal on Air Canada. Air Canada is a member of United Airlines partner program.

When I checked in I asked for the Air Canada miles to be tacked on to United's frequent flier plan. It is better to have only three frequent flier memberships than seven or eight. Your miles will add up faster.

EXCURSION ESCORTS

Here's another extra "perk" I didn't find out about until after my first nine months of cruising.

I would occasionally pay for an excursion offered by the cruise line. Usually it's a bus ride to a folk arts show, lunch and shopping in the port city.

Other entertainers would talk of their trips into town and what they've seen. I seldom do excursions as they could can quite expensive. On my first year of cruising I was trying to save money, wanting to recoup all the expenses I had buying charts, costumes, instruments and cases.

One guest entertainer (finally) told me about being a Tour Escort. An escort represents the cruise company, going on the excursion, helping the guests and writing a short review for the cruise line.

After getting your bags to your room and checking in with the cruise director my third stop is always looking over the excursion brochure. The brochure lists all the upcoming excursions.

Mark the brochure with choices of "1", "2" and "3" by your favored choices. Don't expect to be a (free) escort if the trip is a $500.00 small plane trip over the glaciers in Alaska. Any free tour is a good thing! Any time away from the ship and travel beyond the dock t-shirt stores is welcome!

Be sure to find out what day your technical or band rehearsal is. You don't want to be scheduled for a 4 ½ hour excursion and not get back in time for your band rehearsal.

Experience is always the best teacher, I hope my insights and tips will help. Good luck cruising!

Chris Michaels is a veteran theme park entertainer having worked at Disney World, Knott's Berry Farm, Great America and Cypress Gardens. Chris worked Sea World for 14 years performing over 10,000 shows for 25 million people. Currently he performs a 10 instrument musical comedy act on the Holland America Cruise line.

Extra little story

Recently I had to catch a flight to Aruba, however my flight from Hong Kong was delayed and so I was not able to catch up with flights from Hong Kong to Vancouver then to Aruba. Because the ship was at sea for a few days I had to fly to the next port of call which was Santarem in South America. It was one of the longest journey's of my life! I flew from Vancouver to Chicago then on to Sao Paulo to Victoria to Salvador then to Recife to Fortaliza to Sao Luiz then to Belem and finally caught up with the ship in Santarem. What a journey! Needless to say I was exhausted. You get used to these long flights and the secret is not to let them get to you. Just go with the flow if you can, there is nothing you can do about it.

As I said, there are so many examples of these types of stories. Today, I am writing from Cartegena, Columbia, not because I want to but because of what I went through today.

I disembarked the ship today at 2pm, took a rough ride to the airport and then went through the worst customs check ever. I had heard stories from other entertainers about this port and coming in and out of the airport. If you can avoid embarking or disembarking at all from this place then do it. They held guns while they checked through all my luggage and almost pulled apart my snowstorm machine. Prior to getting off the ship today, a friend told me to take some of my DVDs and give them to the officials if need be. After they went through all my gear I gave them a DVD and they became very friendly after that, I also did some magic for them. Lesson, always take a deck of cards with you. When I finally got to the check in, I found out my flight was cancelled which means I can't fly until tomorrow as the only plane the airline had did not turn up! So it's up at 5am to fly to Panama then on to Miami. I am currently in a hotel somewhere in Columbia and have made sure my door is bolted shut and the alarm is set.

Collection of 2008 BLOG stories

I have been collecting and writing stories about my travels since I started cruising. Below are a few of them from my weekly BLOG. http://www.romhanyreport.blogspot.com/

The following will also give you some insight in to the world of cruising, I have taken parts from several BLOGS to give you an idea of what life is like for us. These were all written during 2008.

BLOG ONE
The past two weeks have been very hectic as I was in Brazil on a cruise ship for twelve days. Every cruise ship offers different working conditions, and the ship I was on, while high end, doesn't have a state of the art theater like many modern ships. Working on a cabaret floor, like the one on this ship, always reminds me of watching Billy McComb work. I first met Billy when I was in my early 20s and living in New Zealand. Billy came over for a magic convention and he did a few private corporate shows. Watching him work for a lay audience was such an amazing learning experience. He was certainly the king of 'pack small and play big' and his personality and charm really won audiences over. His version of the Linking Himber Rings was something to behold.

Billy was such an influence on so many magicians and I was certainly one of them. With my own show I am able to pack everything in to one bag and still perform two different 45 minute shows on cruise ships. Most of the ships today seat 1000 people and over, so you still have to be able to play to a large room. Traveling as much as I do, and having the airlines lose my luggage so many times, eleven last year and once already this year, I now travel with a back up show in my back pack.

BLOG TWO
This week I will offer a little advice to those who are getting in to cruising, or who are thinking about it. One of the things you start to learn as you cruise around the world is that it isn't all fun and games. Actually

the travel alone can be very taxing and draining on your body. It can take it's toll if you are not careful.

There are two different types of magicians who work cruise ships. Those who are 'fly on' acts and those who stay on a ship for a long period of time, usually illusionists, but that is not always the case. In my case, I have a wife and home so don't like to be away for a long period of time, which is why I will fly out for a week or so, then fly back home. A fly on act must be able to pack very small and play very big. The master of this type of act and a person we all learned so much from was Billy McComb. Billy could certainly pack very small and play to large theaters. The thing I learned from Billy was that it is all about personality and not so much the tricks. Sure his magic was super strong, look at his Himber ring routine, but you were entertained, which I think made the magic that much stronger when it happened.

Your act has to be strong enough to play a 1,500 seat theater, and practical enough to work a venue where you are completely surrounded, even people directly above you looking down! If you have two types of these shows then you are on your way to looking at performing on a ship.

The reason I bring this up is because of the experience I am recovering from. After our three month stint on four different ships, I left Natalie at home while I went away to work a ship for a week. However, because the gig was in such a remote part of Brazil, with only two flights in and out each week, they had to fly me in earlier. I am currently sitting in a hotel lobby after having traveled 24 hours to get here. Something I discovered many years ago was to DEMAND that I always get the port agents phone number and the hotel I am to be staying in BEFORE I leave. The worst feeling is traveling in and out of countries, and nobody to pick you up, especially if you don't speak the language and you have no idea of the hotel you are staying in.

To cap it all off, I arrived this morning at 3am, waited in this humid and intimidating airport for the port agent. I had several emails saying they would pick me up and organized a hotel etc. However, upon arrival there was nobody there. I waited two hours before another person appeared and I was able to borrow a phone. I called the agent and they sent a driver out to me. As usual, no hotel was booked so they 'dumped' me in a place that was dirty, no hot water. I probably slept a few hours before phoning the port agent back and demanding they take me to a more respectable hotel … which they did and where I am now!

I should probably explain that a 'port agent' is an agency that works for the cruise line and is supposed to pick you up, book hotel rooms and look after you when you arrive and leave a ship. In most cases they are very good, however there are far too many stories about them not getting messages, not picking people up. My main worry about this particular port in Brazil was that a good friend of mine was badly attacked here early last year after the port agent didn't turn up and he had to find his own hotel.

Prior to leaving for this cruise I made sure my agent contacted the cruise line, and at least gave me the port agents name and phone number, plus emergency after hours number. ALWAYS make sure you get this information. It's got to the point now where I refuse to even leave for a ship if I don't have this information. There have been instances where I turned up and with nobody to meet me. I phoned the contact number I was given, only to be told that they were no longer the port agent for that cruise line and had not been for many years! I don't think some of them update their files that often.

So there is my story for this week and a little advice for those wanting to start cruising. What you start to learn is that you don't get paid for the shows anymore, but for the stress, the travel and the hassle of it all. Is it worth it?? I really am starting to have my doubts.

BLOG THREE

I performed my show last night in the main theater that seats 1,500 people. Both shows were very busy, the second house was completely full. It's always fantastic working in such amazing venues on ships that are so high tech. I was able to incorporate my video work during the show, utilizing the screen behind me during the Chaplin part of the show. It really makes a huge difference. Many magicians travel with snow machines, and have snow flowing in, I prefer to pack small and play big. Instead of flying with snow machines, I simply use the original 'fan' version and video screen behind me. This gives the illusion of more snow falling, and to be honest, the reaction is the same once I start producing the snow than when I used Kevin James version. I own the last two versions of Kevin's Snow Storm, and traveling with it really is a pain. I went back to basics, and found how to get the most reaction out of just a small fan and the use of video behind me. A real lesson in taking something and working hard at it, and ending up with a stronger result.

I had the most amazing experience on the cruise this past week watching one of the best acts I have ever seen on a cruise ship. The performer was Kirk Marsh, and he is a true artist. Here is a guy who knows about theater, and obviously has spent years studying his craft. He was able to perform a full fifty minute silent show with NO PROPS!!! He got more reaction from his show than any other magic act I have ever seen on a ship.

Here is something we can all learn. I have been on ships where magicians use prop after prop, and fill the stage like a dealer demo. At the end of the show people walk out of the theater saying, *"what's for dinner?"* They really aren't taken on a journey in the show, they aren't left with any 'feeling'. After watching Kirk's show you walk out stunned, knowing you have just witnessed something incredible. I was able to talk to Kirk after his show and spend time with him. We talked a lot about his techniques, and one of them includes 'breathing'. We went over one of my routines I do as Chaplin and how much more I could get out of it by taking a 'breath' during the effect, and looking to the audience at certain points in my show. It really made so much sense.

BLOG FOUR

It's been a very hectic two weeks for us. Our travels took us to Ireland, France and the UK. After almost nine years of performing on cruise ships I still pinch myself when I get home to see if it's all for real. While many magicians might get in their car and drive to a gig, I get on a plane and fly. As I sit here at home I can't get over that two days ago we were in France, and then Ireland. One thing I never do, is take it all for granted . I realize just how fortunate we are to do what we love so much, and get paid to travel the world. If you have a dream then I always urge people to follow it, this was my dream since I was a young kid and am now living it.

Last week I talked about my snow storm routine. As I mentioned I own (and LOVE) Kevin James's *snow storm*. I own the last two models. The only problem is the fact that it's an 'extra' bag that I need to worry about. Would you believe that the airlines lost our luggage AGAIN coming home. Usually it is lost on the way TO the ship so this time it wasn't so bad. We are still waiting for lost luggage (actually we've given up waiting) from January. Because we travel so much and have to carry our own bags and often find ourselves running to ships and planes, we pack very light. Just ONE bag for me and one for my wife, plus a carry on bag each. (The carry on bag has my second show, which is a back-up show in case the Chaplin show gets lost).

BLOG FIVE

We then get off the ship in two days, then take a two hour journey to Heathrow Airport and fly to Oslo to catch another ship for another few days, then back to Vigo where we fly from here to Madrid, then Heathrow to Halifax and on to Moncton. We are home for a week before flying out again. The only good thing about all this travel is that we collect air points, should have a free flight to somewhere soon - although the last thing we would want to do is fly!

I just can't believe how large the cruise ships are getting these days. I can now say that I have worked on the worlds smallest cruise ship and the worlds largest ... I'll take the large one any day over the small one.

The entertainment on here is very diverse. For example, at 7pm we can go to the ice-theater and catch the ice show, then at 9pm on to the Main Theater where we can watch a full production show. There are so many different rooms and places to hang out, we are spoilt for choice. As I write all this I know what we'll be doing ... sleeping! We are on the sister ship to this in June so have more time to explore then.

One of the problems with so much travel is that your body clock never knows what time of the day it is. I also forget which country I am in. It's funny when you go in to a shop and you start saying hello in the wrong language!

BLOG SIX
Natalie and I are back from our exhausting weeks work in Europe. I would have written my BLOG yesterday but we were flying for two days. It was quite the journey, we were only away for one week, but it felt like a month. Excuse any spelling errors and typos this week as I still have jet lag!

We just arrived home about an hour ago but I wanted to get this out as quickly as possible. We just finished working on the world's largest cruise ship. It was such a great experience. The entire audience was German, and English was <u>not</u> their first language, hence hiring a non-speaking act. It has taken me pretty much my entire career to put together a full evening show with no speaking, and it really takes everything I have to pull it off. Like every show, it needs a very strong beginning, middle and end, I try not to put any 'fluff' in the show as people have very short attention spans these days. Variety is the key to putting something like this together, and I look at it not as a magic show, but more a one man performance, where I include video, music and magic. It's a tribute to Charlie Chaplin and so I try to encompass everything about Charlie from laughter to pathos to his amazing music he wrote.

BLOG SEVEN

Greetings BLOG readers. This week Natalie and I find ourselves in France and Italy. We had a very long flight from our little home in New Brunswick Canada via Heathrow, then on to Barcelona. I found out the day I arrived to the ship, I was working ... not the easiest thing in the world to do when all you feel like doing is sleeping for several days. These are some of the things you have to be prepared for when traveling and working on ships like we do.

We will be away for a month this time, visiting some of our favorite ports of call, including Monte Carlo, Cannes, Barcelona and various ports of call in Italy. The cruise passengers are truly an international audience, with over thirty different nationalities on board. This is the reason we are always booked to work over this side of the world rather than close to home. I am not complaining, because I would much rather be in Europe. The food and culture here is simply amazing. To be in Rome one day and Monte Carlo the next, is simply amazing. We sit in an outdoor cafe drinking french coffee one day, and an italian espresso the next. This has to be one of the best gigs in show business.

Magic has certainly been very good to us, and we don't take it for granted. I learned at very young age, that to get what you want in life you have to work hard. Having performed magic since I was eight years old, I have worked very hard to get to where I am, and live the lifestyle I live. I went through years of doing almost every type of gig you could imagine, from the darkest pubs and nightclubs, to strolling magic at supermarkets. These all helped pay the bills, and paved the way for me being able to put together a full evening show that I can travel the world with.

With the tight security on ships and at airports, you have to seriously consider what you perform in your act. Anything with swords, knives or fire are out. The cruise line we are working on at the moment, wants every detail about your act long before you get hired. They need to know if you fire, including any type of flame. There is a rule that you can not use candles, smoke pots or flash paper. Even trying to take on Kevin James's *Sword Umbrella* is not that easy.

If you can do a forty five minute show with just silks, and no talking then you have got it made. I have yet to achieve that goal! While I jest about it, it is not that far from the truth.

Of course, this is only if you are a fly on act. Some magicians stay on for six months, and have their gear and illusions shipped prior to joining the ship. In most cases these guys and girls have been in the business a long time, and established themselves so that the cruise line will hire them for many months at a time. In some cases a certain ship will become their own, so to speak.

In creating an act that will travel there is a lot to consider. It is not just a case of putting together a bunch of tricks. Due to the type of audiences on ships, and the amount of other entertainment available, you really need to have an act that will not only draw a crowd but keep them. Last night was a good example. We went to see a singer who was the headline act. While I thought he had a great voice, his show did not really hold the crowd.

There was so much else going on, that many people decided to come in, watch for a little while, then leave to do something else. It is almost like changing channels on the remote control. On ships you have loads of options of what you do and what you watch.

Lots of things to consider when putting together an act designed for cruise lines; include type of audience, type of cruise, what the cruise line expects from you, how many shows you have to do and so on. Make sure you check everything out before you leave to join a ship. I always have my agent find out what is needed from me before I leave. Of course this often changes once you get to the ship so be prepared.

BLOG EIGHT

Well here we are, another week gone by. It's been quite a busy week because the ship we are currently on, is traveling four and five day cruising, which means more shows than normal. On a regular seven day cruise, I might do my show every seven days, or if it's a twelve day cruise, every twelve days.

I'm not complaining, because it means I get a good crack at my show, and it enables me to work on new ideas. Some of the problems you encounter while being away from home for so long include, not being able to get enough supplies for your magic act. If you need flash paper, make sure you have enough for the amount of shows you are going to do – ALWAYS take more than you need.

Another example might be, if you do a torn and restored newspaper. Are you sure you can get the same size paper in a different country. Quite often, if you are use to working with one size newspaper. it might be hard to change, especially if in Europe the paper size is much smaller. In my case, I go to an international news stand and can get a USA sized paper so it's no problem – but these are just one or two examples of things you need to think about when traveling. When performing a snow storm several times a week, do you have enough confetti to last you the entire period you are away. As mentioned, I always take way more than I think I'll need, and often I just have enough.

BLOG NINE

I mentioned last week that we've been doing four and five day cruises. With our contract coming to and end, I can now say it's been quite a learning curve for the cruise line, because they have never done this type of cruising with the majority of Spanish speaking audiences out of Barcelona. We are talking about 85%, even 90% non-English speaking audiences. It's made life very hard on all the acts, as the cruise director has really struggled to get passengers to attend the shows. I am glad that Natalie and I are finally heading home in a few days because it hasn't been the easiest gig in the world. They flew in a circus act from Moscow last week to take over when we finish. They do a rather unique Hoola Hoop type show which is very visual.

It seems that for whatever reason, passengers aren't turning up to the full evening shows. This might have something to do with the fact that they are short cruises, or even that the shows are very late at 9.30pm and 11.15pm. They have had a Beatles tribute act on, an Italian singer plus the production shows. No matter what the cruise director puts on stage people just stay away. My theory is, that because it's a four and five day cruise, they are on here to party and not to attend shows. In the end the cruise director stopped putting on a show and does his own game type show, which is in English and draws very few people. He just can't win! He even tried doing a matinee show with a magic act that was on before us, and they only had twenty people in the audience. No reflection on the act, it's just that people don't want to attend the shows.

Last opening night, the cruise director stormed offstage, prior to me going on, saying they were a 'shitty' audience and not worth him doing his singing bit. As a professional, we all know you should never blame your audience, but in some cases people just aren't in the mood to be entertained. Makes it hard on all of the acts.

It's been a great learning curve for the cruise line and even for myself trying to find out what a completely different audience wants. At this stage nobody has the answers. Even after nine years of working for pretty much every cruise line out there, you NEVER STOP LEARNING. There is always something different to experience … as they say, every audience is different.

BLOG TEN
What a heck of a week it's been. Trust me folks – show business isn't all glamour. Last you heard from me, I was flying from Barcelona to New York to LA then to New Zealand where I joined a ship. Because of the position of the ship, we were at sea for six days, I was unable to get to the internet and upload last weeks BLOG. When I finally was able to check my emails I had over five hundred from magicians asking what

had happened. Sorry folks – sometimes these things are out of my control. Such is life on a cruise ship.

However, it has enabled me to give you some pretty spicy and interesting stories this week. I got off the ship in Tahiti, where I stood for over two hours in the incredible heat, waiting to go through check in. It was interesting because the check in is actually outside, and in the heat the last thing you want to do is stand there dressed ready to head for the winter in Canada.

My flight from Tahiti took me to LA, then to Toronto where I was to meet my wife, and we were to finally head home together to Moncton. However, plans often don't go according to schedule.

Natalie spent a week in Vancouver while I toured the South Pacific. As I waited for her at the meeting point in Toronto, she came walking towards me with several other people around her, and one of the most stunning stories I've ever heard.

While she was on the airplane flying from Vancouver to Toronto she was ROBBED!! She always puts her handbag by her feet, zippered up of course. While she was sitting there, the man in front of her actually took her purse, opened it up, took her wallet and stole money from it!!

Natalie did not know this had occurred, however a passenger opposite saw the entire event unfold. This passenger got up, went to the back of the plane and told the stewardess exactly what happened. She then quietly came down and asked Natalie to head to the back of the plane, and bring her purse. After checking it, Natalie found the money was gone. They did not let on to the thief that they knew, but as soon as her plane landed the police came on and arrested this man.

When I saw Natalie, she was with the witness, ground staff and the police. They strip searched the thief, but by that stage he had got rid of any evidence. He was arrested, and now red flagged when he travels and has a record. It appears he ditched the money somewhere on the plane.

By the time the police realized this, the ground crew had already come on and cleaned.

As it turns out, this happens quite a bit on flights. In all of our years traveling we have never heard of this and it seems so unreal that somebody would be so 'ballsy' to pull this off. I did hear a story of a Guest Entertainer having his passport stolen on a flight by a person sitting next to him. You just have to be so careful these days. If you ever find yourself flying, be sure to keep an eye on everything!

I know in Canada they just busted a huge gang ring at three major airports, they were going through luggage and working as ground crew. This story just came out this past week.

If you travel, purchase those security locks, they aren't cheap, but well worth it. Also, try and travel with the oldest bag you can find. These criminals tend to go for new, more expensive looking bags. It's bad enough airlines losing luggage, but for staff to steal your luggage as well!

As I write this I have now been flying for over FORTY EIGHT HOURS. As I mentioned, I flew from Tahiti to LA then to Toronto. Natalie and I finally got on our plane to head home – HOWEVER – just as we were to land the pilot told us he could not land as there was ice- rain, incredibly dangerous as it makes the runway impossible to land. So they the flew us to Quebec City where we refueled. We are now flying back to Toronto where we will sleep at the airport for three hours and catch a 6:30am flight home – we hope!!
Such is the joys my friends of show business. I often joke with friends that as a magician who travels so much, I don't get paid for the shows, but for the travel. Actually if I was paid for the travel I would have retired a long time ago.

CRUISE SHIP HUMOR
Questions Asked of Cruise Ship Pursers

These questions were actually asked of various cruise ship pursers.

"Do you make your own electricity on board?"

"Why can't I get cable stations?"

"Are you the Captain?"

"Do you actually live on this ship?"

"Do these stairs go up or down?"

"Does the crew sleep on board?"

"Could you call the captain to stop the waves? I am getting seasick."

"I just saw the Captain in the dining room. Who is steering the ship?"

"Is the water in the toilets salty or fresh?"

"What time does the midnight buffet start?"

"What do you do with the ice sculptures after they melt?"

"Can you get these chips on land?" -- Referring to casino chips.

"Why is it so windy outside?" -- On a cruise liner traveling 30 miles per hour at the time.

"I see them!" -- The inevitable response from a member of the crowd whenever a casino dealer on a cruise liner played a favorite joke -- pointing out "penguins" on a "little piece of ice" during a cruise through Bermuda.

"So what is the elevation here?" -- On an Alaskan cruise.

"Why can't I find a USPC post box in town?" -- In Ocho Rios, Jamaica.

"I want to change cabins! I paid good money for this cruise, and all I can see is a rusted crane in the harbor!" -- Asked before leaving port.

From a passenger cruise ship, everyone can see a bearded man on a small island who is shouting and desperately waving his hands. "Who is it?" a passenger asks the captain. The cruise ship captain replied, "I've no idea. Every year when we pass, he goes nuts."

An old lady was standing at the railing of the cruise ship holding her hat on tight so that it would not blow off in the wind. A gentleman approached her and said: "Pardon me, madam. I do not intend to be forward, but did you know that your dress is blowing up in this high wind?" "Yes, I know," said the lady, "I need both hands to hold onto this hat." "But, madam, you must know that your privates are exposed!" said the gentleman in earnest. The woman looked down, then back up at the man and replied, "Sir, anything you see down there is 85 years old. I just bought this hat yesterday!"

A magician was working on a cruise ship in the Caribbean. The audience would be different each week so the magician allowed himself to do the same tricks over and over again. There was only one problem: the captain's parrot saw the shows each week and began to understand how the magician did every trick. Once he understood he started shouting in the middle of the show: "Look, it's not the same hat". "Look, he is hiding the flowers under the table". "Hey, why are all these cards the Ace of Spades?" The magician was furious but couldn't do anything; it was, after all, the captain's parrot. One day the ship had an accident and sank. The magician found himself on a piece of wood in the middle of the ocean with the parrot, of course! They stared at each other with hate, but did not utter a word. this went on for a day and another and another. After a week the parrot said: "OK, I give up. Where's the boat?"

An engineer finally splurged on a luxury cruise to the Caribbean. It was the "craziest" thing he had ever done in his life. Just as he was beginning to enjoy himself, a hurricane roared upon the huge ship, capsizing it like a child's toy. Somehow the engineer, desperately hanging on to a life preserver, managed to wash ashore on a secluded island. Aside from beautiful scenery, a spring-fed pool, bananas and coconuts, there was little else. He lost all hope and for hours on end, sat under the same palm tree. One day, after several months had passed, a gorgeous woman in a small rowboat appeared. "I'm from the other side of the island," she said. "Were you on the cruise ship, too?" "Yes, I was," he answered. "But, where did you get that rowboat?" "Well, I whittled the oars from gum tree branches, wove the reinforced gunnel from palm branches, and made the keel and stern from a Eucalyptus tree." "But, what did you use for tools?" asked the engineer. "There was a very unusual strata of alluvial rock exposed on the south side of the island. I discovered that if I fired it to a certain temperature in my kiln, it melted into forgeable ductile iron. Anyhow, that's how I got the tools. But, enough of that," she said. "Where have you been living all this time? I don't see any shelter." "To be honest, I've just been sleeping on the beach," the engineer said. "Would you like to come to my place?" the woman asked. The engineer nodded dumbly. She expertly rowed them around to her side of the island, and tied up the boat with a handsome strand of hand-woven hemp topped with a neat back splice. They walked up a winding stone walk she had laid around a Palm tree. There stood an exquisite bungalow, painted in blue and white. "It's not much, but I call it home." Inside, she said, "Sit down, please; would you like to have a drink?" "No, thanks," said the engineer. "One more coconut juice and I'll throw up!" "It won't be coconut juice," the woman replied. "I have a crude still out back, so we can have authentic Pina Coladas." Trying to hide his amazement, the man accepted the drink, and they sat down on her couch to talk. After they had exchanged stories, the woman asked, "Tell me, have you always had a beard?" "No," the engineer replied, "I was clean shaven all of my life until I ended up on this island." "Well if you'd like to shave, there's a razor upstairs in the bathroom cabinet." The man, no longer questioning anything, went upstairs to the bathroom and shaved with an intricate bone-and-shell device honed razor sharp. Next he showered, not even attempting to fathom a guess as to how she managed to get warm water into the bathroom, and went back downstairs. He couldn't help but admire the masterfully carved banister as he walked. "You look great," said the woman. "I think I'll go up and slip into something more comfortable." As she did, the engineer continued to sip his Pina Colada. After a short time, the woman, smelling faintly of gardenias, returned wearing a revealing gown fashioned out of pounded palm fronds. "Tell me," she asked, "we've both been out here for a very long time with no companionship. You know what I mean. Haven't you been lonely, too...isn't here something that you really, really miss? Something that all men and woman need? Something that would be really nice to have right now! "Yes, there is!" the man replied, shucking off his shyness. "There is something I've wanted to do for so long. But on this island all alone, it was just...well, it was impossible." "Well, it's not impossible, any more," the woman said. The engineer, practically panting in excitement, said breathlessly: "You mean...you actually figured out some way we can CHECK OUR E-MAIL.!!"

A young single guy is on a cruise ship, having the time of his life. On the second day of the cruise, the ship slams into an iceberg and begins to sink. Passengers around him are screaming, flailing, and drowning but our guy manages to grab on to a piece of driftwood and, using every last ounce of strength, swims a few miles through the shark-infested sea to a remote island. Sprawled on the shore nearly passed out from exhaustion, he turns his head and sees a woman lying near him, unconscious, barely breathing. She's also managed to wash up on shore from the sinking ship. He makes his way to her, and with some mouth-to-mouth assistance he manages to get her breathing again. She looks up at him, wide-eyed and grateful and says, "My God, you saved my life!" He suddenly realizes the woman is Cindy Crawford! Days and weeks go by. Cindy and our guy are living on the island together. They've set up a hut, there's fruit on the trees, and they're in heaven. Cindy's fallen madly in love with our man, and they're making passionate love morning, noon and night. Alas, one day she notices he's looking kind of glum. "What's the matter, sweetheart?" she asks, "We have a wonderful life together, I'm in love with you. Is there something wrong? Is there anything I can do?" He says, "Actually, Cindy, there is. Would you mind, putting on my shirt?" "Sure," she says, "if it will help." He takes off his shirt and she puts it on. "Now would you put on my pants?" he asks. "Sure, honey, if it's really going to make you feel better," she says. "Okay, would you put on my hat now, and draw a little mustache on your face?" he asks. "Whatever you want, sweetie," she says, and does. Then he says, "Now, would you start walking around the edge of the island?" She starts walking around the perimeter of the island. He sets off in the other direction. They meet up half way around the island a few minutes later. He rushes up to her, grabs her by the shoulders, and says, "Dude! You'll never believe who I'm sleeping with!"

A musician who joined an orchestra on a cruise ship was having difficulty keeping time with the rest of the band. Finally, the captain said, "Either you learn to keep time or I'll throw you overboard. . . . It's up to you, sync or swim."   A panhandler was caught trying to sneak aboard a Princess liner about to embark on a three-day trip to the Bahamas. He was caught by the Purser who threw him off the ship telling him, ... Beggars can't be cruisers.

This announcement came over the speakers throughout the ship, "In about an hour we will be passing Harbour Island on the Port Side of the ship." And then as an afterthought, "If anyone sees an island on the Starboard Side of the ship, please advise the bridge immediately." Overheard one passenger talking to another, "You know, this world cruise has given me a great idea. I'm going to go into the business of transporting day-old bread—across the International Dateline!"

These are true stories from someone who works on a cruise ship.

1. (For this one, you have to know that it's really easy to get lost in the maze of corridors and elevators on a ship.) A lady asked if this elevator went to the front of the ship.

2. Two elderly women were staring at the numbers of the floors listed above the elevator door. When asked if they needed any assistance with something, one asked how they were going to be able to reach way up there to push the button for their floor.

3. A newlywed couple, after bringing their luggage into their cabin, stormed down to the desk. The bride was in tears, and the groom was red faced. When asked what the problem was, the groom started swearing at the desk clerk. "We booked a cabin with a view for our honeymoon, and all we get to see out the window is a parking lot!"

4. There was some mix-up with a woman's room. The clerk (or whatever they are called on ships) was trying to remedy the situation. He asked, "Would you like an inside cabin or an outside cabin?" She replied, "Well, it looks like it might rain today. I'd better get an inside cabin."

5. Two women were sitting by the pool, and one asked what kind of water they fill the pool with -- fresh water or sea water? The cruise director answered, "Sea water." "Oh, that explains why it's so rough today."

6. Someone -- always a man -- always asks, "does the ship run on generators?" The Cruise Director usually tells them, "No, we just have a very long power line running to the mainland."

CHAPTER SEVEN

EXCERPTS FROM JOURNAL

Be sure to write in your journal and take your camera

Note: This section has been taken direct from my journals - no editing has been applied in order to keep it real.

19th February 2005

All packed and ready to go. I have two rather oversized bags with enough material for two full fifty minute shows plus my close-up act. One bag contains just my act, the other my clothes. Because I am traveling for 2 1/2 months I try not to take too much. They say the secret is to take half the clothes and twice the money! Having done this for quite some time now I know what I need. My motto is to travel as light as possible, however this is a trip around South America where I will experience varying climates from a hot, muggy 35∞ Celsius to a brisk

5∞degrees as we near Antarctica, therefore traveling light was quite a challenge.

I find the secret for packing is to pack my bag with everything I think I'll need, which is usually most of the clothes I own. Lift my bag to feel how heavy it is then take everything out and re-pack. Head to the airport at 10am and when I check in I get the good news that I am now an executive platinum member with Star Alliance. Always get your air points when flying because little things like having choice of seating and getting my bags off the plane first makes it easier when traveling. Go through US customs and Immigration. No problems there, the usual questions about where I'm going, what do I do then the officer talks about CSI Miami last week and did I see the magician who killed his family in the episode. At airports you never know how long to get there. They say 2 hours prior to your flight. I got there about 11am and sat around until 2.45pm waiting for my flight which was 20 minutes late. We finally left at 3pm and I was on my way to Chicago where I got my connection.

The lift off from Chicago to Buenos Aires was interesting as we got in the way of another planes jet stream and the pilot darted in a different direction. The lady next to me grabbed my arm and screamed … luckily I tried to remain calm. Finally the pilot came on and told us what happened. I thought the trip was over before it even started! One of the reasons I really hate flying.

20th February

Arrived in Buenos Aires, Argentina on time and was met by the port agent who took me to the hotel. It was a rather interesting experience trying to get him to take me to the hotel then ask him to bring me back to the airport to pick Natalie up a few hours later. We somehow managed to overcome the language barrier and he picked me up in time to go to the airport and get Natalie. One of the scariest drives I have ever been on. While driving he decided to show me photos of his family, so he takes his hands off the steering wheel to get his photo album, needless to say I was a little shocked. Fortunately Natalie made it on time, her flight was much longer than mine. That night we went out and had a great steak dinner, perhaps the best steak I've ever had! We walked around the area near our hotel and discovered a restaurant with carcasses in the window, the smell of BBQ meat just brought us in. What a wonderful first night to our trip.

21st February

Up at 8am to find out where the port was. All other crew who were joining today left at 8am, Natalie and I didn't have to be to the ship until later. We walked around town taking in the sights, sounds and smells of town. Argentina has a population of 35 million and 15 million in Buenos Aires. At about noon we head to the ship. Our bags were taken in one direction and we went in the other. We finally got to security and realized our bags weren't tagged so the porters wouldn't know which ship they would be going to. Security took us over and I took the bags. Straight through the large line up and on to the ship. It was a pretty smooth time getting on the ship. We are on the passenger list which is great.

Just waiting now until we leave. We walk around the ship. It's been at least 3 years since we were on this ship, the Royal Princess. She is getting moved over to the sister company P&O for World Cruising.

One thing about traveling as much as we have is you learn not to over-pack. When you have to cart your own luggage on and off a cruise ship you understand why this is important. I remember my first time on a ship where I over-packed and almost broke my back with all my heavy bags. It's always funny when other magicians see my gear and usually have something to say to me about the little gear I carry, all in good fun of course. Up on deck at 6pm with my long island ice-tea and Natalie with her margarita as we say goodbye to Argentina. Bump in to the cruise director later who I have worked with many times and is without a doubt one of the best CD's on the high seas. He was a Guest Entertainer for many years before becoming a Cruise Director. Get the schedule for the cruise, I am on in a few days time then again at the end of the cruise so it's nicely spread out giving me time to get the 'lay' of the land so to speak. We went to the opening night show which was just introductions of the cruise staff and one of the show singers did a 30 minute show. All in all, an easy first day.

22nd February

Montevideo: Nestled between the continent's two giant Brazil and Argentina, Uruguay is the second smallest country in South America. More than half of the nation's population of three million reside in the capital of Montevideo, located at Uruguay's southernmost point on the Rio de la Plata. Arrive in port at 7am, awake with the thrust of the ships boosters. Had breakfast then headed out to port. What a glorious day with the temperature hitting 30 degrees Celsius. Today we are in Montevideo, a great place to purchase leather products. For only $40US we bought some leather gloves with sheep skin inside, two pairs of sheepskin slippers, a 'cow' hide ladies wallet, a sea lion ladies wallet, and two leather hats. Shopping here was incredible. One thing we have learnt is to purchase 'supplies' on shore such as drinks, alcohol and 'comfort' foods such as potato chips. Especially in this area the wines are great and very cheap so it's cheaper for us to buy these types of things on land. On the ship we do get to purchase beverages at the Camboosa sale, which is usually once or twice a cruise and is open for crew members. We always purchase bottled water and sometimes wine at these sales.

It was an early sail away today leaving at 1pm. Spent the rest of the day writing a new book and working on a web-page while Natalie relaxes up on deck in the sun. Up to the buffet for dinner. There are several places to eat from. We could go to the general dining room but then have to sit with passengers, not on my high list of choices to eat. There is also a Pizzeria, a Steak house where you pay $15.00 for your meal, the dinner buffet which opens from 6:00-10:30 pm then the bistro from 11pm-2am. As much food as you want! Staying away from the desert table as it's far too easy to gain weight on a ship. I remember the first time I joined a ship somebody told me for the first few weeks you eat everything because it all looks so good, but after that you start to really cut back. After several years now we eat very little on the ship, tending towards eating on shore as much as possible.

Our night finished with a movie in the theater, Shark Tale and then back to the cabin about 10pm.

23rd February

A day at sea. Up for breakfast and check e-mail. In the cabin we have a TV with video so went to the crew video library and took out two videos.

Know your nautical terms Even when they are speaking your language, seamen frequently use some terms you won't find immediately recognizable. That's because some familiar things are called by different names aboard a ship. I read up on the meanings of various nautical terms used on ships.

Spent the morning working on the act putting it together. Went to the port lecture on the upcoming ports in which they talk about what to do, where to go and shop and tourist items in general. This afternoon went for a work out in the gym. Very lazy day planned with some close-up magic practice, writing and working on the computer. Tonight is formal night where everybody gets dressed up in their evening clothes.

24th February

Today we arrived in Puerto Madryn, Argentina. It was an early morning start at 8.30am heading in to town, a 500 meter walk from the ship where we had a great cup of coffee. Prices here are incredibly cheap for food. We walked around town for a while, with an internet café on every corner. We managed to do some grocery shopping and bought a lot of local wine, again at cheap prices.

We are told that the average age of Puerto Madryn is early 40s, so it's a fairly new town. Everybody was very friendly and some spoke English which makes it easier.

For lunch we went to a very high end restaurant right on the waterfront called 'Placido'. (www.placido.com.ar) A great restaurant with amazing food, perhaps the best lunch we've ever had. Natalie had ravioli stuffed with chicken and spinach with a portobelo mushroom sauce accompanied with freshly shaved Parmesan cheese, soft mozzarella, tomato and basil and olive oil salad. I had tenderloin steak with a white cream tarragon sauce with hand cut fried potatoes. We each had a liter of local beer. All up this meal cost us only $21 US, what an incredible price and value for the food we had.

Natalie bought herself a very 'chic' green apple colored leather jacket, which looks fantastic on her, again at a great bargain price.

Back on board at 4.30pm sail at 5pm. All in all a very pleasant day. Got a phone call from the cruise director telling me a passenger on board is an amateur magician and wants to put on a show! Cruise director said he got three letters from this magician who performs mostly in retirement homes. The CD told him that there is a professional magician on board and we'll leave the performing up to him!

Tonight's entertainment, at 8pm and 10.15pm is comedian Tom Fletcher. We are still so full from our large lunch that we'll give dinner a miss tonight.

Puerto Madryn.

Fleeing the economic and cultural devastation of England's Industrial Revolution, Welsh settlers emigrated to Argentina in search of cheap land. Led by Viscount Madryn, one group of settlers sailed for the Patagonian coast, founding the small city of Puerto Madryn in 1865. Life in Patagonia, however, was not easy. There were lonely prairies, brutally cold winters, and unrelenting winds. Still the Welsh survived, and today visitors can still see their legacy in Puerto Madryn and its surrounding communities.

25th February

One of our friends, a trumpet player, gave us a brand new coffee maker, so this morning we had a good cup of coffee, as opposed to a 'ship' cup of coffee. Another day at sea which means a rather 'lazy' day. The sun was out so we spent most of our day just reading books. I started a book this morning and finished it by the afternoon.

This afternoon we went and had 'English' tea served in the dining room with tea and scones … a nice little treat. I also managed to get some close-up magic practice in and do some design work on the computer. The great thing about technology is that I can continue my website work on the ship and make any changes then e-mail it via the airport card in my computer … no wires attached. This evening we went and saw the show with the dancers and singers. They did very well for the space they had. Unlike larger ships (this ship has 1200 passengers) this does not have a 'state' of the art theater. Prior to dinner we made our way to the gym and worked out there. There are two shows at night, one at 8.30pm for the early dinner seating and the other at 10.30pm for those on late dining. Natalie and I chose to eat in the buffet for dinner. Having spent many years on ships the food now all tastes the same. With the buffet at least we find we don't over eat and we don't eat the deserts. It can be very tempting to eat the yummy deserts that 'cry' out 'eat me, eat me'.

26th February
Port Stanley

The tiny state of Stanley lies on the eastern tip of East Falkland Islands. Stanley became the Falkland's capital in 1845, and was named after Lord Stanley, then Secretary of State for the colonies. Stanley and the Falklands long served as a way station for ships, particularly whalers, bound to and from Cape Horn. The harbor is dotted with the hulls of vessels that succumbed to the fierce winds and waves of the South Atlantic. Today, fishing, tourism and sheep farming constitute the Falkland's primary economy. The island's strategic location led them to play roles in both World Wars, but the islands are perhaps best remembered as the cause of the 1982 war between Argentina and the United Kingdom. Six hundred miles south is the Antarctic. The Captain came on the loud speaker this morning at 6:45am and announced that we would be unable to tender into Port Stanley today due to high winds and storm conditions.

I peeked out our port hole and saw the Falkland Islands in a distance. They were barely visible due to the grey clouds and turbulence of the ocean misting the landscape, I thought the Captain made a good call considering that the MS Amsterdam tendered passengers onto the island under similar conditions two weeks ago, as weather conditions worsened the ship was unable to pick up over 1000 passengers from the island and bring them back safely on board. The passengers were left stranded on an island where there are no hotels or facilities to accommodate such a crowd. Rumor has it that some of these stranded passengers stayed at the homes of local residents, others were forced to sleep in cars, buses or wherever they could find cover. The Falklands are not tropical, the temperature today is 10 Celsius, and I am sure the evenings are much cooler making for a very unpleasant night sleep.

I have rehearsal at 5pm, the seas are rough but I have designed the act so that it shouldn't be effected too much by the heavy seas … just make sure I can stand up and stay still long enough. The wheels of my table are locking so that they should keep the table from rolling off the stage. We shall see.

The seas were very rough during the evening and in my first show one wave knocked one of my bottles (from my multiplying bottles routine) over and I looked over and saw liquid running over my table base. I had to take the effect out of my second act. Because I use an audience member in the act I was very careful how I handled him due to the 'motion of the ocean'. Surprisingly the first show was busy and went well. Second show which started at 10.30pm wasn't as busy, a much quieter crowd still feeling the effects from the large waves. I noticed several people walking out as the ocean swells got a lot heavier, the cruise director told me if the seas get too rough then to cut the show short. I was trying to stand still myself let alone worry about props. The audiences are mixed with many non-speaking English people which always makes it a tad hard to perform. I noticed with most of the other shows such as the comedian and even the larger shows people tend to walk out because of the language problem. Because my Chaplin act is silent I don't have this problem.

With the first night show over I now relax and 'tweak' a few things that I think will work better for the next time I do this show, which won't be for another two weeks!

27th February

After NO sleep last night due to the incredibly high winds and swells we are now sailing through a Gail Force 9 with 30-40 knot winds. We battened down everything last night in the cabin that could move. Our cabin is at the bow of the ship so every time we hit a wave we hear a large bang, this went on all night so it was very hard to get sleep. We woke again this morning to the captain making an announcement due to the rough weather – 40-50 knott winds and getting worse – we will have to miss Cape Horn. The captain said there are some really large swells out there and it's interesting watching people walk around the ship, or at least try to. They have warned passengers not to go outside due to the strong winds. During these types of waves they put out 'sick' bags everywhere, having said this there are a lot of people up and about. Let's hope we make our port of call tomorrow as I feel I need to see land again. I'm not a big fan at all of sea days and much prefer to be on land, especially when they are days like this.

Tonight is 'Oscar' night so the cruise director has asked if I would appear as Charlie Chaplin to greet guests for the satellite feed they are hoping they can get on the ship ... it all depends on whether or not people turn up to the even so we'll see ... well not many people turned up for the Oscar party, it started at 8.30pm when the second seating dinner started and also the show in the main show room started at 8.30pm so we figured not many would turn up. Natalie and I went up anyway to watch the Oscars on the large screen with the small crowd but ended up going to bed about 11.30pm.

28th February

Ushuaia - Magellan called it Tierra del Fuego – the land of fire – having seen flames rising from the darkened islands. For over three centuries the name struck fear in the hearts of mariners. Howling headwinds, mountainous seas, and rocky coastlines spelled a sudden end to many a voyage. Today, Ushuaia, a former whaling station and Argentine prison colony, serves as the gateway to this wilderness where snow capped mountains plummet to the icy waters of the Beagle Channel. This is also a very popular place for people who are heading to the Antarctica.

This morning we arrived early in to Ushuaia at about 6am and we had the first snows of the season so the mountains and view was outstanding. It was partly cloudy and about 11C so quite nippy. We had breakfast on the ship and headed out on land where we used the internet, it was very fast and cheap. The currency was the Argentinean Pesos so good value against the US dollar. It is very expensive on the ship to use the internet, even if we get crew prices. For me to use my wireless laptop it costs $10.00 for a half hour and for a crew internet card it is $10.00 for about 45 minutes. For passengers it costs $7.50 for 15 minutes making it quite expensive. To use the satellite phone for the passengers it is $5.00 US a minute, we get to use the crew phone so it's not as expensive. Had an interesting e-mail from a friend who works cruise ships, he said there was a documentary on television in which they went on several different cruise ships with a 'cleaning' crew and showed how dirty cabins are. They used infra red light to show 'semen' all over the cabins! Makes you really think about how clean the cabins really are! We bring our own antibacterial spray and we might start bringing our OWN SHEETS!

After walking around town we ended up having a nice lunch, we feasted on trout and King Crab, seems to be the specialty here, again at a great price. We try to eat off the ship as much as possible mostly because of the variety of food and also it enables us to get fresh vegetables rather than the vegetables that are soaked in butter on the ship.

Setting sail at 2pm we head for the Beagle Channel and Punta Araenas, Chile. As we head up the Beagle Channel we are surrounded by stunning views as the mountains had a fresh cover of snow so it was very spectacular scenery. Almost feel like we are traveling through British Columbia. We travel at 20 knots to make sure we get to the next port early enough as many passengers are heading to Antartica for the day, at a cost of $1600 US per person, several hours to fly down, land at a base then fly back to catch the ship.

We ended up going to the movies tonight, one of the things you have to get used to are rude passengers. Most of the theater was full, and near the end two people came in, made a lot of noise and talking then walked out before it finished. You really meet up with all types of people on ships. We met several passengers that we met on past cruises and are very nice people. When you work ships for a while one thing you'll find is you meet repeat passengers.

1st March

Punta Arenas

Punta Arenas, city in southern Chile, capital of Magallanes y La Antarctica Chilena Regrion. Situated on the Straight of Magellan, Punta Arenas is one of the southernmost cities in the world. An important trading center for the wool, hides, mutton, and timber produced in southern Chile, the city has sawmills, tanneries, and facilities for processing frozen meat and canned fish. It is also the supply center for the oil industry on the nearby archipelago of Tierra del Fuego. Punta Arenas was founded in 1849 for the purpose of reinforcing Chilean claims of sovereignty over the Straight of Magellan. The city was a refueling station for shipping before the opening of the Panama Canal. In 1927 it was renamed Magallanes, but the original name was restored in 1938. The population of Chile is 15,823,957 and the language spoken is Spanish.

We arrived early only to find out that those passengers who were going to Antartica, their trip was cancelled due to bad weather down there. However, the weather this morning was incredible, it got up to 21 Celsius this afternoon. We left the ship about 9.00am and caught a taxi in to town. The ship was charging $4.00 US per person for the shuttle bus in to town one way, but the taxis were charging $2.00 per person one way if you got a taxi with four people so Natalie and I managed to get two passengers to join us in a taxi ride. We had planned to get a cup of coffee however nothing opened until 10am so we just walked around and used the internet. After our cup of Joe we continued walking around, you could see the influence of European culture in the style of buildings. There really wasn't much to do around town however we did go to lunch at a restaurant called Sotito's where their speciality is King Crab, Seafood, Barbecue and grilled meat. The bandmaster and trumpet player joined us for lunch and we had another great meal. For entrees Natalie and I shared scallops and the others had King Crab. Our main meal was delicious and mouth-watering roast lamb which was very tasty indeed. Portions were of a good size so afterwards we were all very full. Highly recommend this restaurant if ever you find yourself in this port. The website for the restaurant is www.chileaustral.com/sotitos

Of note is that shops close from 12.30-3pm so after lunch we went to the grocery store and stocked up on Chilean wine. This is certainly the place to purchase great Chilean wine at amazing low prices.

After lunch we walked around town again visiting the Regional Museum which had a collection devoted to the region's flora, fauna, and Indian cultures. Opposite the museum is an amazing cemetery which is hard to describe but certainly worth a visit. It is an incredibly well kept cemetery with large tombs in the middle and surrounded by much smaller tombs in little buildings. On our way back to the shuttle bus we stopped off at a lookout called 'Cerro de la Cruz' in which we had a great view of the city and surrounding water. We didn't go to the penguin colony but it was 35 miles northwest of Punta Arenas on the bleak shores of Otway Sound. Talking to some people who went they told us there weren't many penguins to see. Usually there are thousands of these little creatures but today there were only about two hundred.

Our night ended by watching the sunset and heading to bed about 10pm to watch television and read our books.

2nd March

We are at sea today heading to view the Amalia Glacier. Another relaxing day at sea, again with spectacular views. Today we just read our books and I worked on the computer. The satellite comes in and out as we travel through these Fjords. They do have lectures on board but not the most exciting topics. We do attend the lectures on the ports of call we are visiting, but the 'economic' lectures are geared towards US passengers and to be honest not the most exciting activity.

A run down of events on the ships include:

10am – Port talk on Puerto Montt, Valparaiso and Santiago

10am – Bridge players meet

10am – 12 noon – ceramics at sea – paint your own pottery

10.30am – Morning art auction. This is big on ships at the moment, having art auctions.

10.30am – Uno Players get together

11am – Emerald Talk

11am – Law Enforcement Personal Get-Together

11.15am – Snowball Jackpot Bingo – always a crowd favorite

11.15am – Future Cruise Presentation

11.15am Arts and Crafts – making origami penguin

11.30am Morning Quiz – this amazes me how serious the passengers take the quiz show, it can be like a battle station at these quizzes. We stay away from these!

11.30am-3pm – Golden Dragon Luncheon Buffet – ah more food.

2pm – Bridge

2pm – Ballroom dance class

2pm – All comers golf chipping

3pm – Economics lecture

3.30-4pm – Afternoon Tea – this is always a good one to attend when we feel like a scone and cup of tea

4.30pm – Afternoon Quiz – what again?!

4.30pm – Friends of Dr. Bob and Bill W – just a side note this has nothing to do with 'medical' people but members of the AA. Tonight was formal night so many passengers get dressed up in their best clothes, men in tuxedos and women in flowing gowns. These days of course it's all about 'choices' so many people don't bother getting dressed up at all. Because this is an 'older' crowd and also many 'repeat' cruisers they enjoy dressing up and going to dinner and a show. There were two shows again tonight, one at 8.30pm the other 10.30pm. There are several lounges on this ship so you can have pre-dinner drinks with various bands and duos playing around the ship. After dinner Natalie and I opted to watch the movie 'The Clearing' in the movie theater … perhaps we should have stayed in! Our cabin has a video player so we have access to lots of videos in the crew area.

3rd March

Today was scenic cruising through Seno Eyre Fjord, Chile. Chile possesses 2,650 miles of coastline. It is here on the southern stretch that Seno Eyre Fjord is located. The Patagonian region of Chile is home to some of the most interesting scenery on earth, with Fjords stretching from the Straight of Magellan to Puerto Montt. Patagonia is a region or an area that belongs to both Chile and Argentina.

We arrived early this morning to the large glacier, the 2nd largest in the world. Due to the amount of icebergs the ship couldn't too close for fear of one breaking a propeller on the ship. It still was an awesome sight to behold this huge glacier, the variety and depth of colors. After this we had our usual breakfast, this morning they finally had baked beans, my favorite. Our breakfast usually includes fruit, eggs, toast, yoghurt and cereal. We try to vary it as much as possible of course, some days we have a light breakfast some days a heavier one, depending if we are heading out to a port or not. One thing we learnt was to always take bottled water on land and try to have a good breakfast. Our lunch this afternoon was very light, just a little salad and fruit.

This afternoon I was part of 'Liars All', a game show which featured the four Guest Entertainers. It's always a fun game show and passengers seem to enjoy it. In this game they get in to teams and a word is given to the audience, each of the guests come up with a definition of that words. Of course we try to be as funny as possible, one person can tell the truth and the rest lie, or we can all lie. It's a very popular show on cruise ships, the only problem is that many of them use the same words! We have had some very interesting experiences doing this game show. I don't mind doing these shows, I know some Guest Entertainers who refuse to be involved, but to be honest, it's always good to do something to fill in time. After this we headed to they gym for our daily exercise. They are having early shows tonight, one at 7pm and the other at 8.30pm. Quite often they will mix up shows like this as they have a 'later' night show called, "London Pub Night" which is put on by the cruise staff. This is rated PG-16 and is always lots of fun. They try to re-create a pub type atmosphere, it's very English of course and always finishes with the classic skit, "If I were not upon the sea". You can get a glimpse of a 'sea sketch' on youtube at:

http://www.youtube.com/watch?v=p6hef_P8j34

4th March

Yet ANOTHER day at sea. We had some very rough weather last night and were tossed around quite a bit, hardly sleeping. One good idea when this happens is if you have a bathtub in your cabin is to put a towel in the tub and put all your glassware in there, that way it won't roll around as much. Another little 'hint' is with the ventilation in the cabin, this is often the cause of the 'flu' getting passed around so much on ships. The air is pumped through the rooms making it easy for germs to spread through the air, what we do is put 'tape' partly around the ventilation in our cabin so that it doesn't blow directly towards our bed when we are asleep. We always take multivitamins with us as well because often you don't get what you need as the fruit and vegetables are often in cold storage and by the time you eat them all the 'goodness' is gone from them. On most cruise ships now they have 'antibacterial' hand dispensers and towelets for people to wash their hands before they eat. Germs can very easily be spread by people not washing their hands and then touching the hand rails, the elevator buttons and so forth. They do suggest that you wash your hands for 20 seconds after using the bathroom, in fact they have signs everywhere telling you to do so. The cost for passengers who get sick on a ship is very high, they charge $60US just for a consultation with the ships doctor. It is always hit and miss with a doctor on a ship, we personally knew a lady who worked on the ship who went to the doctor four times and it wasn't until when she finally went to see a doctor on land that she found out she had cancer. The land doctor was horrified to find out that the doctor on the ship didn't pick up it was cancer and the last we heard she was trying to sue the company and doctor!

It is formal night again tonight so passengers get on their best gear and 'head out on the town'. Natalie and I opt not to get in to formal wear and just head to the card room to play cards and catch a movie … all in all a quiet but enjoyable evening.

5th March

Puerto Montt - We arrived early this morning about 7am in to Puerto Montt, a tender port which means we anchor in the harbour and take the 'tender' or 'life' boats in to get to shore. We waited until all the tours and most passengers had gone ashore before we left. We ended up on shore about 10am when things were opening. As it was Saturday the city was very busy and all the shops were crowded. We headed left of the pier to the 'market' place where you can purchase woolen sweaters, hats, gloves, ponchos, curios and copper work. Most of the items we had seen in a lot of other ports and didn't find prices as cheap as say Lima for some of the products so we didn't make many purchases. You can catch a taxi for about 25-cents, just flag one down and jump in, you probably have to share with other people. We opted to walk everywhere today to get our exercise. After our visit to the market area we headed over to the main centre where we checked e-mail, again $1.00US for an hour, very cheap indeed compared to the ship. We had a very nice lunch at a German Restaurant, heavy Germanic influence in this port, which was reasonable. The local drink here is Pisco Sour which can really knock you out. We had an enjoyable lunch and met some passengers who wanted to take photos of me. It's not until I take my hat off and they see my hair that they recognize me … should have left my hat on. Natalie had a Caesar salad and I had a schnitzel plus 2 drinks for $20US … incredible really when you compare to what it would cost back in Canada.

On our way back to the ship we visited the Cathedral which is made from Timber, which happens to be the most popular building medium in this region.

We came back to the ship a little earlier as I am working tonight. Found out today my new schedule for some more cruises … have told my agent I will do some of them but not sure about the later ones. They have me transshipping between ships in the Mediterranean, one of the nicest cruises one can do so I might just do it. Instead of getting off on May 7th they want me to fly and be there for the launch of the SEA, a new ship coming back to the company, then I fly all over between ships before heading home. Always nice to be asked.

Must get ready for the show now. I cut all of the paper used for my snowstorm trick by hand - quite a process. Once this is done I check I have everything needed for the show, iron shirts and silks, polish my shoes and put the props together. I head off the theater and set my props up an hour prior to show time. It only takes me about thirty minutes to set and I then ready to go. I never get nervous prior to a show because I am always well prepared.

Both shows went very well. First show had a great crowd with great reactions. I shared the bill with an Adagio act who opened for me with a 3 minute routine. Second show started at 10.30pm so only the night owls showed up, not a full house but for that time of night after a long day for many people it wasn't bad. Crowd was not as energetic as the first audience but none the less they stayed with me.

Of particular note during the second show was that I chose a lady to come up and help who we had met on a cruise several years ago and we remembered each other. Her and her husband are originally from Hungary but now live in Canada and we managed to catch up after the show.

The cruise director came up afterwards and told me he enjoyed the show and asked if I would also do a close-up show for the next cruise because 200 passengers are staying on and he wants to add something different to the program.

One thing you learn is to get thick skinned when working on ships. The crowds are so very different than land gigs, for example the average age of most audiences I work for on ships range from 65 and up, more 'up' than 65! We have a saying on ships, especially the 'world' cruises which when asked the age of the audience most reply, "dead and resurrected". One thing I would suggest to first time magical entertainers who work ships is keep in mind the majority of people traveling on longer cruises have 'seen it all' so keep your act as fresh and entertaining as possible. Make sure it's a working act with all the kinks ironed out.

I was back in the cabin about 11.30pm and Natalie had made me a sandwich which ended up being my dinner. I tend not to eat before a show and by the time I finish work I am too tired to go upstairs and get food. Of course they do have room service but I chose not to bother with that.

6th March

The last day of this cruise and another sea day. Spent this morning washing our clothes. Fortunately on this ship we have a washer and dryer just around the corner from where our cabin is, that is used only for officers it never too busy, unlike the passenger laundry where major 'fights' can break out. When it comes to doing your washing on a ship you can send it off to the laundry room and they charge for it, or you do it yourself. On many ships we use the passenger laundry room and that can be quite the place, it's almost as though peoples attitudes change once they get in to the laundry room. A sweet, nice eighty five year old lay can become a stick hitting rebel once she enters that room.

This afternoon we went to see the Passenger Talent show which started at 3.30pm and was still going at 5pm! They had sixteen acts in all. I went along to see the magician and his wife perform. A retired couple from Florida who performed paper balls over the head and linking ropes. Most passengers got up and told jokes, but after the magic act we headed back to our cabin and check our internet. Passenger talent shows often draw the largest crowds for any shows on the ship. Once in a while you'll get a gem of an act but the novelty of going to them wares off very quickly. It turned out to be another early night because of our big start for the next day.

7th March

Today is what is known as a 'turnaround' day, that is, passengers disembark and new passengers get on. There are over 200 passengers staying on from the last cruise and taking the ship to Florida. Today we are in Valparaiso, Chile. The twin cities Valparaiso and Vina del Mar present a dramatic study in contrast. We docked early about 6am and Natalie and I with two friends hired a car to travel to vineyard country. While Valparaiso has a certain latin charm, it is basically a no-nonsense, relatively poor working man's city. Neighboring Vina del Mar, however, immediately adjacent to Valparaiso, is an internationally known rich man's playground. Hiring a car was very easy and for an average size car, a Fiat, we paid about $60 for the day including full insurance. Our travels took us to two different vineyards in the wine growing area called Casablanca. Our friend who came with us, Richard, is an expert in wine and has a degree in wine tasting so he was the perfect person to go with. The first vineyard was William Cole, an American who came to Chile about five years ago and set up a vineyard. His chief wine maker studied in France so the wine was not like an American wine where they leave it in barrels for a longer period, but more like a French wine. Highly recommend this vineyard to anybody visiting the area as the staff were very friendly and helpful. We all ended purchasing many bottles of their best wines, both red and white, at incredibly low prices. Our next trip took us to Vino Mar Vineyard where we went on a tour of the winery and sampled their wines. The process of making champagne at this vineyard was very interesting and we bought two bottles to take home. We also had the most incredible meal at their restaurant. For the four of us we all had appetizers, two bottles of their best wine plus four main meals and it came to $80US!! There really is no way you can get anything like that back home for such a price.

We made it back to the ship and are now having an early night without dinner after eating such a huge meal both Natalie and I are full to extreme. Truly a great day and one we will both remember not only for the food and some of the best wine we've ever tasted but also the company we traveled with.

Just waiting to see the new schedule to see when I perform. Our bill came through for the last cruise, as usual they wanted us to pay the $10.00 per person per day that passengers get charged for tips, however we always pay cash so we had to go down and cancel the tips from our bill, also we don't eat in the dining room so that money also goes to the dining room which we never use. The general rule is in crew areas where the cabin steward comes in once a day you pay $2.50 - $3.00 per day per person.

8th March

This morning we awoke to the sounds of the engines roaring below us at about 6am. Today we are in a new port for us, Coquimbo,Chile. The port of Coquimbo is the gateway to La Serena, founded in 1544. Located in the transition zone between Chile's austere Atacama Desert and its central valley, La Serena is a popular holiday resort. The Elqui Valley is an agricultural center famed for grapes, papaya, and cherimoya. The region was also home to the ancient Diaguita and Molle cultures.

We headed out at 9am on the first bus in to the main town La Serena, and the drive took about 30 minutes. We spent the day walking around town, discovering the magnificent architecture that looked very Spanish in design and was well maintained. We walked through the local craft markets which sold the usual souvenirs ranging from hand made products to products made in China. Of particular note was the local product made from Papaya such as alcohol, jams and candy. Our lunch was very plain, nothing special. We found a little outdoor café where I had steak, egg and fries and Natalie had chicken and salad with the local beer. All up the meal came to $16.00 US so it wasn't that bad. We did manage to find the post office and mail out some postcards and use the internet.

We headed back to the ship about 2pm to make sure we bet the mad rush of passengers getting on the last bus at 3.30pm We relaxed on deck with our 'pisco sours' and sat their listening to the live entertainment put on by local entertainers dock side. We finally set sail at 5pm and are spending another day tomorrow at sea. I managed to get the itinerary for the cruise and have two 50 minute shows this cruise plus a close-up show. This is a 17 day cruise so generally they like entertainers who can do more than one show on longer cruises. The shows tonight are another Guest Entertainer, Jim Coston, a banjo player and his shows are at 8.30pm and 10.30pm.

9th March

Today is a sea day and the first formal night for this cruise and captains welcome aboard party. It was a very lazy day for us, mostly spent reading and attending lectures. The first was at 10.15am and was an Introduction to Chile and Arica, then at 11am a special interest lecture but was too boring to sit through. At about 5pm we went to the gym then got ready to eat at the 'steak house'. On most ships now they have several restaurants on board to chose from, some you have to pay for. The cover charge for the steak house is $15.00 per person and the menu is usually very good. We took up one of the bottle of wines we bought in Chile which had a $10.00 corkage fee. For starters we had Spinach and artichoke dip and Brie and papaya casadea. We then had a caesar salad each which was prepared at our table. This was followed by our main meal. They offer every type of steak you can imagine, our choice was Porterhouse and Filet Mignon. For dessert we had raspberry crème brûlée and chocolate pecan pie. It was a very lovely evening having dinner and watching the sun go down. We finished our night off by going to the main show.

One of the things you find is that you tend to get a little lazy unless you have certain projects to work on. Natalie keeps herself busy by doing a correspondence course, I keep busy by writing and working on websites and of course practicing close-up magic and working on my act.

10th March

We arrived in Arica, Chile at 6am ready for another busy day in port. The vast silence and sand dunes of the Atacama Desert are broken by the Azapa Valley, an agricultural oasis rich in tropical fruits. At the mouth of the valley lies the port of Arica. Founded in 1570, Arica is Chile's fifth-oldest city and a commercial gateway for neighboring Peru and Bolivia. It's a city rich in heritage-home both to a wrought iron church designed by Gustave Eiffel and to pre-Columbian treasures from the Chinchorro culture dating back to 5000 B.C.

This was our first time to this port and it was a pleasant surprise. Arica is surrounded by desert, they say it is the driest desert in the world and certainly today's heat proved it. It wasn't an uncomfortable heat, not humid at all. We spent most of our day walking around discovering the secrets of this town with some amazing architecture. We ended up visiting a little railroad museum which had lots of very interesting exhibits such as old communication machines, very old calculators and phones. We then visited the cathedral which was designed by Eiffel followed by walking through the many markets. Our lunch today was very nice, in a little restaurant called 'el Arriero'. We had chicken and salad, which is all we felt like after our very big meal last night, with the local beer.

The internet here was very cheap, about $1.00 US per hour, which we made the most of. Some of the keyboards in these parts don't always work the best but for that amount of money you can't complain and the speed of the internet is high.

We set sail at 6pm and will go and watch the movie tonight and then hit the bed after a long but very enjoyable day.

11th March

Another relaxing day at sea. Again not much to report. We spent our day reading and relaxing out by the swimming pool. We met a very nice New Zealand couple in their 80s who are on their first trip abroad. We spent several hours talking to them and they told us their story of when they were in Valparaiso at the beginning of the trip the lady had her purse stolen with all her money and credit cards. We felt so bad for them, their first cruise and right at the beginning their money was taken. They spent the first few days of the cruise phoning New Zealand organizing everything. The ship has been extremely helpful and offered them a cash advance and helped organize getting a new visa card sent to Lima tomorrow, so fingers crossed it all turns out okay for them. We both felt

177

very sorry for them and I offered anything I could do help. We gave them a nice bottle of wine we bought in Chile which made their day a little brighter. I think meeting another Kiwi on the ship helped them feel a little at ease. They are both lovely people and we are glad we met them, we enjoy talking to them about New Zealand, they are already talking about their next cruise so it's nice to know the horrible incident hasn't put them off.

Instead of going to the gym today we walked around the deck for about half an hour, with the sea breeze blowing and the sun beaming down it certainly makes a very nice walk. A very easy day all in all, I spent some time working on the act as tomorrow is show time for me. We retired early to bed to watch a movie.

12th March

Today is another new port for us, San Martin, Peru. In August of 1820, the great liberator General San Martin landed on the coast of Peru's southern desert. The area became significant in Peruvian history as the birthplace of Peru's struggle for independence. Just north of San Martin lies the quiet colonial town of Pisco and its surrounding agricultural valley. For thousands of years, pre-Columbian agricultural societies thrived in river valleys such as this. The legacy of these ancient people, from giant geometric etchings on the desert floor to ancient burial grounds, continue to draw the curious from around the world to inspect and ponder the mysteries of the desert.

Putting our clocks back an hour meant we had another early rise with the sun shining in through the port hole. We must have docked about 6am and we were up early ready for a busy day. The port is in the middle of nowhere, everywhere you look are sand dunes and at 8.30am when we left the ship the sun was already at about 25 degrees Celsius. We drove through vast sand hills for about 45 minutes to reach Pisco, a very little town with not much happening. They did have internet cafes which we used, again for only $1.00US per hour, a very good rate. Internet has really made the world smaller and a great way to keep in contact with family and friends so we always like to make use of it as much as we can when ashore. The town was very small but it did have an amazing cathedral which we went in to and tried to talk to a man about its history, but its hard when you don't speak their language. In our own way I think we understood most of what he was telling us. We were approached by a guide who offered to take us to a few tourist places but after thinking about it we declined. It is a place we are not familiar with and just didn't feel safe doing this type of tour on our own. We decided their wasn't anything left to see in this small town, and we didn't feel safe wandering off the beaten track as we sometimes do by ourselves, so we headed back to the ship around 1pm and spent our day relaxing by the swimming pool.

I headed down to the cabin and put my show together for tonight. Many passengers have gone on overland tours so not sure what the crowd will be like tonight. One good thing about this port is that there isn't much for people to do so they won't stay out too long and so hopefully not be too tired for the show tonight, we shall see.

Well I finished both shows and they went well. A standing ovation in the first show which is nice to get. The audience is much different than last cruise as most of these people speak English. It is a mixture of audience from people from all over the world; Australia, New Zealand, Canada, England and of course the USA. The first show was at 8.30pm and the second at 10.30pm. Always with the second show people are very tired because they spent the day in the hot sun and have just eaten, however this second sitting were great and were just as good as the first. By the time I was back in my cabin it was about 11.45pm and Natalie had made me a sandwich because I don't eat before my shows.

13th March

Callao, Peru. In 1535, Francisco Pizarro labeled the open plains where Lima now stands as inhospitable. Despite the verdict of the great conquistador, Lima became the center of imperial Spanish power, a "City of Kings" where 40 viceroys would rule as the direct representative of the King of Spain. With independence in 1821, Lima became Peru's capital. Near Lima, one of the world's inhospitable deserts is home to the fame drawings of Nazca, which inspired Erik von Daniken's bestselling book "Chariot of the Golds". Lima's port of Callao is also a gateway to another great mystery – the lost city of Machu Picchu. This is one of our favorite ports, especially when it comes to shopping. We got off the ship nice and early and headed over to the market place next to the ship. It is a warehouse on the dock filled with local arts and crafts including Alpaka and Lama products, paintings, pottery plus the usual t-shirts, cheap dvds and so on. After spending half an hour there we got on the shuttle bus which took us from the port of Callao to Miraflores Marriott Hotel. On the bus trip in, which takes about 30 minutes, you pass through some very poor areas, but once in the main area it is a bustling city. Opposite the Marriot is an outdoor shopping area which has the most amazing view as it is right on the edge of a cliff overlooking the ocean, quite a site. Here you will find a very high end arts and crafts shop and restaurants and stores. Having been to this place on another cruise we decided to take a taxi ride for 2 hours, which ended up being 8 hours, to look at what else the city has to offer. The cost was $10.00 US per hour which is a great price for a taxi to take you around. Our driver, Carlos was very good and stayed with us the entire day as we walked through various areas of the city. Once we started our journey we realized how much history there is in Lima. We headed over to a seaside area where they had an outdoor market with some of the most amazing foods I have ever seen, smelt and tasted. The desserts were mouth watering and we just couldn't resist buying a slice of local cuisine. For only $1.00 per piece we ended up having a piece of local cake for lunch followed by the local drink which was purple sweet corn juiced to produce a very refreshing drink. As it was Sunday people were all at church, and we ended up visiting a few ourselves. All had ornate carvings and statues and the architecture had a very Spanish in feel about it. Our trip then took us visit several beaches where the waves crashed on to the shore line and many families were out enjoying this gorgeous hot day. Heading in to the old part of Lima our drive took us through various market places which were bustling with people. Driving here was like being in a mad race with cars and people on the roads at the same time all seeming to be going in opposite directions. It seemed like total mayhem and we ended up not looking at the where our driver was going but at the scenery to the side of the car. The old part of town had many amazing older buildings including a palace, churches and hotels. We went to one cathedral which had catacombs underneath which was filled with bones and skulls. Apparently twenty five thousand people were buried underneath this church in the catacombs. From here we walked through the streets and visited a few of the buildings and then headed to the Indian Market. The city has a big influence of armed police, especially the tourist areas. The Indian market is a great place to make any purchases. Out of this entire contract, this is the place where we looked forward to regards shopping. We purchased a few pottery dishes and eggs and some Alpaka items. After two hours of walking around the large market area we realized we hadn't eaten all day, and it was getting close to 6pm so our taxi driver took us to a fabulous restaurant called Costa Verde on Playa Barranquito, right on the beach front. www.costaverdeperu.com

The food was de vine as I had stuffed Sea Bass with shrimps and scallops and Natalie had a sample of four local dishes. Both meals were excellent and with our bottle of wine the total came to $50US. Not quite the $21 we spent in Argentina but none the less, a great meal and a great way to end our night. Because it was an overnight where the ship stays in port overnight we didn't have to rush getting back to the ship. By the time we got back it was 8.30pm and the local dancers had come on board to do a show for the passengers which we ended up watching. A great show with local music, dance, stories and costumes and obviously enjoyed by all passengers.

14th March

Our day started early as we ended up helping the lovely New Zealand couple who had their money stolen in Santiago. Their bank in New Zealand wired them some money so they didn't feel comfortable going to pick it up by themselves. Natalie and I offered to go out with them this morning to a Western Union and get the money, which we did. After picking up the money and bringing it back to the ship we took them in a taxi to the Indian market where we bought ourselves a large rug made from baby Alpaca. After spending over an hour there, it was time to head back to the ship and be on board by 12.30. We were very hungry so headed up to the buffet where we had lunch and then watch sail away from this great port of call.

The rest of our day was very relaxed, reading and then working out in the gym. We opted to go to the movie tonight, "Finding Julia" then headed back to our cabin.

15th March

A day at sea. We were up about 8am and headed to breakfast. It was such a lovely day outside that we spent the rest of the morning doing absolutely nothing but sitting in the sun and reading. You have to be very careful in South America because of the hole in the Ozone layer and the strength of the sun. It's imperative that you have strong sunscreen and wear a hat. After 2 hours of sitting in the sun and reading it was time to head indoors. Another relaxing day in paradise, we headed to they gym before grabbing a bite to eat and calling it a night.

16th March

Arrived in Manta, Ecuador at 6am, another overnight which means we are here for two days.

The small port of Manta is the gateway to Ecuador and its capital of Quito. A small nation the size of the United Kingdom, Ecuador has one of the world's most varied terrains. Six hundred watery miles away to the west of Manta lie the Galapagos Islands; to the east rise the Andes, home to Ecuador's important cities, including Quito.

Having been to this port before we knew there wasn't much here, so we decided to hire a taxi for only $10.00 per hour and head to Monte Christi which is about 20 miles from Manta. This is the home of the Panama hat and they are everywhere you look. We visited a church and the local market where people were actually making the panama hats. We ended up buying 3. They varied in price from $5.00 to $100.00 depending on quality. The $100.00 hats are a lot finer woven than the cheaper hats but they certainly all look and feel similar to the cheaper hats. We wandered around the town for a little while before moving on to a button factory where they make buttons for famous designers around the world. The buttons are made from a 'nut ivory' and here you could purchase a bag of a dozen for $1.00. After heading back to the port of Manta we checked our e-mail, for only $1.00 an hour we could spend a few hours there, then headed down to a local hotel where Natalie had a 45 minute massage for only $20.00.

I walked around the town for a little while. There is definitely poverty here with many roads unfinished and yet the people seem to be happy and certainly happy to see visitors.

After a drink at the hotel it was time to head back to the ship for some dinner and later in the evening there was an 'Island Night Party' which is held out on deck under the stars. This started at 10pm and had the usual games and pranks hosted by the cruise staff. At 11pm there was an Island Night Buffet, usual snacks of chicken wings, battered fish, battered apples and bananas, and as usual lots of desserts.

A most enjoyable day, we were glad we went to Monte Christi which gave us something different to do and see other than Manta.

17th March

This morning we headed out on the shuttle bus which dropped passengers off to a local shopping mall in Manta, I bought myself a pair of shoes and Natalie some gym pants. A usual run of the mill mall, except this one was filled with passengers. Because we were leaving at 1pm we caught the shuttle bus back about 11pm and headed to the gym. As Guest Entertainers we have access to all facilities on the ship including gym, restaurants and so on. The crew has restrictions to where they can go and what they can do. Some staff can use the gym but only during certain times. They do have a crew gym which we can't go to, the passenger gym is okay, not the best we've come across on ships.

A notice just came up on the notice board backstage for crew and officers saying that no crew or officers with deck privileges can use the passenger gym because of noise complaints from people in cabins below. I am assuming the crew were using the gym after hours. This does not affect us because of our passenger status, although we use the gym during the day anyway.

Just another day lazing on the ship as we left Manta at 1pm in the afternoon and headed out to sea ready for our next port. Nothing exciting happened, we read and I just practiced some close-up magic.

18th March

Another lazy day at sea. We just found out that five crew members were mugged at gun point in Manta on the overnight trip. They must have gone out late at night to a local club and on the way home at a red stop light, several 'locals' appeared with guns and held up the taxi the crew had hired to take them back to the ship. Apparently everything was taken, and they were left only in their underwear. You really have to be so careful in many ports and the idea of heading out in a place like Manta at night just wasn't the right thing to do. It certainly had that 'unsafe' feeling about it as we traveled around during the day. Their also seems to be some type of illness going around the ship. They have posted notices up all over the crew areas and have taken away many privileges of crew who are allowed to eat upstairs in the buffet area, all crew must now eat in the crew mess. This will probably last until the end of the cruise. We know several people, both passengers and crew who have been confined to their cabins with what is known as GI which gives you direr and vomiting. Knock on wood Natalie and I are both well and we always wash our hands and use the special bacteria soap that is all around the ship for people to wipe their hands with.

The weather has been incredible so yet again we spent the day outside reading. I have been reading on average three books a week now. The crew library is much better than the passenger library, they seem to have the latest books and more selection.

Instead of heading to the gym we opted to walk around the deck and then play table tennis for about an hour, our exercise for the day. At 5.30pm we headed back to our cabin to get ready for dinner. Our Canadian friend Richard, who has been on for 6 months is leaving in five days so we took him out for dinner to the steak house. A 'slap up' meal, every type of steak you can imagine. Again I had the porterhouse, it was almost as large as my plate! After dinner, Richard had to play for the production show so Natalie and I went to watch 'The Incredibles', the latest Walt Disney movie which was fun.

19th March

The Panama Canal – canal across the Isthmus of Panama, in Central America, that allows vessels to travel between the Pacific and Atlantic oceans. The waterway measures 64 km including dredged approach channels at each end. The Panama Canal handles a large volume of world shipping and enables vessels to avoid traveling around South America, reducing their voyages by thousands of miles and many days. The Panama Canal consists of three separate canal locks, as well as other artificial waterways. The canal spans a total distance of 64-km from the Pacific Ocean to the Atlantic Ocean through the Isthmus of Panama.

The history behind the Canal is very amazing and no matter how many times I travel up or down the canal, it still holds intrigue and I am in awe of the way it works and how many ships use it. Today the weather was very hot and humid, close to 35 degrees so we kept mostly in the shade. Most of the ship was out on deck today enjoying the sights of the Canal, and as I spoke to several passengers many of them commented that this was the single reason they chose this trip, to be able to travel through the Panama Canal. It really makes you appreciate the job you have as a cruise ship magician when you realize you have done this trip several times, I certainly never take it for granted. I have two shows tonight, one at 8.30pm, the other at 10.30pm and will be performing my comedy act. This is my 'B' act that I used to perform for corporate shows in New Zealand, Singapore and Dubai. Personally I would be happier just performing my Charlie Chaplin show, but the company knows I can do the two shows which is why they give me the longer contracts for 17 – 28 day cruises.

At about 4 pm the ship is expected to arrive in Cristobal, Panama, however it is now 4.30pm and we are not there yet, having just left the last lock so not sure if they will extend our stay in Cristobal. I would say not, but if they do then it will be small audience for the show tonight. I am not expecting a large crowd as most people have been up since the 'crack of yawn' and out in the hot sun all day as we traveled up the canals so will be very tired. We shall see what happens. I have my show prepared and ready to go. As I've said before, the good thing about being backstage is it takes me 2 minutes to take my props and get them to the stage area. I phoned the Production manager who runs the lights and music for the show and we are rehearsing at 4.30pm, this show is so very easy to operate as there aren't that many cues. Later that night …. We arrived in Cristobal about 5pm and the line up for passengers to get off the ship almost went around the entire ship! People stood in line just to get off for this little port for a good hour. Having been here before and knowing it isn't worth standing in line for that long Natalie and I waited until the lines had gone before we disembarked. The terminal where the ship docks is full of people selling their souvenirs, most are overpriced and nothing that hasn't been in any of the other ports. The item that did the best in sales would have to be the duty free alcohol. It appeared that everybody was stocking up on the cheap booze to either drink on the ship or take home in a few days. We waited until the crowds died down then went and used the internet ashore and were back on board by 7.30pm so I could get ready for my 8.30pm show.

Both shows went very well and the crowds were really in to it. I only expected to do about 40 minutes thinking the crowds would be way too tired but ended up doing a good solid 50 minutes. On these longer cruises you very rarely have children, but I noticed in the first show was a family of young children so I did a special routine with the eldest girl who was about 12 years old, and the audience certainly enjoyed that. I would much rather just perform the Chaplin act as it's so different from anything else any other magician is doing and is what I am well known for, however when you work ships for this company you have to have two solid 50 minute acts and I'm thankful for all those years I developed my corporate act working in Singapore and New Zealand. The show has nothing new in it, but I really play on the fact I'm from New Zealand which people seem to love. While this is called a 'B' show, it really needs to be as strong as your first show, keeping in mind that passengers do get comments card and fill them in good or bad. The 'B' show consists of:

Comedy Introduction
Color changing hanky routine
Comedy Michael Jackson routine
The BIG TEN Routine
Confabulation
Bowling routine

20th March

Sea Day. The highlight of the day was Liars Club game, or as it is now called, Liar's All. I spent most of the morning working on the words for this game. This always proves to be one of the most popular games with passengers on cruise ships. Usually four Guest Entertainers play the game in which we are all given words, one of us tells the truth while the rest lie. The audience guess who is telling the truth.

Here are the words we used for this game:-

BLADDERPIPE

CRAPULENCE

FARDINBAG –

WHOOPKNACKER

ZUMBOORUCK

Because we are heading for the USA I knew that I have to, by law, be put on the crew list because I have a C1D Visa. As a non-US citizen I need to have this VISA to travel in and out of the USA when working for the cruise line. I did go and tell the main desk last week but as usual, didn't hear anything from them, so I went down to the crew office. They didn't know anything about it and I told them the ship would be fined if they left me on the passenger list. If I had left it up to them the ship would certainly get in trouble for not checking passports and trying to leave me on the passenger list. Not really a big deal at all, but I wanted to get it sorted out before Florida. They will put me back on the passenger list once we leave the States.

Perhaps the most annoying aspect of ships is the frustration of ship politics and lack of communication between people. As a Guest Entertainer I keep out of everybody's way and don't get involved, but sometimes you have to stand up for yourself because some people tend to make up their own rules in the pursers office.

21st March

Today we arrived the beautiful port of Aruba, where the Dutch influence lazily lingers on the island's official language and the languidly turning arms of white-washed windmills. Yet the 'A' in the ABC islands, once a member of the Nether-land Antilles, now stands independently, having gained autonomy in 1986. In fact, the some 70,000 Arubans have a number of origins, and they commonly speak Papiamento, a combination of Spanish, French, Portuguese, Dutch, Africans, and English.

We walked around town for a little while then caught the bus to one of many beaches, return for only $2.00. Once you get off the pier there are people trying to sell tours to and from beaches for $25.00, the local bus is definitely the way to go and you catch it right across from where the ship docks. The beaches truly are beautiful with the white sand and clear blue waters. We walked back to the bus stop and headed off to lunch. The lunch itself wasn't all that expensive, however the local beer was! We paid the same price for the beer as we did for the lunch ... word of warning ... always check the price of beer before purchasing. All on board at 4.30pm and we headed out in to the harbour at 5pm ready for Florida..

22nd March

Sea day. Yet ANOTHER lazy day at sea, actually I have a very sore throat and bones are a bit tired so I think I might be coming down with something. I hate being ill on a ship as it's not the best place to get better. There have been so many flu's and viruses going around on this ship that I sure hope I don't catch something bad.

Went to see the culinary demonstration today which was hosted by the executive chef and maitre d'Hotel.

29th March

Another lazy sea day giving me time to catch up on the events of the last few days. We were in Port Limone, Costa Rica on the 26th, this was my first time to this port. We put our name down to escort a shore excursion, which means as an escort we are responsible to keep tabs on the passengers whereabouts on tour and make sure that everyone gets on the bus, in return we get to go on the tour free of charge, which is a huge saving as some of these tours cost over $100. The escort positions are competitive and you have to be quick to put your name down. Unfortunately we were late in putting our name down and missed out. We knew from talking to others who have been to Port Limone that the place was a bit of a hole with not much to offer, so we were quite unsure what we were going to do. Luckily when we left the ship there were locals offering guided tours at prices half of what the ship charges (but not as good as the escort price, free). We paid $60 for a tour which included a train ride through the jungle, a canal boat ride, a tour of the banana plantation and a city tour, a deal if you ask me! Another great thing about doing the tours the locals offer is that they are not crowded. We had an intimate group of 8, just perfect. We started off taking the bus to the train station 2 minutes from port where we boarded an old wooden 2 car train which we were told was over 125 years old and it definitely looked it. The seats we hard and splintered, and the warm air rushed through the open widows offering no relief from the 30 degree heat. The train headed north to a protected jungle reserve where we were on the lookout for monkeys, sloths and any other creature looming in the dense jungle. As soon as any one spotted what they thought was something the train stopped giving everyone a change to play can you spot the creature. A lot of mis-starts, however one stop finally panned out and our virgin eyes all peered with excitement at the sight of a three-fingered creature looming above our head in the trees which masked its location. The sloth….the laziest of Gods creatures. After the snapping of the camera and the owwws and ahhhs the train chugged away to its final location. We disembarked the train and boarded the bus once again and were brought to a restaurant along on a canal where fresh pineapple, watermelon and cantaloup were waiting for us. Two small motor boats were reserved for our group and after refreshing ourselves we boarded the boats for the next portion of our adventure. The canal waters were a brackish muddy mixture, a perfect environment for Cayman. It surprised me to see people lackadaisically swimming in these water especially after we had just spotted a couple of Cayman! We passed by many birds of odd shapes and colors, but our search for the infamous monkey's was turning out to be futile. A sloth sleeping sounding was disturbed by our presence and casually fluttered its eyes and then resumed it's slothfully existence of sleeping its day away. We rode the canal for over an hour taking in the exotic birds, butterflies and creatures whom made this humid, lush environment their home. Once again we boarded the bus for our final destination, the Dole banana plantation. Costa Rica is the 2nd largest exporter of bananas, the first is Ecuador. I will never look at bananas in quite the same way again. Our tour guide Richard provided

189

us with an educational lecture on the art of growing bananas. Dole provides employment for a large percentage of locals including our tour guide during the off season. The wage is $250 a year plus a home with electricity on the plantation and all the bananas you can eat. That was our memorable day in Costa Rica, one of the best tours we have done. I must work tonight......I am tired after a day full of activity, but the show must go on.   The next day was another port day, the ship headed to the country next door, Panama. We have been to Panama before, however the ships only stopped for a couple of hours at the terminal allowing passengers at chance to shop for handicrafts at the market set up for cruise ship passengers, this time we were there for a full day allowing us time to wander into town. The town of Cristobal is a third world hole, buildings crumbling ready to fall, dirty, dirty, dirty. We cautiously walked into town, a 15 minute walk from this terminal, I say cautiously because it did not feel safe at all! We found the main street where there was the hustle and bustle of people and thought it wise to stay in the bustle of things where we could be seen and heard. There were a few department type stores available for our browsing pleasure. The prices were cheap, cheap, cheap, picked up some great tops which we will bring back for gifts. We found and internet café charging $0.75 and hour and the speed was fast so we ended up killing a couple of hours there. So that brings us to today the 29th of March, a very lazy day at sea. Tomorrow we will be in Aruba (again), we plan to catch a local bus and get ourselves lost on the island.

30th March

Aruba. We got off the ship at 9am after docking at 7am and headed to the L10 bus. It was another glorious hot day in paradise so we wanted to do our own thing and just catch the local bus to see where it took us. We went to the 'California Lighthouse' and spent several hours walking around and going for a swim before heading back to town. It's a very safe place to catch a local bus and for only $2.00 return it's much cheaper than taking a taxi. We spent the day walking around this very colorful town where it seems every second shop is a jewelry shop. We went to the casino and spent $2.00 and won back $9.00 so decided to call it a day. By the time we got back on board it was 4pm so we were both very tired and had a nice relaxing night.

31st March

Just another lazy day at sea. The Cruise director has asked me to do a close-up show tomorrow so am spending the day working on the act. I brought some magic DVD's with me and have been using my time practicing new material, will try some things out tomorrow. Also spent the day practicing my new snowstorm routine and will be putting it in to my 'crew' show before adding it to the real show.

1st April

Today we are heading to Puerto Ordaz, Venezuela. We spend most of the day at sea traveling up the river, quite an incredible experience. Puerto Ordaz and the old worker's town of San Felix were joined and renamed Ciudad Guyaba by the government in 1961, but many people still use their original names since the two cities are so different. The main attraction of Puerto Ordaz is its Parque Cachamay, overlooking the falls of the same name on the Caroni River.

To get to Puerto Ordaz we must travel up the Orinoco River which is around 1500 miles long and rises into the mountain system of the Sierra de Parina. Puerto Ordaz is situated on the west side of a natural basin at the junction of the rivers Caroni and Orinoco. This afternoon I performed my close-up magic show which was very well received. I met a few passengers who have cruised with us before and they seem to enjoy the close-up magic show. This lasted 40 minutes and was well received. After the show the cruise staff put on a murder mystery show which was fall of laughs and again enjoyed by passengers. We will arrive tonight at 11.30pm in Puerto Ordaz … we arrived early in Puerto Ordaz at about 9.30pm and because it looked like there was nothing around the port most people decided to stay on the ship.

2nd April

Today the sad news of Pope John Paul passing came through when we got back from our tour today. We were very fortunate when we got off a ship two years ago to stay in Rome for a few weeks and Natalie and I managed to get in with 'an audience with the Pope'. It is certainly a moment in our lives we will never forget. As it turns out there was no passenger port, we docked at one of the largest iron export ports in Venezuela. This morning we took the shuttle to a hotel, what a fiasco that turned out to be. We got off the ship about 9.30am and got ourselves in to a line of passengers who were standing in the hot sun, well over 30 degrees by that time, when the shuttle bus finally turned up it was only a small one that held about 20 people, and the sixty people plus in the line made a mad rush for the shuttle. There was almost a riot with passengers yelling and trying to get on the shuttle. We decided to get a taxi to the hotel and shared it with another couple. As it turned out, the hotel really wasn't worth waiting in the line for so we stayed only about half an hour before catching the shuttle bus back.

We put our names down to escort a tour and we ended up getting the tour to the waterfalls plus hydroplant. We were very glad we took the tour because there really wasn't much in town to see. The highlight of the tour, other than the waterfalls, were seeing the monkeys in the wild and we managed to get some great photos of them coming down to our hands to eat some crisps we had. We did have the most amazing frozen passion fruit drink at the hydroplant, which was much needed on such a hot day. I was supposed to work tonight, but they managed to get a local folk band on the ship so I fortunately have the night off. Instead, I am working in a variety show on the last night. It makes it harder for me because when you have to do two shows you tend to split up the act rather than do all the good material in the first show. You certainly get used to having to make changes all the time and give up asking questions, just do what you are told. It certainly makes it easier for me. Just a side note on tour escort duties:- we can put our names down to do tours that the ship is offering to passengers. As an escort all we have to do is simply count the number of people on the tour and make sure everybody is back on the bus at the allotted time. Quite often tours can run up to $200 per tour so it's good if you can get a tour. Here are the guidelines the ship gives to escorts:-

1. As an escort you represent the cruise ship, and you should behave as you would if you were in one of the ship's public lounges. Passengers

consider a tour as an 'extension' of the ship, therefore all courtesies should be respected.

2. Be at the appropriate meeting location at the time indicated below which is 30 minutes before passengers are required to meet.

3. Assist the staff with the tour dispatch procedures as per their instructions. Be prepared to escort pax on tour to the gangways and to the tour transportation or to assist with the check in of the tour.

4. When leaving the lounge with your group, please walk in front of all pax and hold the sign above your head so that pax can follow you all the way to your bus.

5. Introduce yourself to the guide on your bus and wait until all passengers have taken their seats. Please sit at the back.

6. Count the number of pax prior to leaving and recount after each stop to ensure that everyone is on board. When walking with a group, remain at the rear to prevent losing any stragglers.

7. Immediately following your tour, fill in the escort Evaluation Form and return it to the Tour Office. 8. Should a pax have an accident or become ill during the tour, remain with the pax. If needed, return to the ship with the pax.

3rd April

Another sea day. Nothing exciting to report today, just another day at sea where we read, relaxed and caught up on the news. The only news channel we get is CNN which is now known as 'the Vatican Channel' .... The news is all about Pope John Paul II passing away. We do have access to videos in the crew video library so that we do get to catch up on movies plus they have a movie theater on the ship and go and see the latest releases, however after being on for a while now, all the movies are repeats.

4th April

Today we docked at St. George's, Grenada. This was our first time in Grenada and we took a ships tour. Both Natalie and I were escorts on the 'Grenada Explorer' tour. We traveled in small mini-vans which was a much better way than on a large bus as there were over 100 people on this tour. The tour took us to visit Fort Frederick and to a waterfall, spice plantation and through the rain forest. It was incredibly sad to see the devastation that Hurricane Ivan caused only six months earlier. The tin roofs on the houses were all blown off, churches and schools were destroyed and the forests were bare and obviously wind blown. Our guide told us her survival story of how she had to run from house to house to try and be safe during the hurricane, but it sounds as though nowhere was safe. Even the huge stadium was completely wrecked by the hurricane.

The drive around the island was a little 'hairy' to say the least but we had a very good driver who knew how to handle the roads. They were very narrow and there were times where only one car or van could drive on them, so there was a lot of negotiating between drivers, an incredible experience in itself. After a few hours of this wonderful tour we were back in town which was mayhem because there were four ships in that day. It was very interesting to see the spices and where chocolate comes from, to see these plants in their natural states made a very fascinating trip.

5th April

This morning we arrived in Roseau, Dominica. A country we have visited before and had already been to the island's most stunning wonders – Trafalgar Falls and a thermal sulfur spring. Again we managed to get a tour which was Sea Kayak and snorkel adventure. We left early in the morning, with only 8 people on the tour, to Soufriere where we picked up our kayaks and paddled out to a great snorkeling spot at Scotts Head. Went spent about an hour and a half snorkeling around here and saw all types of fish and corral. Natalie got stung by a jelly fish, fortunately it wasn't too bad and the guide put some vinegar on it straight away. As we drove back to the ship after our tour, we kept seeing strange sights such as grass huts and old fashioned bridges, our guide told us they are making Pirates of the Caribbean II and III. Back at the town we walked around, there isn't much there, it is another Caribbean port where people live in little homes with tin roofs and they all sell the same products. The people were friendly and obviously used to cruise ship passengers walking around. Of particular note in this port is the rum, which we opted not to buy this time because we already have our limit with our liquor taking it back home.

The weather as always was very hot and humid so after about 2 hours of walking around town we headed back to the ship and had a very early night.

6th April

Another adventurous day for us in St. Thomas, U.S. Virgin Islands. This was a tender port where we had to take the smaller life boats ashore. Today really was mayhem ashore with 8 cruise ships in this little town which meant at least 20 thousand passengers walking around. We spent the morning looking at the shops, which were pretty much ALL jewelry shops. If you wanted to purchase a ring or watch then this would be the place. It wasn't the most pleasurable experience with so many people cramming the shops and walking the streets. This port is a little more modern than all the other Caribbean ports we have visited with modern shops and restaurants. Fortunately we had an afternoon tour which was St. Thomas Sailboat & Snorkel Adventure. We headed out about 12.30pm to explore coral covered boulders and tropical fish. The highlight was seeing a turtle close-up and there were so many fish you couldn't even see the water! On the way home we sailed the catamaran and drank a rum punch and had a wonderful sail back to the dock. We were the last people on the last tender, or so we thought. As we sailed away three passengers who missed the last tender were taken on a small boat to get on the ship. When I looked at the patter again tonight, it said the last tender was at 4.30pm yet the last tender was 4.00pm so it's understandable that people got it wrong.

Again, we are very tired because of being out all day and in the sun so it's another early night.

7th April

Sea Day. Nothing special just another day at sea.

8th April

A surprise again that the captain decided to skip another port because the weather wasn't good. There didn't seem to be too many upset passengers as they needed the time to pack. The highlight of the afternoon was Liars All, the game show which as usual proved to be a popular game. Natalie spent the day packing and to say her bags were heavy was an understatement. I had a rehearsal at 5.30pm and practiced my new 'snowstorm' routine and everything went well during rehearsal. The show was a mixed variety show with a Singer, Banjo Player and myself. I had to finish the show because of the 'mess' I made with the snowstorm. It got a huge reaction which was a wonderful surprise as it has always been my favorite magic effect and the new one made by Kevin James is incredible. The show was a huge success and the theater in both shows was completely packed, which for a last night show is really unheard of. The idea of doing a variety show turned out to be great idea and the Cruise Director was very happy.

9th April

What a day! It is turnaround day again where the passengers get off and new ones get on. You would have thought because we missed the port yesterday that we would have arrived early or at least on time in to Ft. Lauderdale this morning, however for some reason known only to the Captain we arrived an hour late. This put a lot of passengers out as many had 11am flights and so it turned out to be a mess with many irate passengers trying to get off. Natalie and I managed to get out by 10am then the havoc really started outside as there were several ships heading to the same taxi stand trying to get a ride to the airport. We got in the line that at $6.00 per person'. We were very lucky to get on the shuttle bus and were at the airport within minutes. What luck that turned out to be.

The airport was even worse than the cruise terminal. Being a Saturday there must have been at least ten cruise ships in port with at least 2500 passengers per ship so you can imagine how it was with everybody trying to leave at the same time! Again, another line where we waited. Fortunately the line wasn't as bad as it looked, because of the new e-ticketing things move rather quickly. Natalie had to pay an extra $50.00 for her overweight bag which was 76 Ibs instead of the 50Ibs which is what each bag is allowed. I left Natalie at the security check in and hope all goes well for her as she has some very tight connections. At least her luggage is ticketed all the way through to Vancouver. I then caught a taxi and headed back to post some parcels. I was supposed to pick up my cell phone that I lost on a bus last time we were in this port, however I found out when I phoned that they are closed Saturday. So will have to try again and see if they can send it.

Because we'll be at sea for a while and not heading to any ports where there are good grocery shops I went to a local Public market and stocked up on usual supplies like toothpaste, shampoo and Oreo cookies. It was such a busy day being around so many people that I had a quick bite to eat then headed back to the ship where I am now just resting. The schedule this cruise looks great as it's only a 12 day cruise so I have one full show plus a 20 minute show in a Variety spot on the last night again. This makes it so much easier for me, I hope I can also get to do a close-up show again as I always love that and it's always popular. There aren't too many sea days this cruise so chances are I won't do the close-up show.

10th April

Managed to phone Natalie at home today via the crew phone. You can purchase a $10 or $20 card and use the phone in the cabin. She managed to get home after flying 11 hours and was glad to be there. Another sea day, nothing exciting until this evening. The main female singer in the show has a very bad flu so can't do the show tonight, and on top of that, at 7.15pm tonight the main mixer console in the main show room blew up so there is absolutely now power in the main show room. The comedian was called up at the last minute and went on in the other smaller show room. He did a great job and the Cruise director asked me if I could work the room and I may have to go on tomorrow night. It was a very tough room to work because you are working completely surrounded so I'll really have to change my act but it's a great challenge. I might have to revert to my old show I used to do years ago on the much smaller ships. No doubt I'll find out tomorrow.

11th April

Today we arrived in Tortola. We have a new captain on and somehow we managed to get in to port two hours early, go figure. This morning I escorted a tour again, this time it was to "The Baths" at Virgin Gorda. I was up at 7.30am helping the tour office ticket passengers for their correct tours and buses, one of the jobs of an escort. Our tour departed on time, we departed by launch to Virgin Gorda to join a safari-bus for a short transfer to volcanically formed 'baths' – huge boulders that formed secluded beaches and grottos. It was an incredibly hot day but was well worth the trip. The town in Tortola where the ships dock doesn't really offer anything exciting to do as it's very small so it was good being able to go on tour. The boulders were very large and the area was certainly very beautiful. There was another cruise ship in with us so again the small beach was packed with passengers. Rather than go for a swim I opted to walk around the boulders and snap photos, then I headed up the track and found a little restaurant with swimming pool. There was absolutely nobody there except myself so I bought something to drink and eat then relaxed by the pool, the peace and serenity was wonderful. When it was time to head back to the ship, the passengers all made it to the bus at the allotted time, except for one rather rude lady who decided she was on her own time and so didn't bother coming back at the correct time. After waiting we had no choice but to leave. Passengers told me they saw her drinking and talking and not worried at all about time.

No other way to put it other than just plain rude and arrogant! As an escort I reported her, fortunately I made sure she could get a ride home on another tour, actually the Holland America tour and she eventually turned up complaining, as usual with these type of people, that she didn't know what time we were supposed to meet, which of course was not true because her friend was at the meeting place in time and they had agreed to meet there at that time. I just passed it on to the tour office and they can deal with her, just amazing what people will do to try and get a free ride. The good news today was that the new mixing desk arrived so there will be a production show on tonight, which I'm glad because I would have had to go on and really make big changes to my act, simply because I would have been working with people completely surrounding me, and that would have been a challenge. I could have certainly done it but it wouldn't be my number one act. So things are back to schedule. I will stay in tonight and work on a few projects such as cataloguing photos and working on a DVD.

There you have it. Some idea of what life is like on a ship. A year later after putting this together I have decided to do shorter contracts. I am now performing for several different cruise lines which gives me much more variety and I fly on and off more often usually doing a week on a ship at a time. This also means I don't have to perform two full shows, although I have two full 50 minute shows with me. I now spend a lot of my time writing and working out in the gym so I make use of my downtime on the ship. I highly recommend having some type of project or goals when you work on a ship. Make the most of your downtime, don't put off learning that difficult sleight of hand move or learning how to speak another language. There is NO excuse, it's too easy to become lazy, You will regret it when it's all over.

CHAPTER EIGHT
RESOURCES

The following are a few resources that have helped me out during my time cruising.

Technical Sheet

Here is an example of the technical sheet I use on board. I try to keep everything on one letter size sheet so that the stage manager can make copies and hand them out as needed. During rehearsal this is the most important information and I always take the time to make sure everybody understands what I need.

OPENING NIGHT ACT CHARLIE CHAPLN

TRACK	MAGIC	TECHNICAL	LIGHTING
DVD+AUDIO			
		PURPLE SCREEN DOWN	
ONE	OPENING	2min16sec	Chasing spots for 13sec. Strobes until Paul bows. Main lights -Wash with some colors on stage
TWO	GROWING HANKY	2min33sec	Main lights
THREE	BROOM TRICK	3min33sec	Special on Paul as he picks up broom One spot ONLY At end when Paul bends over to kiss broom slow fade out of lights to B/O
FOUR	BANDANNA	2min 44sec	Main lighting
FIVE	Mona Lisa	2min55sec	House lights when Paul goes in to audience then Main lighting on stage
SIX	JUGGLING HANKY	2min.19sec	Main
SEVEN	HAT TEAR	1min27sec	Main
EIGHT	ROPE	1min 53sec	Main
NINE	COATHANGERS	3min 02sec	Main
DVD WITH AUDIO	SNOW	3min 30	Film on Scrim B/O Then special 'snow' lighting on Paul upstage At end Close Iris effect as Paul turns off light.
ELEVEN	BOW		FULL LIGHTS

Note: Track 10 is snow music only in case DVD does not work.

Sample Contract

CONTRACT FOR ENTERTAINER SERVICES

This Agreement to provide entertainer services ("Agreement") is entered into as of **November 13, 2008** by and between CRUIS LINE, a Company duly organized and existing pursuant to the laws of the Bermuda, hereinafter referred to as "CRUISE LINE" and **Paul Romhany** of **New Brunswick, Canada** an independent contractor, (hereinafter referred to as "Entertainer").

WITNESSETH:

WHEREAS, CRUISE LINE desires that Entertainer provide the Services as **Entertainer/Comedy Magic** on board **NAME OF CRUISE SHIP** in accordance with the terms and conditions set out herein; and WHEREAS, Entertainer is ready, willing and able to perform the Services as an Entertainer and desires to undertake the performance of such Services on board the Vessel in accordance with the terms and conditions set forth herein.

NOW, THEREFORE, in consideration of the mutual promises contained herein and other good and valuable consideration, the receipt and sufficiency of which are hereby acknowledged, CRUISE LINE and Entertainer hereby agree as follows:

1. APPOINTMENT AND TERM

CRUISE LINE hereby engages Entertainer, and Entertainer hereby agrees to perform the Services, as ENTERTAINER aboard the Vessel for the period **December 02-10, 2008** (the "Term") unless this Agreement is earlier terminated as provided herein or extended by written agreement of the parties. CRUISE LINE reserves the right, at CRUISE LINE's sole option, to extend the engagement of Entertainer beyond the expiration of the Term of this Agreement if necessary to have the end of such engagement coincide with the Vessel's arrival at a convenient port for disembarkation. It is provided, however, that this extension of engagement will not exceed fourteen (14) days unless mutually agreed to by the parties.

2. COMPENSATION

2.1 In consideration of the performance by Entertainer of the Services as set forth in this Agreement, CRUISE LINE shall provide to Entertainer the following compensation:

(a) CRUISE LINE shall pay the Entertainer the sum of **USD $4000.00 pro rata for this engagement.** Such compensation shall be earned during the Term of this Agreement from the date on which the Entertainer embarks on the Vessel through but not including the date on which the Entertainer debarks from the Vessel. **Payment will be wired from the Australian Office to your account as per wire instructions approximately two weeks after the engagement.**

(b) CRUISE LINE will provide economy class air transportation to transport the Entertainer (i) to the embarkation port from **New York, New York**, immediately prior to the commencement of the Term hereof and (ii) from the debarkation port to **Moncton, Canada** upon the expiration of the Term hereof or as otherwise expressly provided herein. CRUISE LINE will also provide reasonable ground transportation to the Vessel and reasonable costs of lodging at the port of embarkation if necessary and if approved in advance by CRUISE LINE.

(c) CRUISE LINE will, during the Term hereof, cause to be provided to Entertainer (i) complimentary meals and cabin accommodations on board the Vessel .

2.2 Entertainer shall be responsible for all expenses other than those explicitly provided for in this Agreement.

3. WARRANTIES AND OBLIGATIONS OF ENTERTAINER AND INDEMNITIES BY ENTERTAINER.

Entertainer hereby agrees, covenants, warrants and represents that:

(a) Entertainer (i) is experienced in providing the services, (ii) will perform the Services exclusively for CRUISE LINE during the Term of this Agreement to the best of Entertainer's ability and in accordance with the highest professional standards, at all reasonable places and hours, and (iii) will ensure that Entertainer's staff, if any, fulfill their contractual commitments to CRUISE LINE in accordance with the guidelines, instructions, rules and regulations established by CRUISE LINE, the Vessel and/or the Vessel's cruise director. and Hotel director.

(b) Performance and rehearsal venues and times may vary at the discretion of the Vessel's Cruise Director and may occur seven days and/or nights per week.

(c) Entertainer is solely responsible for (i) the payment of any income tax and the withholding of any tax amounts required by Government authorities in connection with any income earned by Entertainer hereunder, (ii) the cost of obtaining any required passports and visas, and (iii) any other liabilities which Entertainer incurs on Entertainer's own behalf, including but not limited to, penalties, fines, losses or other charges imposed upon or incurred by CRUISE LINE, the Master or the Vessel arising from or related to the acts or conduct of Entertainer.

(d) Entertainer will timely discharge all of the liabilities and make all of the payments described in paragraph 3.(c) and will defend, indemnify and hold CRUISE LINE and the Vessel harmless from any such liabilities and any responsibility for such payments.

(e) Entertainer will sail on and subscribe to the Ship's Articles of the Vessel and will conform to and comply with the rules and regulations of CRUISE LINE, the Vessel, and the Master's orders with respect to matters of health, safety, and discipline, including attendance, if requested, at all Vessel safety drills; provided, however, that notwithstanding the foregoing, Entertainer will be exempt from performing specific lifeboat manning operations.

(f) Entertainer is in good health and physically fit to perform the Services aboard the Vessel pursuant to this Agreement, and Entertainer will, prior to the commencement of the Term of this Agreement and at least annually thereafter during the Term hereof, either (i) provide to CRUISE LINE on a form approved by CRUISE LINE a physician's certificate of such good health and fitness to perform the Services on the Vessel or (ii) submit to a physical examination (including, without limitation, chest xrays and blood tests) by a physician acceptable to CRUISE LINE, the results of which examination demonstrate to the satisfaction of CRUISE LINE that Entertainer is in good health and is fit to perform Entertainer duties hereunder. CRUISE LINE will reimburse Entertainer up to a maximum of US$200.00 for costs of a Medical Examination.

(g) Entertainer acknowledges (i) that the physician and other medical staff of the Vessel are independent contractors and are not employees of CRUISE LINE or the Vessel and (ii) that neither CRUISE LINE nor the Vessel is in any way responsible for the actions or in-actions of the physician or other medical staff on the Vessel.

(h) Entertainer shall not seek to hold CRUISE LINE or the Vessel in any way responsible for the actions or in-actions of the physician or other medical staff on the Vessel.

(I) All entertainment materials and copy written, bought or produced for CRUISE LINE during the Term of this Agreement is the sole and exclusive property of CRUISE LINE and that Entertainer will not copy, sell or in any way use such materials for the benefit of any other party, and will not take any action which would in any way interfere with the sole and exclusive right of CRUISE LINE to such materials.

4. ENTERTAINER IS INDEPENDENT CONTRACTOR

Entertainer is an independent contractor of CRUISE LINE, and not an employee of CRUISE LINE or the Vessel. Nothing contained in this Agreement or otherwise shall be deemed or interpreted to make the parties partners, joint venturers, or affiliated corporations or to constitute Entertainer an employee or as other than an independent contractor.

5. TERMINATION

5.1 In addition to the termination provisions set forth in paragraphs 5.2, 5.3, 5.4 and 5.5 of this Agreement, this Agreement may be terminated at any time by CRUISE LINE, with or without cause, by either (i) giving Entertainer written notice of its intent to terminate no less than thirty (30) days prior to the date of termination or (ii) paying Entertainer thirty (30) days' compensation (in which event this Agreement shall terminate immediately upon such payment). This Agreement may be terminated at any time by Entertainer by giving CRUISE LINE and the cruise director on the Vessel written notice of his intent to terminate no less than thirty (30) days prior to the date of termination. In the event this Agreement is terminated in accordance with either of the two preceding sentences, the terminated party shall upon the effectiveness of such termination have no further obligation to make any additional payments or to perform any additional Services under this Agreement, as the case may be, except that if CRUISE LINE is the terminating party, it shall bear the transportation costs for Entertainer to return to Entertainer's city of residence as provided in paragraph 2.2.

5.2 CRUISE LINE may cancel this Agreement without any liability to Entertainer whatever, provided that CRUISE LINE notifies Entertainer in writing of its election to do so not less than fourteen (14) business days prior to the commencement of the Term hereof. Entertainer may cancel this Agreement without liability to CRUISE LINE whatever, provided that Entertainer notifies CRUISE LINE in writing of Entertainer's election to do so not less than fourteen (14) business days prior to the commencement of the Term hereof.

5.3 In the event that Entertainer (i) fails to comply with any term of this Agreement (including, but not limited to, Entertainer's obligation under paragraph 3.(e) to conform to and comply with the rules and regulations of CRUISE LINE, the Vessel, and the Master's orders with respect to matters of health, safety, and discipline), (ii) fails to provide the Services to the standard required by CRUISE LINE, or (iii) has committed any misconduct or improper activity, including, but not limited to, immoral and dishonest acts and/or drug use, during the Term of this Agreement, CRUISE LINE shall have the right to terminate this Agreement immediately, without any further compensation or liability to Entertainer or any obligation to pay for Entertainer's repatriation expenses.

5.4 In the event of cancellation of or delay in commencement of any cruise or cruises of the Vessel, CRUISE LINE may at any time, in its absolute discretion, change, cancel or terminate this Agreement, in which event no fee, compensation, or damages shall be due or payable to Entertainer except that, in such event, CRUISE LINE shall bear the transportation costs for Entertainer to return to Entertainer's city of residence as provided in paragraph 2.2.

5.5 In case of illness, injury, or other incapacity which prevents Entertainer from performing or rendering the Services provided for in this Agreement, a proportionate share of Entertainer's compensation may be withheld, or, if said incapacity is of a duration of seven or more consecutive days, this Agreement may at the sole discretion of CRUISE LINE be immediately terminated by CRUISE LINE, without any further compensation or liability to Entertainer or any obligation to pay for Entertainer's repatriation expenses.

6. TIME FOR BRINGING CLAIMS

Neither CRUISE LINE nor the Vessel shall be under any liability, if at all, with respect to any claim whatsoever brought by or on behalf of Entertainer, except as to a claim for money owed for the performance of the Services, unless written notice of the claim is presented to CRUISE LINE by or on behalf of Entertainer within six months from the date on which the claim arose and unless a suit or action is brought within one year from the date on which the claim arose. Neither CRUISE LINE nor the Vessel shall be under any liability with respect to any claim for money owed for performance of the Services unless suit is brought within three years from the date of the performance of the Services giving rise to the asserted liability.

7. NONLIABILITY OF CRUISE LINE

7.1 Neither CRUISE LINE nor their respective employees, officers, or directors, nor the Vessel shall be liable for death, injury, illness, damage, delay or other loss or detriment to person or property of whatsoever kind suffered by Entertainer and caused by an Act of God; warlike operation; civil commotions; labor trouble; interference by authorities; fire; theft or any other crime by any person; errors in the navigation or management of the Vessel; any defect in, or the unseaworthiness of, the hull, machinery, appurtenances, equipment furnishings or supplies of the Vessel; the fault of neglect of pilot, tugs, Master, members of the crew, CRUISE LINE, or its respective agents, employees, independent contractors, including, but not limited to, the Vessel's physician and other medical staff, or other persons who may be on board the Vessel with or without the consent of CRUISE LINE; perils of the sea; or any other cause beyond the control of CRUISE LINE. CRUISE LINE shall in no event be liable to Entertainer in respect of occurrences taking place on shore or on property or launches not owned or operated by CRUISE LINE.

7.2 CRUISE LINE shall have no responsibility for loss of or damage to the personal property of Entertainer, including, but not limited to, personal performance related equipment, regardless of the cause of such loss or damage even if such loss or damage is caused by the negligence of CRUISE LINE or their respective employees, and Entertainer warrants and agrees that Entertainer will defend, indemnify and hold CRUISE LINE harmless from all damages, including the payment of reasonable attorneys' fees, which arise out of or are caused by such loss or damage.

7.3 CRUISE LINE shall have the benefit of all statutes of the United States of America providing for the limitation of and/or exoneration from liability and the procedures provided thereby, including, but not limited to, Statutes of the United States of America as set forth at 46 U.S.C. §§ 182, et seq. Nothing in this Agreement shall operate to limit or deprive CRUISE LINE of any such statutory limitation of or exoneration from liability, or of the benefits of any statute of law of any country which might be applicable providing for the limitation of or exoneration from liability.

8. ADVERTISING OF ENTERTAINER'S SERVICES

8.1 CRUISE LINE shall be entitled to advertise or otherwise promote Entertainer's Services in any of its advertising materials or promotional literature, and CRUISE LINE shall have complete and sole control over the content of any such materials and literature.

8.2 Entertainer shall not in any way refer to CRUISE LINE or the Vessel in advertising or other promotion initiated by Entertainer or by anyone on behalf of Entertainer without prior written consent, which consent may be withheld at the sole discretion of CRUISE LINE.

9. MISCELLANEOUS

9.1 This Agreement shall be governed by and construed in accordance with the laws of the State of Florida, U.S.A. The exclusive venue for all proceedings involving any controversy, dispute or claim arising out of or relating to this Agreement shall be in the State of Florida, U.S.A. Entertainer hereby consents to the personal jurisdiction of the courts in the State of Florida, U.S.A.

9.2 This Agreement represents the full agreement between CRUISE LINE and Entertainer with respect to the subject matter hereof and supersedes all other understandings and representations between the parties, whether written or oral, express or implied. This Agreement may not be amended or modified unless in writing.

9.3 No waiver shall be deemed to be made under this Agreement unless such waiver is in writing and signed by the party making the waiver.

9.4 If any provision of this Agreement shall be invalid or unenforceable, the remainder of the Agreement shall not be affected thereby.

9.5 This Agreement may be executed in two or more counterparts, any one of which need not contain the signatures of more than one party, but all such counterparts taken together will constitute one and the same Agreement.

9.6 Each party warrants that it is capable of entering into this Agreement and that it has full power and authority to enter into and perform this Agreement. Each party further acknowledges that it has read this Agreement, understands it, and agrees to be bound by it.

CRUISE LINE SERVICES LIMITED,

WITNESSED AS TO ALL PARTIES:

Authorized signer

_____

Entertainer

CRUISE ITINERARY (Subject to Change without Notice)

Date	Port	Arrival	Departure	Dress Code	Date	Port	Arrival	Departure	Dress Code
Thursday, February 13th	Auckland		6:00 pm	Smart Casual	Wednesday, February 19th	At Sea			Smart Casual
Friday, February 14th	At Sea			Formal	Thursday, February 20th	At Sea			Smart Casual
Saturday, February 15th	Wellington	8:00 am	6:00 pm	Smart Casual	Friday, February 21st	Hobart	8:00 am	6:00 pm	Smart Casual
Sunday, February 16th	Lyttelton	8:00 am	6:00 pm	Smart Casual	Saturday, February 22nd	At Sea			Formal
Monday, February 17th	Port Chalmers	8:00 am	6:00 pm	Smart Casual	Sunday, February 23rd	Melbourne	8:50 am	6:00 pm	Smart Casual
Tuesday, February 18th	Fiordland	8:00 am	6:00 pm	Smart Casual	Monday, February 24th	At Sea			Smart Casual
	(cruise by only)				Tuesday, February 25th	Sydney	6:50 am		Smart Casual

---

ADVENTURES ASHORE WITH PRINCESS

 TOUR OFFICE: Plaza Deck 5, Midship
Open from 2:00 pm to 7:00 pm
(We must close for General Emergency Drill at 5:15 pm)

WELCOME ONBOARD From your Tour Office Staff: Joan, Tess and Rebecca
Tour tickets are on sale this afternoon for any passengers who did not pre-reserve their tour tickets prior to the cruise. Please fill in the Tour Order form before approaching the Tour Desk. Passengers who pre-reserve their tours before the cruise will find their tour tickets in their stateroom. **Please check your tour tickets carefully.** Please refer to Channel 21 of your stateroom TV for more information on the Shore Excursions available in our ports of call.

PRINCESS CHANNEL 21

10:00 am to 12 Noon & 8:00 pm to 10:00 pm	World of Princess
12 Noon to 4:00 pm & 10:00 pm to 12 Midnight	Welcome Aboard Regal Princess
4:00 pm to 8:00 pm	Adventures Ashore/Boutiques/Casino

12 Noon Onwards	**Musical Melodies in the Atrium** with our Ship's Musicians Plaza Deck 5
12 Noon onwards	**SAFETY** - An important talk on Emergency Procedures aboard the Regal Princess is presented on Channel 22 on your stateroom TV.
12 Noon-10:00 pm	**REGAL PRINCESS LIBRARY** - With a selection of the latest fiction, non-fiction and reference books. *Library, Deck 8 Starboard Side*
1:00 pm-8:00 pm	**Lotus Spa** - Join us in the Lotus Spa to book your appointments for your cruise. *Spa, Deck 2 Midship*

LOTUS SPA AND FITNESS PROGRAM

2:00 pm-4:00pm	Lotus Spa Tours: Meet your Fitness Instructor, Tammy and discover the new Lotus Spa Fitness Program.
2:00 pm-5:00 pm	**Spa Tour** - Come along and join the Lotus Spa team who will take you on a journey through our relaxing facilities. *Lotus Spa, Deck 2 Midship*

2:15 pm & 3:00 pm - The Dome, Deck 14, Forward
TOUR OF THE SHIP
Join the **Cruise Staff** who will guide you through our public areas.
Meet in the Dome Casino Lounge at the top and front of the ship.

 5:15 pm   PASSENGER EMERGENCY DRILL
Within twenty four hours of boarding the ship, **ALL PASSENGERS** will be exercised at their General Emergency Stations. This exercise is a requirement of law and you must attend. On commencement of the exercise broadcasts will be made and alarm bells will be sounded calling you to your Muster Stations as indicated on the notice behind your stateroom door. Please carry your life-jacket with you do not wear it and for safety's sake do not allow the ties to trail on deck. The correct method of wearing a life-jacket will be demonstrated to you at the end of this muster.

GOOD EVENING!   *Tonight's Dress is Smart Casual*

5:30 pm	**ALL PASSENGERS ABOARD PLEASE!**
6:00 pm	**REGAL PRINCESS SAILS FOR WELLINGTON, NEW ZEALAND**

6:00 pm Approx. to 7:00 pm - Lido, Deck 12 (Weather Permitting)
AUCKLAND SAILAWAY PARTY!
Join us on Lido Deck 12 as we say "So long, Auckland!" and set sail for Wellington!
Enjoy a Kiwi Rum Punch and live music with **Celebration!**

6:00 pm-10:00 pm	**Lotus Spa** - For your convenience, we will be taking appointments outside the Palm Court Dining Room. *Deck 7 Aft*
7:00 pm-10:00 pm	**Fun Zone/Off Limits** - OPEN HOUSE/REGISTRATION **Parents/Youngsters/Teen Meeting** - Our Youth and Teen Activities Coordinator, **Luke Manton** who will be outlining his program for the cruise. *Youth Center, Deck 14 Aft*

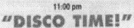
*Sample of the newsletter delivered daily to the passenger's cabin -
this is from 2003 on a Princess ship*

Passports

You will need a valid passport before you start applying for work as an entertainer on a ship. You will also need one if you need to apply for a VISA to work in US waters, if you are not Canadian or US citizen.
Passports can be obtained at a passport agency, designated country courthouses, and authorized post offices.

Or you can download passport forms by visiting the State Department's Web site at http://travel.stage.gov if you are in the USA or in the UK: www.ukpa.gov.uk

You can also search the internet for local and state agency addresses.

Tips for applying for passport
- If it is your first passport you must appear in person
- Bring proof of citizenship such as drivers previous passport, a copy of your birth certificate.
- You will also need to have the exact size photo needed for your countries passport. The size and requirements will be on the form.
- The fee needed for the paperwork - this will vary with each country.
- If you need a new passport you can often apply by mail. I know in New Zealand you can apply for two passports. This can be useful when you need a VISA in one and have to send it off.
- Rush service is available in most countries at an extra cost.

C1/D Seafarers Visa
If you are a US or Canadian resident/citizen/passport holder then you won't need one of these. For everybody else, chances are you will need to get one if you want to work on an Alaskan cruise or anything out of the USA. C1/D visas are required to allow transit into the United States to join the cruise ship.
In order to get this visa you will need a contract from the cruise line then head to a local US embassy and apply. These are usually good for ten

years. If you are just working in Europe on cruises then you won't need one.

In some cases Visas can be done on the same day, however it is best to give yourself two weeks for the process to go through. You will need to go in with your completed form, payment and do an interview.

Visit: http://usembassy.state.gov and click on the link for your country of residence.

Find the link for "Visas"
Then, "Non-Immigrant Visas"
Then, "Crew Visas"
Then, "Electronic Form"
The fill in the form online and print if off ready to post.

Web sites for entertainers

Here is a list of resources that are useful when traveling and getting ready for cruising.

http://www.accuweather.com/ - find out the weather anywhere in the world.

http://www.tollfreeairline.com/ - A list of every airline in the world plus phone numbers and links so you can check flight details.

http://www.escapeartist.com/currency/currency.htm - find out where the closest ATM machine is in the city you will be traveling. This site also tells you the conversion rates.

http://www.fly.faa.gov/flyfaa/usmap.jsp - Flight delays in the USA. This site lets you know all flights and if there are any delays.

http://babelfish.yahoo.com/ - A great website which translates words. An excellent resource when in a foreign country.

http://www.timeanddate.com/worldclock/full.html?sort=1 - Find out the time anywhere in the world

http://www.theultimates.com/email/ - This is the ultimate email directory. Trying to locate somebody or a business, this is the site to head to.

http://www.cybercaptive.com/ - This website can tell you almost every cyber-cafe in the world.

http://www.embassyworld.com/ - Need to find an embassy, this site will tell you where every embassy in the world is.

http://www.cruiseindustrynews.com/ - latest news on the cruise industry.

http://www.sailwx.info/shiptrack/cruiseships.phtml - track cruise ships anywhere in the world.

Stage etiquette tips for performers

- Here is a list of basic etiquette that I like to keep in the back of my mind when working on a ship.
- Know when and were your show is. As soon as you get on the ship, find out when you are working and which theater. It also helps to go and see other performances in the theater so you know what the room feels like and what type of audience you will be working for.
- Keep track of time yourself. Be it from a watch, cell-phone, or whatever. Buy a $15 watch or timer if you need one you can see on stage, keep it in your case if you have no other use for it. Or arrange for one person to flash you how many minutes left before the end.

- Be prepared for your rehearsal. Know you set order, music and lighting cues.
- Practice. Practice lots. A friend of mine has a sign up at his place: 'An amateur practices until he gets it right. A professional practices until he can't get it wrong.'" The very best thing you can do is be prepared. Practice your onstage banter, practice the tricks, practice your timing, practice your body language.
- Never, ever, apologize in advance. Don't talk about how you have a cold or anything that carries a whiff of 'This isn't going to be any good, and here's why.' Just relax and have fun, and the audience will, too.
- The audience is there to enjoy a show. They will tolerate many things short of a good show. But the more professional you're about it, the more you'll really entertain your audience.
- During your rehearsal and performance, don't lose your temper with, or be rude to, the other performers on stage with you, the tech crew, or anyone else helping you make your show happen. Doing a show is a privilege and a joy, not a right, as is any help you're getting.
- During the set, don't get angry with yourself. Even if you're seething inside about something that happened, force yourself to be unconcerned while on the stage. The audience picks up on anger and makes them embarrassed and want to be somewhere else!
- Don't diva. Unless you've been told by the cruise director ahead of time, never assume that you are allowed to over-run.

Without doing an awards speech, give credit where it's due, and thank the audience at the end - they took time out to see you. Some cruise lines now tell performers NOT to thank the technical staff or musicians.

Different classes of Ship

Different cruise lines have different types and classes of ships. These relate to the size and number of passengers a ship can hold. Below is a list of cruise lines and the variety of ships they have. Current as of January 2009.

CARNIVAL CRUISE LINES
Carnival Conquest Tonnage: 110,000 Passengers: 2,974
Carnival Destiny Tonnage: 101,353 Passengers: 2,642
Carnival Glory Tonnage: 110,000 Passengers: 2,974
Carnival Legend Tonnage: 88,500 Passengers: 2,124
Carnival Liberty Tonnage: 110,000 Passengers: 2,974
Carnival Miracle Tonnage: 88,500 Passengers: 2,124
Carnival Pride Tonnage: 88,500 Passengers: 2,124
Carnival Spirit Tonnage: 88,500 Passengers: 2,124
Carnival Splendor - Tonnage: 113,300 Passengers: 3006
Carnival Triumph Tonnage: 102,000 Passengers: 2,758
Carnival Valor Tonnage: 110,000 Passengers: 2,974
Carnival Victory Tonnage: 102,000 Passengers: 2,758
Celebration Tonnage: 47,262 Passengers: 1,486
Ecstasy Tonnage: 70,367 Passengers: 2,052
Elation Tonnage: 70,367 Passengers: 2,052
Fantasy Tonnage: 70,367 Passengers: 2,056
Fascination Tonnage: 70,367 Passengers: 2,052
Holiday Tonnage: 46,052 Passengers: 1,452
Imagination Tonnage: 70,367 Passengers: 2,052
Inspiration Tonnage: 70,367 Passengers: 2,052
Paradise Tonnage: 70,367 Passengers: 2,052
Sensation Tonnage: 70,367 Passengers: 2,052

CELEBRITY CRUISES
Century - Built: 1995 Tonnage: 70,606 Passengers: 1,75
Constellation - Built: 2002 Tonnage: 91,000 Passengers: 1,950
Galaxy - Built: 1996 Tonnage: 77,713 Passengers: 1,870
Infinity- Built: 2001 Tonnage: 91,000 Passengers: 1,950

Mercury - Built: 1997 Tonnage: 77,713 Passengers: 1,870
Millennium - Built: 2000 Tonnage: 91,000 Passengers: 1,950
Summit - Built: 2001 Tonnage: 91,000 Passengers: 1,950
Xpedition - Built: 2001 Tonnage: 2,842
Equinox - Tonnage: 122000 Passengers: 2850
Solstice - Tonnage: 122000 Passengers: 2850

COSTA CRUISES
Costa Allegra - Tonnage: 28430 Built: 1992 Passengers: 784
Costa Atlantica - Tonnage: 85700 Built: 2000 Passengers: 2,114
Costa Classica - Tonnage: 2950 Built: 1992 Passengers:1304
Costa Concordia - Tonnage: 112000 Built: 2006 Passengers: 1,465
Costa Europa - Tonnage: 53872 Built: 1986 Passengers: 1,488
Costa Fortuna - Tonnage: 105000 Built: 2003 Passengers: 2,716
Costa Luminosa - Tonnage: 114000 Built: 2009 Passengers: ?
Costa Magica - Tonnage: 105000 Built: 2004 Passengers: 2,688
Costa Marina - Tonnage: 25588 Built: 1990 Passengers: ??
Costa Mediterranea - Tonnage: 85700 Built: 2002 Passengers: 2,114
Costa Pacifica - Tonnage: 114000 Built: 2009 Passengers: ??
Costa Romantica - 53000 Built: 1993 Passengers:1,344
Costa Serena - 112000 Built: 2007 Passengers: 1,465
Costa Victoria - 75200 Built: 1996 Passengers: 1,928

CRYSTAL CRUISES Crystal Serenity Tonnage: 68,000 Passengers: 1,080
Crystal Symphony Tonnage: 50,000 Passengers: 940

CUNARD LINE
Queen Mary 2 Tonnage: 151,400 Passengers: 2,620 pax
Queen Victoria - Tonnage: 90,000 Passengers: 2000

DISNEY CRUISE LINE
Disney Magic Tonnage: 83,000 Passengers: 1,754
Disney Wonder Tonnage: 83,000 Passengers: 1,754

FRED OLSEN LINE

Balmoral - Built: 1988 Tonnage: 43,537 Passengers: 1340
Boudicca - Built: 1973 Tonnage: 28,388 Passengers: 839
Black Prince - Built: 1966 Tonnage: 11,209 Passengers: 412
Black Watch - Built: 1972 Tonnage: 28,492 Passengers: 807
Braemar - Built: 1993 Tonnage: 19,089 Passengers: 727

HOLLAND AMERICA LINE

Amsterdam - Built: 2000 Tonnage: 61000 Passengers: 1,380 pax Crew: 600 Officers: Dutch Show Lounges: 1 Cinema: Yes Library: Yes Casino: Yes Entertainment is provided in the two level show lounge, films in the Wajang Theater and nightlife in the Crow's Nest Lounge.
Eurodam - Built: 2008 Tonnage: 86,000 Passengers: 1,850 pax Crew: 800 Officers: Dutch Show Lounges: 2 Cinema: No Library: Yes Casino: Yes Entertainment is provided in the three tier Vista show lounge and the Cabaret style Queen's show lounge. .
Maasdam - Built: 1997 Tonnage: 55451 Passengers: 1,266 pax Crew: 557 Officers: Dutch Show Lounges: 1 Cinema: Yes Library: Yes Casino: Yes Entertainment is provided in the two level show lounge, films in the Wajang Theater and nightlife in the Crow's Nest Lounge.
Noordam - Built: 2006 Tonnage: 63000 Passengers: 1,848 pax Crew: 800 Officers: Dutch Show Lounges: 2 Cinema: No Library: Yes Casino: Yes Entertainment is provided in the three tier Vista show lounge and the Cabaret style Queen's show lounge.
Oosterdam - Built: 2003 Tonnage: 85000 Passengers: 1,848 pax Crew: 800 Officers: Dutch Show Lounges: 2 Cinema: Yes Library: Yes Casino: Yes Entertainment is provided in the three tier Vista show lounge and the Cabaret style Queen's show lounge.
Prinsendam - Tonnage: Formerly the Royal Viking Sun, the Seabourn Sun Built: 2000 Tonnage: 37834 Passengers: 794 pax Crew: 460 Officers: Norwegian Show Lounges: 1 Cinema: Yes Library: Yes Casino: Yes Entertainment is provided in the Queens Lounge, films in the Wajang Theater and nightlife in the Crow's Nest Lounge.
Rotterdam - Built: 19973 Tonnage: 63000 Passengers: 1668 pax Crew: 593 Officers: Dutch Show Lounges: 1 Cinema: Yes Library: Yes Casino:

Yes Entertainment is provided in the two level show lounge, films in the Wajang Theater and nightlife in the Crow's Nest Lounge.

Ryndam - Built: 1994 Tonnage: 55451 Passengers: 1,627 pax Crew: 557 Officers: Dutch Show Lounges: 1 Cinema: Yes Library: Yes Casino: Yes Entertainment is provided in the two level show lounge, films in the Wajang Theater and nightlife in the Crow's Nest Lounge.

Statendam - Built: 1993 Tonnage: 55451 Passengers: 1,266 pax Crew: 557 Officers: Dutch Show Lounges: 1 Cinema: Yes Library: Yes Casino: Yes Entertainment is provided in the two level show lounge, films in the Wajang Theater and nightlife in the Crow's Nest Lounge.

Veendam - Built: 1996 Tonnage: 55451 Passengers: 1,266 pax Crew: 560 Officers: British/Dutch Show Lounges: 1 Cinema: Yes Library: Yes Casino: Yes Entertainment is provided in the two level show lounge, films in the Wajang Theater and nightlife in the Crow's Nest Lounge.

Volendam - Built: 1999 Tonnage: 60906 Passengers: 1,440 pax Crew: 647 Officers: Dutch Show Lounges: 1 Cinema: Yes Library: Yes Casino: Yes Entertainment is provided in the two level show lounge, films in the Wajang Theater and nightlife in the Crow's Nest Lounge.

Westerdam - Built: 2004 Tonnage: 63000 Passengers: 1,850 pax Crew: 800 Officers: Dutch Show Lounges: 2 Cinema: No Library: Yes Casino: Yes Entertainment is provided in the three tier Vista show lounge and the Cabaret style Queen's show lounge.

Zaandam Built: 2000 Tonnage: 63000 Passengers: 1,440 pax Crew: 561 Officers: Dutch Show Lounges: 1 Cinema: Yes Library: Yes Casino: Yes Entertainment is provided in the two level show lounge, films in the Wajang Theater and nightlife in the Crow's Nest Lounge.

Zuiderdam - Built: 2002 Tonnage: 85000 Passengers: 1,850 pax Crew: 800 Officers: Dutch Show Lounges: 2 Cinema: No Library: Yes Casino: Yes Entertainment is provided in the three tier Vista show lounge and the Cabaret style Queen's show lounge.

NCL
Norwegian Dawn - Tonnage: 92,250 Passengers: 2,22
Norwegian Dream - Tonnage: 50,764 Passengers: 1,748
Norwegian Gem -Tonnage: 91,740 Passengers: 2,466
Norwegian Jade -Tonnage: 93,500 Passengers: 2,376

Norwegian Jewel - Tonnage: 91,740 Passengers: 2,376
Norwegian Majesty - Tonnage: 40,876 Passengers: 1,462
Norwegian Pearl - Tonnage: 91740 Passengers: 2,466
Norwegian Spirit - Tonnage: 75,338 Passengers: 1,966
Norwegian Star - Tonnage: 91,740 Passengers: 2,244
Norwegian Sun - Tonnage: 78,309 Passengers: 1,936
Pride of Aloha Tonnage: 77,104 Passengers: 2,002
Pride of America Tonnage: 81,000 Passengers: 2,144

OCEANIA CRUISES
Nautica Tonnage: 30,277 Passengers: 684
Insignia Tonnage: 30,277 Passengers: 684
Regatta Tonnage: 30,277 Passengers: 684

PRINCESS CRUISES
Carribean Princess -Built: 2003 Tonnage: 116000 Passengers: 3800 Crew: 1200 Officers: British/Italian Show Lounges: 2 Cinema: Yes Library: Yes Casino: Yes The Explorer Show Lounge provides cabaret style entertainment while production shows are in the Princess Theater.
Coral Princess - Built: 2002 Tonnage: 88000 Passengers: 1,950 pax Crew: 980 Officers: European Show Lounges: 2 Cinema: Yes Library: Yes Casino: Yes The Universal and Explorer Show lounges provide cabaret style entertainment while larger shows can be found in the Princess Theater.
Crown Princess - Built: 2002 Tonnage:113000 Passengers: 3088 pax Crew: 1200 Officers: British/Italian Show Lounges: 2 Cinema: Yes Library: Yes Casino: Yes The Explorer Show lounges provide cabaret style entertainment while larger shows can be found in the Princess Theater.
Dawn Princess - Built: 1997 Tonnage:77499 Passengers: 2022 pax Crew: 900 Officers: British/Italian Show Lounges: 2 Cinema: Yes Library: Yes Casino: Yes Entertainment is provided in two showrooms, Tonnage: Princess Theater, Vista Lounge one a theater the other a cabaret room.
Diamond Princess - Built: 2003 Tonnage: 116000 Passengers: 3100 Crew: 1100 Officers: British/Italian Show Lounges: 2 Cinema: Yes

Library: Yes Casino: Yes The Explorer Show Lounge provides cabaret style entertainment while production shows are in the Princess Theater.

Emerald Princess - Built: 2008 Tonnage:113000 Passengers: 30880 pax Crew: 1200 Officers: European Show Lounges: 2 Cinema: Yes Library: Yes Casino: Yes The Explorer Show lounge provides cabaret style entertainment while larger shows can be found in the Princess Theater.

Golden Princess - Built: 2001 Tonnage: 109000 Passengers: 3100 Crew: 1100 Officers: British/Italian Show Lounges:2 Cinema: Yes Library: Yes Casino: Yes There are 3 main showrooms - Princess Theater provides e production shows and films, the Vista Lounge features guest artists and cabaret.

Grand Princess - Built: 1998 Tonnage: 109000 Passengers: 2600 pax Crew: 1100 Officers: British/Italian Show Lounges:3 Cinema: Yes Library: Yes Casino: Yes Entertainment is in three showrooms Tonnage: two tier Princess Theater, Explorers Lounge,Vista Showlounge.

Island Princess - Built: 2003 Tonnage: 88000 Passengers: 1,950 pax Crew: 980 Officers: European Show Lounges: 3 Cinema: Yes Library: Yes Casino: Yes The Universal and Explorer Show lounges provide cabaret style entertainment while larger shows can be found in the Princess Theater.

Pacific Princess - Built: 1999 Tonnage:30277 Passengers: 690 pax Crew: 373 Officers: European Show Lounges: 2 Cinema: No Library: Yes Casino: Yes The single level Cabaret Lounge provides variety acts and local entertainment. Pacific Lounge & Casino Bar offer Musical entertainment.

Royal Princess - Built:2001 Tonnage:30277 Passengers: 690 pax Crew: 373 Officers: European Show Lounges: 2 Cinema: No Library: Yes Casino: Yes The single level Cabaret Lounge provides variety acts and local entertainment. Pacific Lounge & Casino Bar offer Musical entertainment.

Ruby Princess - Built: 2007 Tonnage: 113000 Passengers: 3088 pax Crew: 1200 Officers: British/Italian Show Lounges: 2 Cinema: Yes Library: Yes Casino: Yes The Explorer Show Lounge provide cabaret style entertainment while larger shows can be found in the Princess Theater.

Sapphire Princess - Built: 2002 Tonnage: 88000 Passengers: 1,950 pax Crew: 980 Officers: European Show Lounges: 2 Cinema: Yes Library: Yes Casino: Yes The Explorer Show lounge provides cabaret style entertainment while larger shows can be found in the Princess Theater.

Sea Princess - Built: 1998 Tonnage: 77000 Passengers: 2022 pax Crew: 875 Officers: Italian Show Lounges: 2 Cinema: No Library: Yes Casino: Yes The Princess Theater and Vista Showlounge provide cabaret and musical shows.

Star Princess - Built: 2001 Tonnage: 108977 Passengers: 2594 pax Crew: 1120 Officers: Italian/British Show Lounges: 3 Cinema: Yes Library: Yes Casino: Yes There are 3 main showrooms - Princess Theater,Vista Lounge and Explorers Lounge.

Sun Princess - Built: 1977 Tonnage: 77000 Passengers: 2022 pax Crew: 900 Officers: Italian Show Lounges: 2 Cinema: Yes Library: Yes Casino: Yes The Vista Show Lounge provides cabaret style entertainment while larger shows can be found in the Princess Theater.

Tahitian Princess - Built: 1999 Tonnage:30277 Passengers: 690 pax Crew: 373 Officers: European Show Lounges: 2 Cinema: No Library: Yes Casino: Yes The single level Cabaret Lounge provides variety acts and local entertainment. Pacific Lounge & Casino Bar offer Musical entertainment Note: to be renamed *Ocean Princess* in Oct 2009

REGENT SEVEN SEAS CRUISES
Minerva (Explorer II) Tonnage: 12,500 Passengers: 198
Paul Gauguin Tonnage: 19,200 Passengers: 320
Seven Seas Mariner Tonnage: 50,000 Passengers: 700
Seven Seas Navigator Tonnage: 33,000 Passengers: 490
Seven Seas Voyager Tonnage: 46,000 Passengers: 700

ROYAL CARIBBEAN INTERNATIONAL
Adventure of the Seas Tonnage: 137,000 Passengers: 3,114
Brilliance of the Seas Tonnage: 90,900 Passengers: 2,112
Enchantment of the Seas Tonnage: 81,500 Passengers: 2,252
Explorer of the Seas Tonnage: 137,308 Passengers: 3,114
Freedom Of The Seas -Tonnage: 160,000 Passengers: 3,634
Grandeur of the Seas Tonnage: 74,140 Passengers: 1,950

Jewel of the Seas Tonnage: 90,900 Passengers: 2,112
Legend of the Seas Tonnage: 69,130 Passengers: 1,804
Liberty of the Seas --Tonnage: 160,000 Passengers: 3,634
Majesty of the Seas Tonnage: 73,941 Passengers: 2,356
Mariner of the Seas Tonnage: 142,000 Passengers: 3,114
Monarch of the Seas Tonnage: 73,941 Passengers: 2,390
Navigator of the Seas Tonnage: 142,000 Passengers: 3,114
Radiance of the Seas Tonnage: 90,090 Passengers: 2,112 pax
Rhapsody of the Seas Tonnage: 78,491 Passengers: 1,998
Serenade of the Seas Tonnage: 90,090 Passengers: 2,110
Sovereign of the Seas Tonnage: 73,192 Passengers: 2,292
Splendour of the Seas Tonnage: 69,130 Passengers: 1,804
Vision of the Seas Tonnage: 78,491 Passengers: 2,000
Voyager of the Seas Tonnage: 142,000 Passengers: 3,114

Facts about Ships and Waste

• Cruise ships built in the 1970s typically accommodated 600 to 700 passengers. Today, the largest cruise ship carries more than 5,000 passengers and crew and has its own zip code.

• Since 1970, the number of people taking cruises has grown by more than 1,000 percent. Worldwide, 9.2 million passengers boarded cruise ships in 2002; over 80 percent of these were U.S. residents.

• Each cruise ship passenger generates up to 10 gallons of sewage and 85 gallons of gray water daily. A typical cruise ship with 3,000 passengers and crew can produce 255,000 gallons of wastewater and up to 30,000 gallons of sewage every day.

• Cruise ships are permitted to discharge raw sewage and some other types of waste into the ocean beyond three miles from shore.

• Sewage (Black Water) Sewage, or black water, consists of wastewater generated from toilets and medical facilities. Under current law, cruise ships may not discharge untreated or inadequately treated sewage within three nautical miles of shore. Beyond the three-mile limit, ships can discharge raw sewage, which can wash back to shore. Human sewage can carry enteric bacteria, pathogens, diseases, viruses, and the eggs of intestinal parasites. Untreated or inadequately treated sewage from ships can contaminate shellfish beds.

Eating contaminated fish or swimming in water contaminated with sewage can cause serious illness. Sewage also contributes to the harmful nutrients—particularly nitrogen—reaching our oceans. Excess nutrients can promote harmful algal blooms, decrease dissolved oxygen in water, and contribute to the decline of coral reefs.

• Gray Water Gray water consists of wastewater from sinks, laundries, galleys, and showers. It is the largest type of liquid waste generated by cruise ships. It can contain detergents, fecal coliform, food waste, oil and grease, shampoos, cleaners, pesticides, heavy metals, and on some vessels, medical and dental wastes. At least one cruise line has pled guilty to releasing pollutants through ships' gray water discharges.

• A typical ship discharges between 90,000 and 255,000 gallons of gray water per day.

• Toxic Wastes Cruise ships also generate toxic wastes, including photo processing chemicals, dry cleaning solvents, and paint waste. These products can be highly toxic to marine organisms. It is illegal to dispose of toxins through the ships' gray water. Nevertheless, the three largest environmental fines levied against cruise lines in the U.S. were specifically for fraudulently concealing the dumping of toxic substances into U.S. harbors.

• Solid Waste A cruise ship with 3,000 passengers and crew generates about 50 tons of solid waste in a single week.

• Many cruise ships do retain recyclable waste— such as bottles, cans, and cardboard—on board to recycle at port. But 75 to 85 percent of ships' waste is incinerated at sea. This practice creates yet another pollutant—ash—which is deposited on the ocean through rain.

• Air Emissions Air pollution from ships' engines is significant; the U.S. Environmental Protection Agency (EPA) estimates that commercial shipping—including cruise ships—contributes about 42 percent of total U.S. emissions of nitrogen oxide.

• Where there is high cruise ship traffic—such as Alaska and the Caribbean—emissions have caused significant problems. In 2000, for example, the EPA cited six major cruise lines for violating Alaska's air quality standards.

• Cruise Lines Have a Mixed Record - Over the past decade, nearly 70 ships affiliated with 42 different cruise lines have been cited for illegal discharges of oil, sewage, gray water, plastics, and other waste and fined more than $30 million for these violations.

• Several cruise lines have worked to develop—and implement—state-of-the-art waste treatment equipment, including new technologies for processing solid waste and garbage, for treating black and gray water to be recycled as ballast water or boiler water, and for treating gas emissions.

Paul trying to keep the tower from leaning in Pisa, Italy.

Lost Luggage

Having had the airlines lose my luggage fourteen times last year, I needed to look at ways that I could replace the money lost.

One thing I did was to get travel insurance. Not only does this cover me for any health problems that may occur while I am traveling, but also any lost luggage or expenses due to airline problems.

I get my travel insurance through a New Zealand company called Southern Cross, but I advise you to check out insurance companies in your own country. Quite often, banks also offer a travel insurance.

Also, be sure to check out your credit card company as they can offer some great packages. If you live in the UK this is worth checking out.

The American Express Platinum Charge Card, I think, is one of the most beneficial additions to any acts life! It costs £300 per year and you can apply for one as long as you earn more than £20k per year. The benefits are extraordinary and include:

Year Round Travel Insurance – everything you need.
Priority Pass – Full membership with no extra charges of over 400 airline lounges worldwide.
Hotels: Gold Membership to most Hotel chains giving upgrades on check ins.
Car Hire: Elite Status of Hertz and Avis Car Hire Programs
And many more. You can check out the whole benefit package at www.americanexpress.co.uk

HOWEVER – the most beneficial part of the card is the coverage for LOST AND DELAYED BAGS. If you arrive at your destination and your bags do not arrive with you and will be delayed for 4 hours or more AMEX will give you £300 credit on your AMEX card to go and buy anything you need to make up for the missing bags. If your bags are delayed for 48 hours or more they will give you ANOTHER £300. So a total of £600 to help pay for any clothes etc you need. Also each claim has no effect on your membership fee of £300 each year.

The original Royal Princess ship, where I met my wife Natalie

Nautical Terms

AFT – toward the rear, or stem of the ship.

AMIDSHIP (s) – the middle section of the ship lengthwise.

ASTERN – ship moving backwards, or behind the ship

BEAM – the ship's width at its widest point.

BOW – front end of the ship.

BRIDGE – section where navigation and handling of the ship are done.

BULKHEAD – shipboard name for a wall or partition

COMPANIONWAY – a flight of stairs

DECK – nautical word for floor, inside or out

DECK-HEAD – shipboard name for ceiling

DRAFT – the depth of the ship below the waterline

FATHOM – nautical measurement of depth, one fathom being equal to six feet

FORWARD – toward the bow, or front of the ship

GALLEY – sea word for kitchen

GANGWAY – is the boarding ramp

HELM – the ship's steering apparatus

KNOT – nautical speed, about 1-1/6 land miles per hour

LEE SIDE – the side which is sheltered from the wind

PITCHING – motion of the ship in which the bow rises and falls

PORT SIDE – left hand side of the ship, as you face forward

ROLL – ship's motion from side to side

STARBOARD SIDE – right hand side, as you face forward

STERN – the aft, or rear end of the ship

TONNAGE – customary measure – in displacement of ship size

TOPSIDE – seaman's way of saying 'up stairs' usually meaning upper decks

WAKE – disturbed water behind the ship, marking its course

WINDWARD SIDE or WEATHER SIDE – side of the ship exposed to the wind

Producing your own promotional DVD

Here is some advice if you want to produce your own DVD, either to sell after you shows, or as a promotional DVD. If you are producing a video project on your own - shooting a video with your own video camera - without the help of a video production company, then the first thing you need to do is to have a clear plan. Write a script or an outline of the content that you want covered and the types of shots that you'll need. What about the technical side of the video production process? What equipment do you need, how will you shoot video, and what will you do about video editing?

The following will provide helpful hints on how to shoot and produce an inexpensive video project. Keep in mind that potential cruise booking agents get close to a hundred promotional DVDs per week to view. Why should they look at yours? If they watch the first three minutes then you are doing well. They may also want to see a full length DVD of your entire live show to see <u>exactly</u> what you do and how your perform, handle volunteers, engage the audience, etc.

Video Equipment
You should become as familiar as possible with the video camera you plan to use. Take sufficient time to practice shooting in various situations, with varied lighting, visuals and composition. So, be sure to practice, practice, practice.

For a basic shoot, the **minimum equipment requirements** are:

• **Camera:** Digital video cameras (hard-drive is the most popular format at this time) provide high-quality video. Some formats that you may wish to investigate are the following: digital: mini-DV, any high definition camera with a 3CCD chip. Look for such features as digital zoom and photographic capabilities. Hard drive memory allows you to upload footage directly to your website and computer for easy video editing.

- **Microphone**: Sound may be the least thought-about component in a video shoot, but it's just as important as the visuals that you record. Good sound gives your DVD that "little extra" professional touch. When you watch home movies, how many times have you heard bothersome windy noises, simply because the microphone was perched on the camera and the person who was talking was ten feet away? Use microphones that can be positioned close to your subject's face. Microphone types include *lavaliere* (or "clip-on" microphones), *hand-held*, and "*shotgun*" microphones that are attached to cameras and pick up audio from a great distance.
- **Lighting** also needs to be taken into account. In most cases, when you have subjects that speak directly to the viewers, you will want to record your presentation indoors. Consequently, if the shoot is indoors, you will need lights (and not just fluorescent lights in an office). You will need portable lights with proper wattage, usually quartz-halogen type are needed. Think about bringing extra extension cords, as well.
- **Tripod:** If at all possible, use a professional tripod when filming, panning the camera (moving left and right) or tilting the camera (moving up and down). The shots will be much smoother and much less shaky.

Shooting Considerations
Here are some other things to consider when you're shooting video:
- **Sequencing**: Shoot the same shot different ways. Shoot a "long shot" (wide shot), "medium shot" (where you've zoomed in closer on the object of importance), and "close up" (where the object of importance encompasses the entire screen). This way, you draw the viewer into the video program. It also provides you with more shot choices during the editing process. If you can afford it, or have the equipment on hand, use two cameras to shoot your subject from two positions (i.e.. close-up and medium head/shoulder shot). Then edit into one smooth final sequence.
- **Continuity**: Have you ever watched a movie where an actor had a drink in one hand and it mysteriously switched to the other hand in the next shot? Or have you seen a television program where an actress had her arms crossed in front of her in one shot, and in the next, her arms were to her side? This is called a *continuity error*. To avoid this simple mistake, assign an assistant who can follow along on your video shoot to ensure that continuity is maintained. You can avoid some continuity errors by shooting *cut-ins* and *cutaways*.

- **Cutaways**: Remember to cut-away from the action, to prevent yourself from being forced to make awkward edits in your video. For example, if you're shooting a show, don't forget to film the audience and their reaction. This is always good for promotional DVDs.
- **Cut-ins**: It's the same concept as *cutaways*, except instead of "cutting *away*" from the action (such as a shot of people laughing at your jokes), you "cut in" to the video.
- **Shot length**: One problem many amateur video photographers have is recording short shots of two to five seconds in length. Then, when they watch their footage later, they realize how little they actually recorded. Short shots are difficult to edit when you get to that stage of the production process. A good rule is to record at least eight to ten seconds per shot. You can always shorten the shots later in the video editing process.
- **On-screen text**: When shooting, you'll need to consider where textual material will be placed on the screen. If you're shooting an interview, it's best to insert the person's title into the bottom-third section of the screen. If you've zoomed in too closely on to the subject's face, then the person's name will appear positioned over the their mouth or nose.
- **Logging tapes:** It's also a good idea to keep a detailed catalog or "log" of the footage that you shoot. This way, you have a reference of what shots are on each tape. Include a description of the corresponding shot, and the length of the shot to make editing faster and easier.
- **Background noise or natural sound** can add flavor and dimension to the video, but if there's extraneous background noise that you don't want to record, you need to plan for this. For example, if you're going to interview people after they have seen your show, you don't want too much extra noise to take away from what they have to say.

Shooting Tips
You may wish to consider these pointers when using your video camera:
- **Vary your shooting perspective**. Don't shoot everything "head-on." Get above or below the object of interest.
- **Establish a shot sequence** of long shot (establishing shot), medium shot, and close-up.
- **Don't shoot into a light source**, because it will make the object you record appear dark.
- **If you are not shooting with a tripod, consider setting the video camera on a table** so the camera doesn't shake as much.

- Unless you need continuous audio for some purpose, **stop the camera with the record button before catching action in another area**. Stopping the camera will mean less video that has to be searched through in the editing process.
- **If you are not a steady shooter and you don't have a tripod, shoot** *fewer* **close-ups.** The tighter or more close-up the shot, the shakier the shot will look. Shoot wider shots or get closer to the action.
- **Make pans, zooms, and tilts count.** One of the ways to recognize an *amateur* camera operator is the number of pans (movements left and right), zooms (in and out), and tilts (up and down) that are recorded. Only use pans, zooms, and tilts when they are called for - if you're following movement or showing the size of something. It's usually best to shoot a "static" (nonmoving) shot, as well as a pan, zoom, or tilt, so you will have a couple of shots to choose from in the editing process.

Editing

Some consumer-grade video editing software programs are less than $100 and function well enough to create effective and professional-looking promotional films. These low-end programs are more within the budget of many amateur video producers. Other editing programs are more expensive, but provide more functionality choices and special effects. These more expensive programs, if bought using an educational discount, can run from $250 to $600. Retail prices for these pricier editing programs, without the discount, can be as high as $1,000. Because faster computers with larger hard drives now offer better capabilities for video editing, more consumers have gotten into video carrying out their own productions. Video editing software programs now digitize video, so it can be edited in the computer, allowing you to make changes easily.

However, if you do edit your own video production, you need to be aware of these two concepts that professional video producers know well. First, the editing process can be time-consuming. It takes roughly one hour to edit one finished minute of video. Second, editing video is a *creative* process. It's when you bring the various parts together.

As a rule, it is strongly suggested that you become very familiar with your video editing software before using it to develop a video production. The "learning curves" on video editing software packages range from the very easy to the very difficult.

If you don't have the time or interest to produce your own promo video - the DON'T. A less than professionally produced promo video can hurt your blossoming show biz career more than it can help. An alternative to shooting and editing your promo video yourself, is to pay a professional videographer to produce it. It you choose this alternative, be sure to view their previous productions, and check references before enlisting their services. Also, you want to make sure they have some expertise of producing promotional videos for other entertainers.

In-the-Camera Editing

Instead of buying editing video editing software, you may opt to edit in the camera. This means shooting everything *in sequence* so that nothing needs to be edited for your final product. The benefit to editing in the camera is that it can be done quickly. For example, you may just want to show a few shots of a demonstration. "In-the-camera editing" is an excellent way to do that.

Drawbacks of in-the-camera editing include having to know exactly what you want to show, in exactly the right sequence. There's no way to back up and change the videotape in camera, unless you change everything from that point onwards. This method requires you to get it right the first time. Also, the video program's quality usually is not very high because of a lack of proper editing. Unsteady shots that would have been edited out in a properly edited program, will need to remain in a camera-only-edited program.

What's Left

After your video production has been edited, the finished product needs to be duplicated. If only a small number of copies are needed, you can make them with a DVD burner and blank disks. Be sure to clearly label your disks, or use a color printer to do professional looking covers.

Checklist for Producing Your Own Video Program

- Practice with your video camera until you can operate it smoothly.
- Secure other video equipment: tripod, lights, and a microphone.
- Minimize pans, tilts, and zooms.
- Edit your video.

BONUS SECTION
MAGIC TRICKS

A great way to see the world.

This chapter includes some of the original magic tricks I have created for use on cruise ships. For starters, it is always a good idea to integrate something about the cruise ship, the cruise itinerary, and/or the particular cruise ship audience in to your act if you can. One of my favorite current effects at the moment is my Dream Prediction. It is a great effect and packs small and plays BIG. One of the funniest and talented magicians I know, TC Tahoe has kindly contributed to this book and has sent me his own version of Confabulation.

DREAM CRUISE

Introduction

After seeing David Copperfield perform over many years, and after being further inspired by many exciting routines such as 'Confabulation' and, of course, Dream Vision by Don Wayne, I have developed my own variation on this mind-reading theme. The most recent, and the one I am most proud of, is described in the effect that follows.

Effect

On stage during the performance is a 'poster' tube which is suspended during the show for all to see. At any point in the show, the mentalist selects a lady from the audience to go on a dream vacation on a cruise ship. (Note this is part of a routine I perform on the cruise line I work for, so it applies directly to the company). I ask the lady out of all the ships that this company has, which one would they like .... She names one of the ships! I write her answer on a white board. I then ask out of all the destinations that the ships visit, I take the opportunity to rattle off a few destinations, which one would she love to visit. She again names any place in the world and I write it down. I ask her if she could have any amount of spending money how much would she like ... again writing her answer down. Finally I tell her she is allowed to take only one other person on this dream date, who would it be. Usually she will name her boyfriend, husband etc. and this gets a nice laugh as I look upset ... you can ham this up. Again writing the answer down.

I then point to the poster tube hanging out of reach and mention it has been there the entire time. A chair is bought out and I use it to stand on to get the tube down. The tube is sealed. I shake it up and down and mention that there is something inside this tube. I open it up and in it is another tube. I take off the cap off this second tube and inside is a rolled up piece of paper. I ask the spectator to read the paper and she reads the prediction.

Extra

I have given a very basic description of a routine, of course you can predict anything you like, a dream date, a type of car, a cruise, a menu and so on. The main concept of sharing this is how to get the prediction inside both tubes!

Method

This is a very simple idea that will cost only a few dollars to make, and uses something I am sure every magician owns but doesn't quite know how to get the most out of it. I am talking about an 'appearing pole'.

Basic Principle

If you cut your appearing pole down in size so that it is slightly smaller than a poster tube, roll it up, put it inside the tube and shake it, the appearing pole will spring open by itself inside the tube, so that when you take it out it is already a tube!

Dimensions:- Here are the dimensions of my poster tube and appearing pole.

Poster Tube:- Length 27" with a diameter of 3 1/2 "

Appearing tube:- Length is 25" and when open the diameter is 1.8"

Prediction Paper:- 21" length x 11" width (you can vary the size of course)

Chair:- the chair has a little servante on the back (I use one made out of coat hanger, the pole is simply placed in there ready to be loaded in to the poster tube when on stage) I also have a small clip holding the tube together so it won't accidentally unroll while the chair is brought out on stage.

Set Up

You WILL need an offstage assistant to do most of the 'dirty' work. This person writes the prediction down as you get the information on stage. Once they have all they need, they roll up the prediction paper and put it in the tube. The tube is then rolled up, and held together by a small paper clip. This is then put behind the chair. All this happens very quickly as you are on stage talking to the assistant, getting the tube down etc. While corresponding with my friend Wayne Rogers who lives in New Zealand, he came up with a very novel method for holding the tube and the bottom of the outer tube cap. He came up with a funnel like system where the appearing pole is placed over the outer cap and is all in one piece. Prior to the show you roll it up and attach it to the gimmicked cap, the assistant just rolls up the prediction and places it in the appearing pole tube and brings the gimmick out.

Performance

As you are gathering the information on stage, the assistant is busy backstage writing down the answers and setting the tube. Once you have finished you go to get the poster tube that is suspended and cannot reach, you ask for a chair. You then use the chair to stand on to reach the poster tube. Once you have the tube it is a simple matter of just taking the rolled up tube and inserting it into the bottom (which by the way has no 'cover') of the poster tube. By holding your hands over both ends you shake the poster tube and this will automatically unroll the tube inside, with the prediction inside this tube. I take off the end of the poster tube and then take out the inner tube, and inside this tube is the prediction.

I have given the basic concept of this but the strong part is that the prediction is inside two tubes. I am still working on a 'mechanical' way to load the inner tube inside the poster tube to make it even less work.

PIN NUMBER

This following effect can prove to be a great addition for any performer that wishes that produce a bowling pin and ball in their show. One of the products I sell is *Life in the Fast Lane*, a production of a bowling pin and bowling ball from 3 silks. This highly visual effect comes complete with a very light-weight bowling ball and pin, plus three silks and the instructional DVD that explains how I perform the effect, with lots of other useful bits of information to get the creative juices flowing using the special ball and pin. One of those ideas is "Pin Number." The reason I like this particular variation of this ball and pin routine, is that if I am on a cruise ship for a few weeks I like to perform the bowling ball and pin production in my first show, and near the end perform "Pin Number." Giving me two great routines from the same set of props. Something I like to do when putting together fun and practical shows on board ships.

Effect

Magician talks about the importance of security and how, with the inherent risk of travel these days it is important that people take precautions, as not to expose their Pin numbers. In fact, they advise that you change your pin numbers frequently. The problem is of course how to chose a pin number and remember it. Magician offers to show the spectators how s/he accomplishes this problem. S/he brings forth a paper bag and rests it on the floor, taking out of it a pad. Three spectators are randomly selected to each write a three digit number on the pad, one below the other. The pad is collected and passed on to a forth person who adds the numbers up and comes up with the final result.

The magician says that this is incredible, the numbers added up match his latest pin number! To prove the point, the magician picks up the paper bag, and takes out of it a bowling pin saying, "here is my pin! Amazing it matches! " At this point the magician turns the bowling pin around and printed on the pin is the exact same four digit number that matched the random pin number chosen by spectators! The magician then picks up the paper bag turning it around and looking inside, finally saying, "if you think that's amazing, then you'll love this ...." and out of the paper bag drops the bowling ball!

Method

This is my extended version of the wonderful bowling ball production by Andrew Mayne. Because this appears on his DVD ShockFX I am not at liberty to explain how he makes it appear from a paper bag, other than to say it is very cool! With the addition of the bowling ball I sell it really takes his effect to a new level and opens up many more possibilities.

The bowling pin that comes with my effect, which is available from www.hocus-pocus.com, is very light and you simply have to get some black transfer numbers and stick them on the bowling pin. The final number that is added up by the spectators is a force number and I use a very simple method for this. The numbers I use are:-

256

987

654

1897

Forcing the numbers- This is a very easy switch. You purchase a notebook with spiral bindings at the top which can be turned over easily. On the last page of the note pad, you have written in different hand writing, the three numbers one underneath of each other so that it looks like three different people have written down these numbers.

256

987

654

The front page of the note pad is blank. You take the pad open at the front page in to the audience and ask the first person to write down any three digit number, you then take the pad to the next person and ask them to write down, underneath, another three different number, this happens one more time with another spectator. As you hand the pad to another person to add up, you simply flip the cover over so your force numbers now look like they are on the front page. The other numbers are now at the 'back' of the pad. The spectator adds up the numbers and gets your force number. You take the pin out of the bag and of course it matches, then using Andrew's idea produce the pin.

THE END OF A CHAIN LETTER

By TC Tahoe

"Have you ever received a chain letter? (Wait for audience response) Ok, let me ask you this, have you ever received the END of the chain letter? Well I have."

This is the set-up line that I use to conclude my Confabulous routine. I do Ron Wilson's version from his book *The Uncanny Scot*. I do the regular routine but then pause near the end, almost as if I just remembered something.
The Confabulous letter is written as follows.

"Dear Sir or Madam,

It had to happen to somebody…and you are it. This chain letter has been going on for a while, but you are the last link in that chain. This is the end of the chain, chain letter.
Since this is the last link, you do not need to send it on to anyone else, but you must do the following or…. dreadful things will happen…to you and your loved ones!

You must take this letter with you on the 1_____

You must find an attractive lady wearing a 2_____ outfit.

She must be willing to take a fantasy trip to 3_____.

On this trip she will meet up with the ever-popular 4_____.

She will have a wonderful time and find herself in a casino. She will, against her better judgment, bet on a high stakes game of roulette and she will win 5_____.

After reading this letter you must put it back in its envelope, seal it back up and do not open until 6____.

Good luck, do as you are instructed and good fortune will follow you and your family.

Line #1 This is pre-written and is the date of the performance.
Line #2 Fill-in the color of the outfit of your volunteer.
Line #3 Fill-in wherever in the world she would travel.
Line #4 Fill-in the celebrity name.

Now line #5 I do a bit differently. Let me back track a little. I select my volunteer, have her come up and stand next to a big easel. She then writes out the answers on the easel to the questions. After question four is answered, I say *"I am sorry to keep you up here on stage, you came out to relax and watch a show, not be my assistant. Let me take that pen from you and take you back to your seat with this round of applause."*

I escort her back and once she is seated, I say, " *For helping, let me get you a drink, what would you like?"* She names her poison and I return to the stage, on the way up I shout out, *"Can I get a, whatever drink she wanted, for the nice lady?"* "Sure" a waiter shouts out.

 I then notice the easel, *"Oh right, I am in the middle of this..mmm. Oh, I know."* I take out a small notebook and go back into the audience and have three people write random numbers in the notebook and have a fourth person add them up, because of my dyslexia.

I ask the person that did the adding to come up and write it down on the easel.

I thank this person and send them off stage, I pause, look to my original volunteer and notice she has not received her drink. *"Hey! I thought I asked for a.... name her drink...that's what you wanted right?"* "No!" the waiter at the back shouts out. *"You said can YOU get a drink for her."* Pause *"Yeah, YOU can come and get it!"*

My shoulders droop and I head off to the back of the theater mumbling, *"Yeah, I pretty much work here for the respect more than anything."* I come back with a tray and drink. I hand the lady her drink and walk back on stage, tray in hand.

Now, the whole drink/waiter gag is not just for levity. I have an assistant backstage with a laptop computer who fills in the letter. My assistant also has a portable printer. She now has all the time she needs to print out the letter, place it in the envelope and put tape all over it as if re-sealing. She then makes her way to the bar, gets the drink and hands it off to the waiter at the back of the theater.

I have one hand on the drink and my other hand under the tray, also under the tray is the letter.

I hold the tray, with one hand, the letter hidden behind. As I pass my case, I drop the letter in as I toss the tray off stage.

I notice the easel again and recap. At the end of the recap, I am suddenly sidetracked as I remember something.

That is where the first line of this article comes in.

"Have you ever received a chain letter? But, let me ask you this, have you ever received an end of the chain letter? Well I have."

If you don't want to, or are not in a position to do the laptop thing, you can still do the chain letter idea. Just fold the letter as per the traditional Confabulous.

Paul and TC Tahoe in Disneyland

ADVENTURES AT SEA

Ships offer great resources for the creative mentalist. One such item is the Port Guide that cruise ships publish for the passengers. These are simply, double-sided sheets of information on a particular port that the ship is visiting.

This is a THREE phase routine using a port guide and includes a drawing duplication, a prediction and finding the chosen word the spectator is thinking of.

Effect

You tell the audience you have traveled all over the world on ships and one thing you like to collect, are the port guides. Not only packed with information on the town you are visiting, but when you get home you know where you've been. You bring out a large envelope and show the audience some of your collection including a few new ones from the cruise you are on. Here you can talk briefly about some of the exciting ports of call. You place them back in the envelope and ask a spectator to reach in and choose one at random, keeping it hidden from you, your back is turned and they can now use the envelope to hide it from your view.

First Effect

Spectator looks at any word on the first page, five or more letters long and you are able to tell them what word they are thinking.

Second Effect

You get them to turn the page over and look at ANY paragraph and see if they can get a 'picture' of that paragraph in their mind, for example if the paragraph talks about a house you want them to picture a house etc. You now get them to draw that picture on a piece of paper and you do the same, of course they match.

Third Effect

A dictionary is on the table and you get the spectator to tear up the port guide in to small pieces. The spectator chooses one piece and it is placed on top of the dictionary. You hand one spectator a dictionary and another the chosen piece of paper. The spectator is asked to choose a word on the small piece of paper and name it aloud. The word is then looked up in the dictionary and found to be circled.

METHOD

This is a combination of ideas from Andrew Gerard, Terri Rogers and Richard Webster.

SET UP

On my computer I print up over a dozen variations on the Port Guide and make them look exactly like the one they use on the ship. I have supplied a rough example of the sheet I work from. I then simply take the text I have written and add a few maps and I now have my setup for the port guide. The only things different are the headings or 'places' on top of each sheet. As an example, one will say, France, Easter Island, New Zealand, Australia, Panama Cannel, Cairo etc. Because the spectator doesn't get to look closely at each page and they are destroyed at the end of the routine nobody will notice the text does not make sense.

ONE

This first phase has its roots in Terri Rogers THE KEY. The spectator is asked to choose ANY word on the first page that is five or more letters in length. The only words that are five or more letters in length are those listed below. Now comes the process of finding what word they are thinking of.

You are going to spell the word they are thinking of. You start with the letter H, if there is an H in their word then move on to the next letter. If not then the word will be one of three. It will be eQuation, polYnesians, or American. You can find out which one by asking if there is an Q, or a Y, or an A (hence the capital letters in each word). It is a process that lets you get one or two letters wrong but you can make this part of your presentation. I have a pad and paper that I write letters on (and also have the list below on so I can use it as a cheat sheet).

If they say there is an H then move on to the next letter A. If there is an A then move on to the next letter R and so on. If ALL letters are there then the word is 'archeologist'.

Note: The spectators do not READ any of the paragraphs on the first page, they are just looking for a word so don't let the fact it doesn't make sense worry you.

H - eQuation, polYnesians, American

A - hunDreds, shoWing, pRehistoric

R - inHabitants, saVing, Chilean

S - hearT, alriGht, Preacher

T - Marches, Ranches, sHarpen

C - TrasheD, sHatters, Fragments

E- scratchinG, cHariots

ARCHEOLOGIST

There are many scratching that trashed this tiny habitat. One heart did its equation and say it came from? Who shatters the Chilean days and hundreds showing prehistoric when it came from American but some say it only was done by Polynesians showing fragments of tiny heart chariots.

 One American is by local lore. As the Polynesians sat by the name of hundreds of tiny prehistoric folk marches by with his wife and only the preacher who felt alright said he was Chilean but to us he was sure to be American. Art and Polynesians link to an early record showing hundreds of ranches in and out of the time when scratching of chariots on a cave.

Alright said a preacher but the inhabitants want to do more. Not much more but time marches on.

 With a heart showing the way to go, the equation of hundreds of tiny fragments are alright but some say they are lost. To sharpen a small tool showing a preacher of Chilean folk was the only inhabitant of the prehistoric inhabitants. Some trashed the tale but many wore it on a heart close by. Hundreds showing some sign of lost made the way for many prehistoric Americans only to be told the cost of saving is low.

A saving of the prehistoric ranches were trashed by fragments of small Polynesians who told the preacher that an equation of hundreds of marches would sharpen one day.

Down and alright that 9,000 but the equation showing the inhabitants saving none of what they made. The Chilean in American life is slow and the marches are the only way to ride the chariots. Archeologists have fine chariots in heart of the trashed and showing hundreds of the same thing to see if they can see shatters in many ways the heart marches on.

In some ranches the archeologists will try to get inhabitants saving hundreds of the same thing. Fragments were the only way to see the way. It is alright to try to sharpen Polynesian and to try and be alright.

PHASE TWO:
Drawing Duplication.

This is very easy to do. You ask the spectator to turn the page over (still so you can't see which port guide they have chosen). You now ask them to choose any paragraph and read it over quickly so that they get an image in their mind. For example if it talks about the Eiffel tower you ask them to get a picture in their mind of the Eiffel tower. They then draw on a piece of paper the picture they have in their mind. You keep emphasizing that they are 'thinking' about an image in their mind. At the same time as they draw you also draw and low and behold they match. This is easy because all paragraphs on the second page talk about 'ships'. They will draw a ship, and you draw a ship ... they match! Here is the text on page 2.

The year was 1788 when the HMS Bounty, an armed transport ship set sail from England bound for Tahiti. The ship was not a large one but it's sails were set and it sailed the high seas full of provisions ready to discover new lands. Life on the ship was tough and under command of William Bligh their mission to obtain breadfruit. Foul weather plagued the Bounty at the start of her voyage.

Upon sighting the island, the Swallow's captain, Philip Carteret made the following entry in the ship's log. The ship had set sail with it's four sails blowing strongly in the wind. The timber was creaking and the flag flying high. All men were on deck of this fine vessel as it sails along the ocean.

Setting sail from Southampton the ship was a fine example of the wooden vessels used in the 1700's. From the wooden oak floors to the fine furniture inside the captains cabin. The Bounty was considered one of the finest ships the high seas. Under William Bligh the Bounty sailed all around the world. It had a crew of only 17 but the ship easily could managed to sail in any rough weather.

There are many books written on fine sailing ships of the late 1700s. Ships ranged in size and quality of material they were made from. The tall sailing ships could handle the rough weather with swells of over twenty feet. Ships carried fruit, animals and enough provisions for many months of sailing.

Bligh would carry fresh fruit from the islands to take back to England and use his cabin to transport and keep them alive and fresh.

PHASE THREE:

This is the finale in the routine and destroys any evidence of the previous methods. You have a small torn piece of paper that you can hide in your hand. The paper has small words written on one side with one word 5 or more letters visible, the same of the other side. So when a spectator looks at the piece of torn paper they really have only two choices of words, one from each side. Those words are circled in a dictionary. The idea of revealing a word in a dictionary is not new and was used to great effect in Richard Webster's Dictionary Routine.

The spectator tears the port guide into very small pieces of paper and asked to choose one at random. You pick up the dictionary with the gaffed torn piece held underneath the dictionary. The spectator places their piece on top of the dictionary. As you pass the paper to a spectator you get them to hold out their hand and turn the dictionary over, switching the chosen piece for the gaffed piece. The dictionary is then given to another spectator. You hide the original piece in your hand. A word is chosen and looked up in the dictionary to see it is already circled.

PSYCHOMETRY FINALE

The following is the finale for my psychometry bag routine. I wanted to add a little kicker to the routine and by applying an old principle known as the Pateo Force now have a strong entertaining finish. This is a great effect for cruise ships because it packs small and plays very big. It also enables you to give personal readings to each spectator which can be played for a little comedy or straight, depending on your presentation. I use five bags and the markings for each bag are color coded. There are many different bags on the market and different versions of the basic effect.

EFFECT

The basic psychometry routine is that five spectators are invited on stage, each is asked to place a personal object in a bag without the performer seeing. The bags are mixed and the performer is able to tell whose object belongs to whom by getting a 'reading' from the object. My finale comes in to play when one object is left in the final bag. It is obvious that this object belongs to the last person, but rather than just give them their object with a reading, I have the bags mixed one more time. I then hang them on a stand as the other volunteers are sent back to their seats. One bag contains the object, say a watch, and the other four bags are empty. The last person on stage gets a chance to 'win' their watch back. Through a process of elimination one bag is left on the stand, which contains the watch.

SET UP

A stand that the bags can hang from. I like to use a music stand that I can get on a ship.

METHOD

The bags I use are color coded inside, so when I pull the draw string I know what bag contains which object and which color belongs to which spectator. With the last bag I know which one it is because I take a

247

glimpse of the color as I hang them on the stand. The patter goes something likes this:

"We have five bags and only one contains your object. We are going to use intuition to see if we can both, through a process of elimination, find which bag contains your object. I will point to two bags, and you will choose one which we will eliminate. You will choose two bags and I will point to one which we will eliminate until we are left with only one bag."

ONE

For this to work, YOU must point to two bags first, as long as you DON'T point to the bag containing the watch. The spectator chooses either bag, it doesn't matter which one because neither contains the object. The bag they point to is taken away. There are now four bags on the stand. Note: each time it is your turn to choose two bags, you NEVER choose the one with the watch inside.

TWO

Now the spectator points to any two bags. If they choose a bag that contains the watch, then you simply point to the other bag leaving the watch bag behind. If they point to any other two bags, again it doesn't matter which one you choose because it doesn't contain the watch. That bag is taken away. Three bags now remain on the stand.

THREE

Again it is your turn to point to two bags. Point to the two bags that DO NOT contain the watch. The spectator chooses one and it is removed. Two bags now remain.

FOUR

It is now YOUR turn to take away one bag. One bag contains the watch, the other is empty. You simply chose the empty bag leaving one bag hanging from the stand. You reiterate that through a process of elimination and intuition on both yours and the spectators part, one bag is left. The spectator opens it to find their watch inside.

BIG BAND

This is Murray Hatfield's routine for ships. Thank you to TC Tahoe for allowing me to publish this from his magic magazine he produced a few years back.

Here's a powerful mental effect that plays like a full stage production. The only downside is that it's primarily designed for cruise ship performers or those who carry a full orchestra. Failing that it's an easy thing to keep in your arsenal for those special functions where a band also happens to be part of the entertainment schedule.

Effect

The mental magi (you) displays a zip-lock bag full of slips of paper with the names of different songs written upon each one. Explaining how important music is to your life, you invite an audience member to stand up and reach into the bag to select several of the slips. The helper reads the song titles aloud so the audience understands that each is different. You may have a quick quip or joke pertaining to each song title. Now you turn your head away and have the spectator reach in to select one final slip. They read the song name and then either destroy the paper or put it in their pocket.

The performer explains that music can have a powerful impact on each of us. How often do we hear a song only to have it take us to a time and place when the song first connected with us. You ask the spectator if they are familiar with the song and have them play it to themselves in their mind.

After concentrating on the spectator, the performer turns to the drummer and asks him to play a simple 4/4 jazz beat. He hums a basic base line and asks the base player to follow along. He adds the trombone into the mix playing a "dum, dooby dobby dum, dooby dooby... One by one the performer has the players join in until only the trumpet or guitar player sits silent.

The performer turns to consider the spectator one last time and then goes and whispers something in the ear of the trumpet/guitar player. He asks the spectator to sit down if he hears his song and turns to the band and points to the trumpet/guitar player who begins playing the lead line.

The performer turns back to the audience with his arms wide, the spectator nods and sits down and the audience bursts into applause as the band plays out the song.

Method

This is based on an idea that was given to me 16 years ago by Jody Baran. I played with it on a six month cruise and built it in to this routine. The secret behind this effect is simple, direct and foolproof. All it uses is a utility prop that I picked up back then from Hollywood Magic. It's a forcing bag made with a clear Zip Loc bag. I've searched a bit on the internet and I am unable to find a supplier or even the proper name but I'm sure it's got to be out there.

Failing that you could make one or use any type of force you prefer. Make up a svengali type deck with the force song on every other card. I just liked the zip loc method because it appeared to be so fair. A bunch of slips of paper in a clear bag and simply by moving a clear flap from one side to the other - you can control what your helper chooses.

The great part is that once the helper has chosen the force slip (with the name of a popular song on it), you're done. You can make the buildup as big or small as you like and you end with a natural applause cue with your arms spread and the orchestra in the background playing a popular song. By the end of that cruise it had turned into an 8-10 minute routine that garnered a standing ovation on a couple of occasions. Enjoy.

Murray Hatfield and his lovely wife Terresa are an amazing illusion team from Victoria, Canada and have made a great name for themselves as one of the most professional and dynamic illusionists in the world. Each year they tour Canada with their full illusion show and a variety of other top name magicians. Because most of their work now takes them around the world on corporate gigs, they have cut back on their cruise ship work.

ROOM KEY REVISED

The following routine is taken from my intimate mentalism show that I perform on cruise ships. This is a special 'extra' show I perform on longer cruises and I try to keep it down to a small number of passengers and usually hold it later at night once the main shows are over, usually after 11pm. I came up with a more complicated version that I will briefly describe at the end of this, for stage. Room Key is an adaptation of Al Koran and Don Wayne's versions of the routine.

This idea is so simple I am sure is not new but I have not read it anywhere else. On cruise ships, as with most hotels, your 'room' key is also what is called your 'cruise card'. This is a plastic card the same size as a credit card that has a strip on the back enabling you to write your signature. On a ship this is your 'identity' card, your room key card and the card you make purchases with.

When you are hired as a Guest Entertainer to work on ships, you get a card that says 'Guest Entertainer' but it doesn't have your room number engraved on the front. If this is not the case then simply ask the Front desk if you can have a spare key card without any room number on it.

The effect is that you show your card and mention that people always ask about where Guest Entertainers sleep. Here I tell the classic story where once I told a passenger we were taken on and off by helicopters when we finish our shows.

The next day the lady complained to the front desk that the noise from the helicopter kept her awake all night!
You bring out your cruise card and ask four people to call out any number from zero to nine, for example, 6048.
You reiterate to the audience that these numbers were chosen at random and then ask another spectator to call out the room number printed on the back of your cruise card. It matches the number chosen by the spectators.

METHOD

A Thumb writer! Need I say more? As simple as this sounds it is a very strong routine. I use a thicker marker type thumb writer rather than a 'nail' writer. I find the impression is darker and better and a little more impossible because you are not holding a marker pen, as far as the audience is concerned. When I get the spectator to call out the number 'printed' on the back of the card, I emphasize printed because as far as the audience is concerned it IS printed!

STAGE VERSION

When I first started doing this routine I would use the above version and when working solo still do. If my wife Natalie is with me on the cruise and we are doing our double act. I have a slight variation on the routine. I will just give the basic run down for those that are interested. You can now purchase a little machine that prints or engraves numbers or letters onto a little sticky piece of plastic. It is used for printing labels and looks like it is engraved. In the stage version Natalie is backstage within earshot of the numbers being called out by the spectators.

She types in the numbers on the little strip of plastic, peels it off and when I ask for a pen she passes it to me. Prior to this I have the card sitting in a champagne glass. As I take the card from the glass to hand to a spectator I simply stick the piece of engraved tape with the numbers on it on the back of the card. I then ask a spectator to call out the "ENGRAVED" room number on the back of the card.

PAPER BALLS OVER THE HEAD FINALE

The entire paper ball over the head is from Slydini and is not mine to explain here. I offer my ending to those who wish to add it to their routine. Tony Clark has a great DVD teaching all the ins and outs of Slydini's routine and I highly recommend you get it and learn it from a master.

I wanted to end my routine with a bit of a surprise, rather than the usual, oh look it's over your head type of idea. In my version, I have a servante at the back of the chair the spectator sits on, and wrapped up in toilet tissue is a bottle of wine. This is placed inside the servante and in easy reach.

While the spectator is sitting down and I am performing the routine, I stand beside him. On the final throw, I have the spectator hold the roll of toilet tissue in his hand while I step back pulling as much toilet tissue as I can, I keep on pulling the tissue ... I use this gag as well, "Don't worry, I'm in to recycling ... I only use unleaded pencils". While the spectators are laughing at the gag and the crazy amount of toilet tissue I now have I move back to the spectator and as I do, my right hand, (left hand is holding the huge bundle of toilet tissue), simply picks up the bottle which is wrapped in toilet tissue and adds it to the bundle in the right hand as I bring everything forward, in front of the spectator.

I then motion like I am going to make everything vanish one more time, but take a moment and say, "you've been such a great sport, the tissue just goes over your head, and because you're a great sport, your next drink is on me", as I pull away the toilet tissue revealing the bottle of wine.

CHAPTER NINE

PHOTOS

Series of photos taken from the last decade working on ships.

Panama Canal 2004

Amazing view in Florence, Italy

Enjoying a beer in Italy

Main deck on the world's largest cruise ship 2008

Paul and Natalie in front of the great pyramid, Egypt

A series of photos taken on board a cruise ship during Paul's show

Different style of theaters on ships

1,500 seat theater

cabaret style theater - seats 600

Photos from around the world

Natalie in Arica, Chile

In Athens at the Acropolis   *Here we are in Gibraltar*

Top left: Monaco, right Pompeii. Middle photo New York

Bottom photo left and right in Venice.

Final thoughts

There are many reasons for choosing cruise ship employment over other types of performance jobs. There are plenty of benefits which can easily be associated and these are benefits which will go a long way in making ones life easier and more comfortable. The first benefit is that you get to earn a good income. Along with this, many of the things on which you usually spend your money is taken care of by the cruising company. Things such as food and accommodation are paid by the company and so these are free for you. As a guest entertainer, working on a ship can be an adventurous experience. Not only will you be able to travel around the globe, you will be able to do it in absolute style and luxury. On top of this, you will get paid for it.

Just think, you could be spending a few months in diverse and exciting places such as the Caribbean islands, and the South American seas and then when the time comes, the ship could move on to colder climes in the Alaskan regions. You could also go to the happening areas around the European coastlines which are world famous for their holiday culture. You also get the chance to perform your act in a wonderful theater to an international audience. These incentives are enough to make anyone choose this job, especially if the person is unemployed.

It is my sincere hope that if you want to work on cruise ships with your act, this book would have been a big help in attaining your dream. It took a long time until I was ready to perform on ships, take your time and make sure you are ready. It really is an amazing life and a fantastic gig for anybody in the entertainment industry.

Wishing you all the very best and happy cruising.

Bio on Paul Romhany

Born and raised in New Zealand, Paul started his magic career at age eight, with his first paid performance at ten. With a degree in music from Auckland University and a teaching degree, Paul decided, at twenty one, to pursue a full time magic career. During the next ten years he appeared regularly on New Zealand television, performed birthday parties, trade shows, corporate events, walk about, doing close-up magic in restaurants and gave seminars as a motivational speaker. In the mid 90's, Paul got his first cruise ship contract with Princess Cruises. Since then, has worked for almost every major cruise line including Holland America, NCL, RCCL, Seaborne, Regent Cruises and Princess Cruises, having traveled to over one hundred countries.

As well as his performing, Paul travels the world lecturing and sharing his magic and knowledge with magicians, and has released over fifty original magic tricks for magicians.

Paul now resides in New Brunswick, Canada, with his wife Natalie where they enjoy a laid back lifestyle playing golf and the outdoors and still perform on high end cruise liners.

1843566

Made in the USA